STILL MORE Good Boats

STILL MORE Good Boats

ROGER C. TAYLOR

IM **INTERNATIONAL MARINE PUBLISHING COMPANY**
CAMDEN, MAINE

© 1981 by International Marine Publishing Company
Library of Congress Catalog Card Number 80-84847
International Standard Book Number 0-87742-136-6
Printed and bound by The Alpine Press, Stoughton, Massachusetts

Published by International Marine Publishing Company
21 Elm Street, Camden, Maine 04843

DEDICATION

*To the Memory of My Seagoing Uncles: Fred Taylor,
Dan Larkin, and Fred Buffum, Masters, Respectively,
of a Good Sloop, a Good Schooner, and a Good Catboat*

Contents

Preface

The purpose of this book is to share still more plans of good boats with you. I love to study the plans of a good boat, imagining myself on board her, underway in a variety of conditions of wind and sea, and at anchor in a variety of coves, harbors, and roadsteads. There is encouraging evidence that I am not alone in this sort of boat-plan-inspired daydreaming.

This book is a sequel, encouraged by the moderate success of its predecessors, the titles of which are obvious: *More Good Boats* was published in 1979 and was, itself, the sequel to *Good Boats,* published in 1977. The publisher asked me to say that these books are still in print and "available at your local bookseller's." They each contain the designs for 36 good boats; somehow in this book, I counted wrong, and you get only 35.

Despite the obvious clarity of the above titles, I have been argued with by the staff at International Marine — a staff of which I myself am a part (if this is hard for you to follow, think how confused we staffers are) — some members of which believe that the books, rather than have real titles, simply should be numbered, as in *Good Boats II, Good Boats III,* etc. As author, I

held out against this boring business. "After all," I asked, "whose books are these, anyway?"

"What will you do if there is a fourth book?" they wanted to know.

"How about starting the title with, *'Would You Believe . . .'?''*

Some people have suggested that I shift over to writing about lousy boats for a while. While it's true that such a course change would simplify titling for a bit, still, I don't see the need. Lousy boats get lots of space as it is — in the boating magazine advertisements.

Let's review the differences between a good boat and a lousy boat. A good boat is handsome, able, and seakindly. All boats that don't have those characteristics are lousy boats.

While few people could disagree with such obviously sound definitions, it is when the designs for specific boats are judged to be either good or lousy according to the definitions that the fun begins. Prejudice surfaces; at least it does in my case.

My dictionary defines prejudice as "an adverse judgment or opinion formed beforehand or without knowledge or examination of the facts.'' I am prejudiced against cruising boats designed under the powerful influence of racing rating rules; it is the International Offshore Rule that is currently being so misused. This rule produces boats that are at once light and beamy. They have high sides and ugly sheerlines. They have tiny, skinny mainsails. They are not handsome and they are not seakindly. A few of them have proven to be able in the hands of large, experienced, muscular crews. As I say, I am prejudiced against this type of boat when it is foisted off as a good cruising boat on that increasingly big percentage of the boating public that is unsuspecting.

A year ago I tested my prejudice against IOR-influenced cruising boats by chartering an IOR-influenced cruising boat and going cruising in her with my family. Imagine my relief when all my prejudices stood up beautifully.

She was ugly. When leaving her side in the dinghy, I averted my gaze. When, from shore, I scanned a harborful of boats that included her, I pretended she was not the boat I had come from.

(There is no point in identifying the vessel. Suffice it to say she is a sloop about 45 feet long. She has a favorable IOR rating. I wish no unkindness to her distinguished designer. She is a fine boat for racing under the IOR.)

Her high sides detracted from more than her appearance. The main reason I like to go in boats so much is that I love the water. I was a long way from my love on this 45-footer. We found that the only way to recover an object in the water (fortunately, it was only a hat we were trying to get back) is to do it from the dinghy, to me a remarkable complication for a cruising boat of this size.

The boat's motion was not easy. Being high, wide, and light, she was thrown about a lot. We did not have her in really rough seas, to be sure; I wouldn't want to.

She had to be steered constantly, like an automobile. It was easy steering, granted, for she was well balanced and had a light helm. You could spin her 'round rapidly, a useless maneuver for a cruising boat.

Her rig was hard to handle. With just the mainsail set, she was basically hove to unless it was blowing hard. This made maneuvering in

harbor tedious. She needed a huge, overlapping headsail to sail at all well, and such a sail, with its single-part sheet, put our family to a great deal of hard work.

The IOR-type sloop did have her good points. She had a good turn of speed. (I would not call her fast, though we could not give her a really fair test, since her sails happened to be cut very poorly.) She had good acceleration for such a big boat. She had a vast amount of deck space and a vast amount of space below. She was well laid out, except that most of the bunks were too short.

In sum, I would far rather cruise in the boats on the pages that follow than in an IOR racer. I think it's absurd that most of the current cruising boats rate so well under the IOR.

I should point out that there are two boats in this book that do not meet my definition of a good boat. They are certainly able and seakindly, but they are not handsome. They are included because each was designed for a special purpose and each would carry out her special purpose very well indeed. I refer to the engineless sailing-rowing-trailering cruiser Dovekie and to the lifeboat-for-cruising-boats Derby Dory. There is genius in these designs.

My crusade for good boats hasn't had much effect on the mass marketing of boats. That's the great limitation of the mass marketing system; it can't react to obvious common sense. In any event, good boats are no more popular now than they were in 1972, when I started showing (a small part of) the world examples of good boats. Yet they are no less popular, either, thanks to the efforts of designers, builders, and sailors who don't cater to the mass market.

Mostly crusading is a discouraging procedure, but I did reap great encouragement recently when I discovered a young student of yacht design who had drawn plans of a ketch with a gaff mainsail and jib-headed mizzen and had drawn in, as big as life — he said because he had read about it in *Good Boats* — from his main gaff to the head of his mizzen mast, a vang. Knowing that I was partly responsible for that simple, sensible pencil line made my minor crusade for vangs seem suddenly worthwhile. (I know it's only a small thing, but we crusaders have to take succor where we find it.)

Thank you to the designers whose plans grace these pages. It is your work that is worth crusading for.

Thank you to the publishers and photographers who have allowed reproduction of their graphic property in this book.

Thank you to Kathleen Brandes, Bruce White, and Nan Kulikauskas for editing this book and putting it together. Thank you to Pat Feener for typing a lot of dictated words that are becoming all too familiar.

The chapters in this book are closely based on articles that have been published in recent issues of the *National Fisherman,* the *Small Boat Journal,* and *WoodenBoat.* Thank you to Dave Getchell and Jim Fullilove of the *National Fisherman,* to Jim Brown of the *Small Boat Journal,* to Jon Wilson of *WoodenBoat,* and to the people who work for them, for their expert presentation of the articles to many readers. And thank you to the readers who have written me about specific boats, correcting and adding to my knowledge of them to the benefit of the text that follows.

The crusade continues. My plea to designers, builders, and sailors is: Let's have still more good boats.

Roger C. Taylor
Camden, Maine

Prologue

DRYING SAIL

Before I was ten, I was captain of a 32-foot yawl. No prodigy, I was given merely a temporary command.

Pop gave me the chore, after a rainy night or a muggy spell, of drying sail on the *Brownie.* There was no thought of throwing off the mooring pendant, of course, yet I was placed in sole charge of the vessel with the responsibility for loosing — even half-hoisting if I wanted to — her sails and then, when they were dry, for refurling them.

I'd row out right after breakfast, before the sun got to steaming things too much, half a mile from our cove to the yawl on her mooring in the river. Oyster beds and general silting kept us from moving her closer to the house. She was far enough away from the family hearth so that when you were out on board her, you really felt as if you were on your own.

One of the best things about the chore was that I was allowed to row out to the *Brownie* in The Cruising Dinghy, instead of having to use my somewhat cranky punt, the *Mahoskus.*

The Cruising Dinghy rowed just beautifully. She was a small, light boat built like a canvas-covered canoe. She was short, with a lovely, curving bow and a wide transom that helped her carrying capacity but kept her from being really beautiful. She seemed to me like an exquisite little lifeboat, perhaps because her bow was so ''sea fendy.'' You could row her fast into closely spaced, steep little river waves and she'd spit 'em off rat-tat-tat.

We called her The Cruising Dinghy because when we went cruising in the *Brownie,* we hoisted her out with the mizzen boom and lowered her into the cradle of the yawl's V-shaped boomkin. One Christmas she became known as The Old Dinghy, because Mother took the liberty of putting beside the tree a brand New Dinghy, a heavy, clumsy boat by comparison, but one that didn't leak.

There was no fender of any kind on The Cruising Dinghy, so my first worry — for every perquisite of command there are a dozen worries — was, by all means, to keep her from bumping. Pop would have detected immediately the evidence of a lubberly landing the next time he came on board.

Sail-drying days often had fresh, puffy northwesters. A northwester was a major worry. I think my lifelong mistrust of northwesters must have started when trying to cope with them drying sail in the *Brownie*.

The object of the game, of course, was to set as much sail as possible so as to create the illusion of being underway. Considerable current ran in the river, so the vessel lay to the tide most of the time. Whether she was headed upstream to the ebb or downstream to the flood, a northwester put her on a beam reach. That meant if I hoisted much of any sail, she could catch a puff from aft a ways (northwesters are notoriously fickle), gather way, and ride up on her pendant. I knew that sailing 'round the mooring would be observed from the house and would probably result in my being relieved of my command. Northwesters were frustrating.

Usually the jib was unbent and sent below when the yawl was on her mooring, so the only sails to dry were the fore staysail, big gaff mainsail, and jib-headed mizzen. The sails had come, years before, from the old Wilson and Silsby loft in Boston. They were made of heavy, gray canvas. That is, I suppose they were made of white canvas, but the whiteness had long since been replaced by a generally weather-beaten look, relieved by a few darker gray areas of — despite our best efforts — mildew.

The first thing to do was slack the lee backstay, in case you forgot it before starting the mainsail up. Such a detail would probably escape notice ashore, but then again, it might not.

Next, slack the three sheets and take up a bit on the three topping lifts. Check to see that plenty of slack has been left in the outhauls.

I approached the casting off of the stops with a mixture of the excitement of loosing sail and the foreboding that I would have to furl the sails again as neatly as I found them.

Each sail had its own personality. The mainsail was scary to hoist very far for fear she'd start to sail, but the gaff climbing horizontal and silent was majestic, the halyard blocks allowing a small boy to hoist heavy spar and sail, magic. After hoisting the gaff up as far as I dared, I'd peak it up a bit. Then it was aft to the mizzen mast to take some of the slack out of the vang. Being captain, I could make these nice adjustments exactly to my own liking.

The mizzen you could hoist right up if she

happened to be lying head to wind (rare delight), but on no account were you to put any strain on the luff of a damp sail. More often it was a case of hoisting it enough so that the drooping leech was well clear of the water.

The fore staysail was absurdly easy to hoist halfway up its stay.

It was an allowed custom when drying sail on the *Brownie* to leave the halyards as they fell, rather than coil them down. The theory was that nothing was going to happen to foul them during the hour or two it took to dry the sails. Seeing the piles of rope strewn about the deck 'round the masts brought a luxurious sense of dissipation, a feeling not often present on the yawl.

While the sails were drying, I had plenty of time to revel in the many intricacies of my command and in the independent status it brought me.

I could take the thin, wooden cover off the compass, set inside a box-like thwart Pop had built for it across the cockpit forward of the wheel. "How does she head?" I'd ask myself, and, reading the card against the lubber line, answer, "West by south, a half south," or whatever. Underway with Pop, compass reading and steering by compass were heavy burdens intolerable of error, but alone on the mooring, I could enjoy the compass as casually as conscience would allow.

I could turn the steering wheel, unsupervised, and, opening the little hatch above the steering gear, peer into the dim lazarette and line up the lug on the gear barrel exactly amidships, indicating that the rudder was in like position.

I could lift off the big mahogany hatch to the engine room and drop down into its gray coolness and its smells of machinery. I could gently roll the flywheel of the Redwing, trying to imagine what complicated gyrations of hidden moving parts caused its resistance. I could uncoil the hose to the brass bilge pump, feed it out the engine-room hatch and over the side, take maybe three or four strokes before it would suck (the exact number to be reported to Pop on my return ashore), and then carefully bring it back on board with a minimum of dripping.

Or, I could loll in the cockpit, whistling carelessly, and watch the dinghy make her little bow wave in the tide. I could go forward, lie down on the bow, and look over the side at the mooring pendant and forefoot making their steady way through the water.

I could watch lowly motorboats go by, enjoying the obvious jealousies of the boys on board them, for surely they could see that someone their own age was the captain of a big, complicated sailing vessel.

I could slide back the heavy, varnished companionway hatch, take out the single vertical board, and nonchalantly go below, feet down the familiar ladder, hands on the hatchway as long as they could reach, and eyes peering down the river, until they went "under." I could unhook the hatch in the forward end of the cabin house and reach up to prop a little stick under its windward edge for extra ventilation. The rehooking of this hatch before leaving the vessel was not to be taken lightly.

I could wipe off the front of the one really fancy thing in the boat, a white enameled Shipmate stove, It always had a little dust on its hinges, latches, and oven-door lettering, and it was very satisfying to make it gleam. Invariably I would lift a faded, blue seat cushion, open the locker in the seat beneath it, and pull out a piece of cedar, split and cut for the Shipmate. It had come from the old dead tree overhanging our shore, but you'd think it was from China by the smell. Pop liked the smell of cedar firewood too, but if he were on board, you wouldn't dream of getting out a piece just to smell it.

I could pump a cup of water at the galley sink, being careful not to waste a drop.

I could take the covered ashtray on deck and carefully dump Pop's cigarette ashes overboard to leeward.

I could even stretch out in the quarter berth for a few minutes.

I could sit in lordly splendor on the port seat at the cabin table (the starboard seat was Pop's), reach out the brass dividers from a long, mahogany box on the cabin shelf, a box with ivory hinges that Pop said he got at Edgartown on a cruise to the Vineyard once, and plan elegant cruises on a chart of distant waters.

All too soon, the privileges of command gave way to duty.

I used to furl up from forward aft. The staysail was easy; it was "my" sail underway, so I was accustomed to dealing with it. The mainsail was heavy for me. I couldn't pull the leech aft nearly as hard as Pop did. I'd have to tie up the big sail reasonably well with two or three stops and then start along again, pulling and punching, trying my best to work a fairly tight final roll between gaff and boom. Furling the mizzen was fun, because much of it was out over the water. You could stand on one side of the boomkin and lean your belly over the boom. I always hoped a motorboat would go by while I was out on the boomkin furling the mizzen.

When I had furled the sails as well as I possibly could, I would go over the entire vessel making sure I had put everything back exactly the way it was when I came on board, as if it were important that no one should be able to detect that I had been there. The final job was to check for Irish pennants.

Then, I would row away ashore, admiring the handsome yawl and hoping her furled sails would look all right.

Drying sail in the *Brownie,* I wouldn't have traded places with the captain of the *Queen Mary.*

1/ The Rozinante

> **Length on deck: 28 feet**
> **Length on waterline: 24 feet**
> **Beam: 6 feet 4 inches**
> **Draft: 3 feet 9 inches**
> **Sail area: 348 square feet**
> **Displacement: 6,600 pounds**
> **Designer: L. Francis Herreshoff**

Ted Sprague and I made each other a deal that neither one of us could refuse. Ted keeps a Rozinante in Rockport, Maine, but until he retired, he had to put bread on the table by working at his engineering job out in Ohio. I learned via boatyard gossip that he was to be separated from his boat for the summer, and since I have always wanted to sail a Rozinante, it wasn't long before I was on the phone to Ted, making him the sacrificial offer of looking after the lovely little lady for the season. Ted is a thorough boatman and knows well that it is far better for a boat to be used, kept clean, and kept ventilated than to sit forlornly on a mooring with no one to wipe away her tears. At any rate, fortunately for me, Ted said I could be the caretaker for the Rozinante canoe yawl *Arete*. Wow!

When I think back 10 years from now on the rare experience of sailing the *Arete*, I know very well the lasting impression that will leap to mind. It will be looking aft at that delicate, pointed stern slipping through the water. If you would have a boat, my friend, get one with a pointed stern.

There. As far as I am concerned, the preceding paragraph says enough about the Rozinante to put her right into the Hall of Fame. Nothing more need be said about the Rozinante, particularly in light of the fact that she is a heroine in that wonderful book, *The Compleat Cruiser,* written by L. Francis Herreshoff, her designer. But you know how publishers are. They always want more. All right, Mr. Publisher, here come more details about the great Rozinante and what she can do. But please, please let's not any of us lose sight of that lovely stern slipping along through the water. It represents peace.

The Rozinante brings to mind a violin, in a general sense because she is so perfectly designed and made for her intended purpose, and in the literal sense because of the lovely wood in her and because of her very delicate and finely tunable rigging. Underway, you find yourself tiptoeing around making gentle adjustments to things. It took me a long time to realize she wasn't going to break.

Mr. Herreshoff referred to her type as a canoe yawl, yet her rig is clearly ketch. He explained all this in the first of his series of articles about the Rozinante that was published in *The*

L. Francis Herreshoff on the roof of The Castle with Marblehead harbor in the background. (Muriel Vaughn)

Rudder and reprinted in his book *Sensible Cruising Designs:* ''This little yacht is a small double-ender of a type that used to be called canoe yawls, and in the 1890s was a very popular type in England for cruising some of their delightful waterways like the Clyde, Firth of Forth, Humber, Mersey, and of course the Solent in days gone by. The canoe yawl is sort of a descendant of some of the sailing canoes that were used in these waters for cruising during the previous decade. The name 'canoe yawl' simply means a boat with a sharp stern that is larger than the usual sailing canoe, or about the size of what was called a yawl boat in those days. Admiral Smyth in his *Dictionary of Nautical Terms,* 1867, describes a yawl as 'a man-of-war's boat resembling the pinnace, but rather smaller; it is carvel-built, and generally rowed with twelve oars.' The term 'canoe yawl' in its day had nothing to do with the rigs these pretty vessels used, for among them there were sloops, ketches, yawls, luggers, and cat yawls . . . .''

Mr. Herreshoff goes on to say that a canoe yawl ''should be a good sea boat and a fast sailer under a small sail plan.'' And, as a matter of fact, those are exactly my next most lasting impressions, after the stern of the Rozinante. I was

amazed at her ability to cope with rough water and always surprised that her seemingly tiny working sails could get her along so well.

One of the many pleasant things about the Rozinante is that you can see and enjoy the shape of her while on board, because she's open all the way through. If you don't pile too much gear in the ends of her, not a good idea anyway, you can see from the cockpit right up into the shape of her bow and right back into the shape of her stern, as she carries you dancing along.

The boat is 28 feet long on deck, with a waterline length of 24 feet, a beam of all of 6 feet 4 inches, and a draft of 3 feet 9 inches. Her sail area is only 348 square feet. Her displacement is 6,600 pounds, and her lead keel weighs 3,360 pounds.

She has very fine lines throughout, with a nice hollow at the waterline both in the bow and at the stern. Her sections are really fairly straight, especially forward, for such a shapely hull.

The sterns of the various Rozinantes I have seen look quite different from each other. The knuckle in the sternpost has to be shaped exactly as called for in the lines drawings, and the rake of the sternpost has to be set precisely as Mr. Herreshoff drew it, else the looks of the boat will be spoiled. On a couple of the Rozinantes I have seen, the knuckle is a bit too pronounced and the sternpost doesn't have quite enough rake. These boats lack the superb grace of the design as represented by Ted Sprague's *Arete*.

She has a very nice sheerline. I didn't measure, but I have a hunch that the *Arete* has just a tiny bit less sheer in her stern than Mr. Herreshoff drew. Both from on board the boat and from alongside in a dinghy, her stern doesn't seem to spring up quite as much as expected.

I will give only the essentials of the Rozinante's construction, since the details are given by Mr. Herreshoff in *Sensible Cruising Designs*. The planking he specified is either ¾-inch mahogany or ⅞-inch pine or cedar. Frames are steam-bent white oak, 1¼ inches by 1¼ inches. The wood keel is 12 feet 4 inches long by 2 inches thick and 14 inches wide, of white oak, yellow pine, or Philippine mahogany. Stem and sternpost are 4 inches thick by

2 ¾ inches wide at the inner faces, of white oak or hackmatack, or could be laminated of either white oak or Philippine mahogany. Floor timbers are 1 ½ inches thick, varying up to 8 inches deep, of white oak. Deck beams are 1 inch by 1 ½ inches, but 1 ½ inches by 1 ½ inches for three extra-strong beams, two at the forward and after ends of the forward deck hatch and one at the after end of the cockpit, the first beam abaft the mizzen mast, to be of oak, ash, or elm. Clamp is 1 inch by 2 ¼ inches "or more," of spruce or Douglas fir, "if possible in one length." Shelf is 1 inch by 1 ¼ inches of the same material as the clamp. Deck is tongue-and-groove strips ¾ inch thick by 3 inches wide, of fir, spruce, soft pine, cypress, or California redwood, covered with canvas. Cockpit coaming and house sides are each 19 feet long and ¾ inch thick of mahogany or oak (the former is far superior for this use, in my opinion). House beams are ⅝ inch by 1 ⅛ inches of oak, ash, or elm. The top of the house is ½ inch thick tongue-and-groove of pine, spruce, or Port Orford cedar, covered with canvas. Cockpit floor is teak slats, 1 inch wide by ¾ inch thick, spaced to leave an opening of ¼ inch between slats. Cabin sole is ¾ inch thick of soft pine, cypress, California redwood, "or other suitable wood." Cockpit seats are ¾ inch thick by 12 inches wide by 6 feet 6 inches long of soft pine (the *Arete's* seats are mahogany, which is elegant).

The deck and top of the house on the *Arete* are not covered with canvas. They are covered with an entirely different kind of material, one without the ancient tradition that canvas enjoys. Now it may surprise you to learn — it certainly surprised me! — that the use of this upstart replacement for canvas was condoned by L. Francis Herreshoff. In the chapter on the Rozinante in *Sensible Cruising Designs,* he wrote, "Fiberglass decks are said to be very good if painted with a non-skid paint." It really says that, right on page 83!

The *Arete* was very nicely built by Smith and Rhuland down in Lunenburg, Nova Scotia, in 1969. One departure the builders made from the plans is noticed quickly on coming aboard by all true Rozinante aficionados: there is a nicely rounded cap along the top edge of the cockpit coaming. This is an improvement, for you inevitably walk on that edge at times, and it also gives you a nice handhold when standing up in the cockpit facing to weather with the boat well heeled over.

A glance at the Rozinante's construction plan shows what a simple boat she is. True to her canoe yawl heritage, she's really just a big open boat partially decked over. With her stripped-out simplicity and her lack of an engine, her cost, Mr. Herreshoff estimated, would be about five-eighths that of the normal cruising auxiliary of the same size. One of the drawbacks to the design is the narrowness of her side decks in way of the cockpit. You can see in the construction section drawing just how little boat there is outboard of the cockpit coaming. Sitting on the weather side of the cockpit, you can't see the lee rail except at the bow and stern, and this mars somewhat the very great enjoyment of watching this boat work her way through the waves. Also, if she's being pressed and you wonder if she finally may have her lee rail down, you have to get up and lean over to leeward to see. (She seldom has.)

The mooring, kindly loaned to the *Arete* for the summer by my neighbor, Dr. Dana Sheldon, was out in the Sherman Cove part of Camden Harbor, where the views of hills and bay are spectacular but where considerable surge works in across the ledges when the wind is in the south. Working around on the *Arete's* deck was a bit precarious at first. She has a quick little roll and jump at times, and it does take time to get used to her narrowness. You keep thinking there will be more deck out there on which to catch your balance than there really is. Once, I actually stepped out over the coaming — onto nothing at all. Thank goodness for that cap on the coaming edge! I came to the conclusion that the most likely time to fall off the *Arete* is when she's at the mooring.

And her tiny, narrow stern deck is a bit precarious for working on the mizzen. A good, stout mizzen topping lift is important, because now and again you find yourself lurching against the boom when you're furling the sail and she's jumping a bit.

Then there is the problem of getting out onto that afterdeck from the cockpit. The *Arete's*

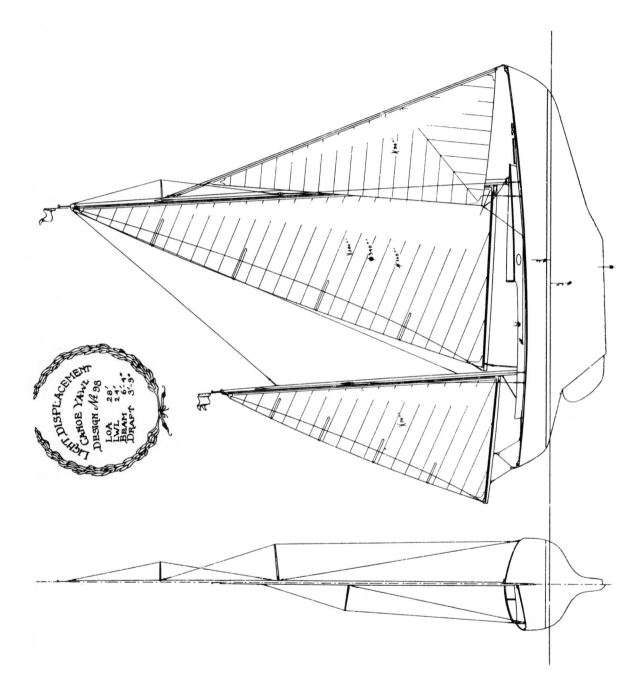

Francis Herreshoff explained that the term "canoe yawl" has nothing to do with rig. (Sensible Cruising Designs by L. Francis Herreshoff, International Marine Publishing Company)

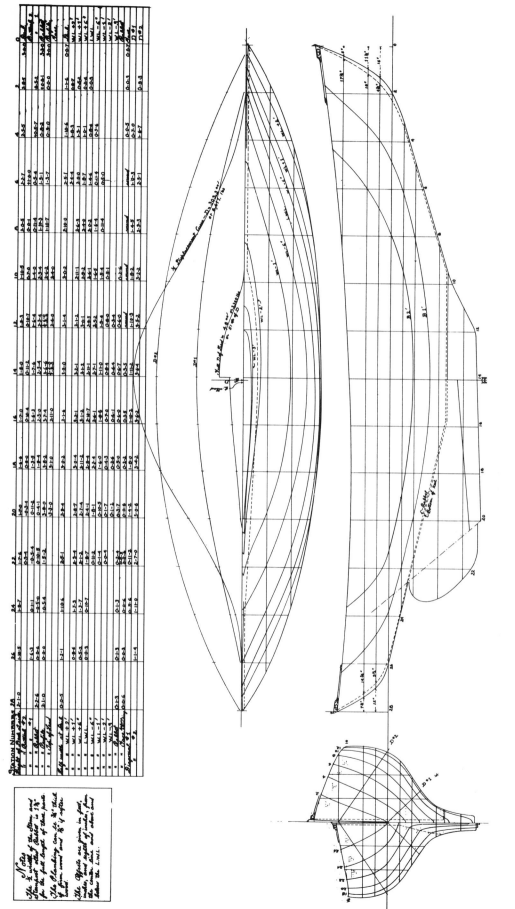

The Rozinante has a delicately balanced set of lines. (Sensible Cruising Designs by L. Francis Herreshoff, International Marine Publishing Company)

main backstay doesn't go to the mizzen mast as shown on the plans, but rather comes down to a two-legged bridle running to chainplates on the rail just abaft the mizzen shrouds. At times the mizzen mast, its shrouds, and the backstay bridle seem designed as a most effective obstacle course to keep you off the stern of the boat. I finally got pretty good at wriggling through and under, and by the end of the summer all that rigging hardly slowed me down at all.

There is no place on board a Rozinante to stow a dinghy. On such a small, narrow vessel you just have to put up with towing a boat. Why can't some genius design an inflatable dinghy that's truly easy to blow up — and deflate — and really rows well?

The big, deep cockpit of the Rozinante is fantastic. Its convenience and security more than make up for the boat's lack of deck space amidships. Just to begin with, it's a fine, secure, sheltered place in which to work at the mooring. Spread out tools and materials to your heart's content, or use the place for a sail loft down out of the wind. Mr. Herreshoff said the Rozinante's cockpit could take six comfortably for sailing; well, I'll go four, but when I use that word "comfortably," I mean people really have room to stretch out or move around a bit without falling over one another.

The thwart across the after end of the cockpit just abaft the mizzen mast is very nice to sit on and steer when she's not heeled over too much. When Weldon described the Rozinante to his friends in *The Compleat Cruiser,* he said this thwart was placed three inches higher than the cockpit seats so that the helmsman could see over the heads of his crew. In the *Arete,* the thwart is only one inch higher than the seats, but it is surprising how much even that small difference makes. In any case, it's good to have a choice of steering seats so you can sit facing forward or to leeward, just as you please.

The cockpit coaming slants outboard at an angle of eight degrees. Mr. Herreshoff designed the cockpit seats to rise coming inboard by that same angle so that the seats and coaming would form a right angle. The *Arete's* seats are nearer to level than that and are most comfortable, but I think they would be even better as the designer decreed.

The cabin doors are stowed away when not in use on slides under the forward ends of the cockpit seats. There's a hook at the back to keep them from sliding back out when the boat heels; Mr. Herreshoff designed a wedge arrangement for this same purpose that would be even handier than the hooks, which require a bit of kneeling down and looking and feeling back up under the seats to secure. About my biggest criticism of the *Arete* is that the lower pintles on her cabin doors should be longer so when you put the doors back on you can start the lower gudgeons on their pintles first, and then line up the upper ones, rather than having to line up both at once. I got really frustrated at times doing this in the dark in the Sherman Cove surge. I tell you it was a terrible hardship. The whole thing was probably the builder's fault rather than the designer's, for Captain Nat Herreshoff knew this trick, and I feel sure it wasn't wasted on his son.

The *Arete* has a big diaphragm pump permanently installed in the bilge at the forward end of the cockpit, discharging through a gate valve fitted at the waterline on the starboard side. This is a wonderful rig. The handle to the thing stows in clips under the after end of the starboard cockpit seat, so that if he needs to, the helmsman can be pumping the bilge in five seconds without leaving the tiller. The pump would not move as much water as a bucket, but it would certainly help out a lot, and would clear the bilge below the sole quickly.

For ground tackle, the *Arete* has a pair of yachtsman's anchors, one of 25 pounds and one of 15 pounds. Pete Culler used to say to put down your heavy anchor and sleep peacefully, and that is just what we did. Both anchors were stowed under the seats in the cockpit with stocks folded and together with their rodes if we weren't doing a lot of anchoring, and if we were, the 25-pounder was lashed on deck away forward with its stock hanging over the rail and snugged right up into the bow chock.

Mr. Herreshoff gave no companionway hatch to the Rozinante, saying it would cost $150 to build (a couple of decades ago), "and I would duck my head many times for that sum." The *Arete* has one, and I must say it's a very nice arrangement in the Rozinante. It makes a fine place to stand and watch her go.

The top of the *Arete's* companionway hatch,

and also of her forward deck hatch, are made of a thick, strong, transparent plastic. Aesthetically, these hatches leave much to be desired when compared with varnished mahogany, but they do let a tremendous amount of light below, and the transparent forward hatch, in particular, transforms what would otherwise be a dim forepeak into a bright place where even missing sail stops can be found. The place where my open canvas bag of oilies and boots was stowed happened to be right under the forward hatch, and it was somehow comforting in fine weather to be able to glance down there and see foul weather gear at the ready as I walked past. I guess I would prefer to keep the transparent hatch forward but to have a nice mahogany slide aft where you need the additional light less and where you see and use the hatch more.

The glass ports in the sides of the house look nice and let you look out from below. And, sitting on the weather side of the cockpit with the boat heeled over, you can look into the cabin and down through the lee porthole to watch the foam from the bow wave flash by. This makes up a little bit for the lee rail being hidden behind house and coaming.

Below, the after end of the *Arete's* cabin is taken up with considerable structure. At first it seemed to me that too much of the cabin was given over to this galley paraphernalia, but I later came to appreciate what is a considerable amount of solid storage and work space in so small a boat. On the starboard side is a big, deep icebox that kept cubes for five days in the Maine summer. There was also a flat for the usual two-burner kerosene stove. On the port side was a nice little sink with a wobble pump drawing water from a big (maybe as much as 20 gallons) water tank beneath it. On each side were counter space, lockers, and drawers. With all the food and cooking gear stowed away for a cruise, you still had one whole big, deep drawer in which to stow ship's gear, a first-aid kit, and a few simple navigational instruments.

Mr. Herreshoff designed a comfortable chair in one after corner of the cuddy. It was made like a canvas beach chair with the canvas forming seat and back in one piece and following roughly the contour of the hull. A neat arrangement, and one that I think would be an improvement in the *Arete,* for she has no truly com-fortable place to sit and read below. For use north of Cape Cod, Mr. Herreshoff said, she ought to have a small coal-burning stove in the other corner. I heartily agree with this, and we sorely missed such a wonderful contrivance on at least a couple of occasions.

Forward, the *Arete* has the so-called double bunk of the Rozinante design. I never have figured out why everybody calls this a double bunk, what with the mainmast growing right up out of the middle of it. Anyway, it's most comfortable, whichever side of the mast you choose to sleep on.

The *Arete* has a W.C. under the bunkboards. It's a neat, out-of-the-way installation, but we found it so out of the way that we seldom used it, even after I cut handholds in the bunkboards (with Ted's kind permission, of course) so we could reach through to open and shut the intake and discharge valves. The bucket was far more convenient than the W.C. And, for males, even more convenient than the bucket was the lee rigging, main shrouds in moderate weather to take advantage of the mainsail as a curtain, and mizzen shrouds in heavy going because of the security of standing inside the coaming on the cockpit thwart (one advantage of the narrow side deck).

The fellow in the construction drawing smoking his pipe and doing his chores up in the fo'c's'le under the forward hatch looks more comfortable than he really is, I suspect. She's fairly cramped up in there.

It takes time, even in a small, simple boat like the Rozinante, to learn the best positions for doing things. It wasn't until near the end of the summer that I learned where to sit when getting lunch underway on a rough day. What you do is you put a cockpit cushion on the sill between cuddy and cockpit and brace your knees on the lee cabinet. You're secure, you can reach everything in the galley, and you can easily pass the results of your labors out to those eager hands.

My first impression of the *Arete's* spars and rigging was that everything was too light, but I was thinking in terms of the length of the boat rather than in terms of her displacement and sail area. The sails are small, for she is so easily driven that little power is needed to move her. Everything on the boat is so diminutive that you find yourself handling halyards and sheets daintily between thumb and forefinger (you can raise the pinky or not, as you wish).

Her mainsail has an area of 180 square feet, the jib has 98, and the mizzen, 70.

Quite complete details of spars, fittings, standing rigging, and running rigging are given by Mr. Herreshoff in *Sensible Cruising Designs.* To give an idea of the scale of things, the mainmast is 4½ inches by 3½ inches at the deck. Hardly massive. The rectangular spars are not as good looking to my eye as are round spars, but they are certainly less bulky.

The strut on the after side of the mizzen mast steadies the spar, which has no partners, since it stands in the open cockpit.

I'd be sorely tempted to raise both booms on the Rozinante by about three inches. The main boom does a little more head knocking than it ought to, and raising both booms would improve visibility to leeward. When steering from the thwart, I found myself peering to leeward through the crack between the foot of the mizzen and the boom.

Mr. Herreshoff's sail plan for the Rozinante shows the springstay making to a turnbuckle aloft on the mizzen mast. On the *Arete,* the springstay led to a rope tail rove through a fairlead on the side of the mizzen mast at the same position as Mr. Herreshoff's turnbuckle and then down to a cleat near the foot of the mast. This is a great rig. It was almost as much fun to play with that springstay as it is to play with the vang on a gaff. On the wind in a breeze, if the mizzen was luffing along lazily, taking a bit more strain on the springstay would flatten the sail right out and put it to work.

The halyards and sheets are all in the cockpit — with the exception of the jib sheets, which belay awkwardly on the outside of the outward-slanting coaming. Mr. Herreshoff shows no winches on the boat, of course, but the *Arete* has a small pair of jib-sheet winches mounted on the outside of the coaming, and I must say they are most handy. Perhaps a good rig would be that fancy kind of winch, right on the top of which you can belay the sheet. It's an awkward reach to the cleats on the outside of the coaming when she's driving along well heeled over and you go to cast off the lee jib sheet to tack.

The main sheet comes right to a cleat on the forward side of the mizzen mast, which just couldn't be handier. Its height on the mast produces just the right angle for the sheet so that no traveler is needed. The mizzen sheet comes in through a hole in the after end of the cockpit coaming and belays next to the tiller.

The *Arete's* jib may have been a bit shorter on the luff than the jib Mr. Herreshoff drew on the Rozinante's sail plan. At any rate, I let the tack of the sail up about eight inches off the deck, which made the sheet lead right, kept the sail a little drier when punching to windward, and, above all, improved visibility on the lee bow.

The *Arete's* only light sail is a small spinnaker, but she is not rigged with spinnaker gear. We set it a couple of times tacked down to the stemhead as a ballooner, but it was more of a conversation piece than anything else. We seldom felt the need for light sails. On the wind or reaching, the working jib seems to be plenty, and she is able to get along quite well with it. Well off the wind, we found that you ought to either head up high enough to just fill the jib, or else run right off wing and wing. Running before it with the jib blanketed and main and mizzen on the same side, the mizzen just about completely kills the mainsail. A good sail for the boat would probably be a balloon jib hanked onto the stay to pole out for running. Then you'd want to take in the mizzen.

We found the *Arete* would carry full sail to windward comfortably until it was blowing perhaps 18 or 20 knots. Then we'd take in the mizzen, and with that much breeze, she'd still have just the tiniest bit of weather helm under jib and mainsail. Then, if it kept breezing up, somewhere between 20 and 25 knots depending on whether we were feeling lazy or ambitious, we'd reset the mizzen and take in the mainsail. This is a rather drastic reduction of 110 square feet; if you were racing her, you would instead reef away, say, 50 square feet of the mainsail.

But jib-and-mizzen turns the Rozinante into a wonderfully easy-to-handle cruising boat that will sail well — including going to windward — in 20 knots of breeze or more. At 40 knots if it kept breezing up, you'd want a further reduction, and this could be made by reefing away, say, 25 square feet of the mizzen. For that, you'd want earings and reefing laceline all rove off, so that the sail could be reefed without leaving the cockpit. (I am going on about all this because the Rozinante is such a wonderful seaboat it is a shame to leave her tied up in heavy weather.) Then, for that really hard chance, it would be good to have a storm jib with an area of, say, 65 square feet. Under storm jib and reefed mizzen, she would be showing only 110 square feet of sail, and I think she'd be among the last boats of her displacement to be kept from working to weather in frightful wind and sea conditions.

Yet another advantage of Mr. Herreshoff's ketch rig in his canoe yawl is that she lies to very handily head-to-wind with the mizzen sheeted flat and nothing else drawing. I don't mean this as a heavy weather tactic. *In extremis,* she'd be better off running under bare poles dragging most of the rope on board (from amidships on each side, not from that delicate stern). But in any normal weather, if you want to stop for lunch or a nap, just take in jib and mainsail, sheet the mizzen flat, and let her lie quietly head-to-wind. Or, if singlehanded, when you come flying into a harbor and want to catch your breath before anchoring, round up, drop the jib, let the main sheet run, sheet the mizzen flat, and let her lie head-to-wind while you stow the jib below and get the anchor all ready to let go. All you need is a little clear space to leeward, for of course she'll go slowly astern. Or, when picking up the mooring, as soon as it's aboard, sheet the mizzen flat and she'll go straight astern until she takes up on the pendant instead of sailing all over the place. Or, when getting underway from an anchor when singlehanded, set the mizzen and sheet it flat, pick up the anchor and get it all washed off and stowed away while she goes slowly astern, then put on the rest of the sail and fill away. That mizzen transforms a prancing thoroughbred into a docile farm horse with the feed bag on.

The Rozinante's tiller arrangement is strange and peculiar. The tiller doesn't swing freely back and forth but instead hits the mizzen mast. You have to lift it a couple of inches to get it to clear the mast. And you have to reach behind the mast even to get your hand on the

thing! It all seems quite awkward — at first. But then you begin to get used to it and rather than trying to push the tiller through the mizzen mast, you get in the habit of automatically lifting it to clear. And you begin to realize that 99 percent of the time the boat is sailing along with a bit of weather helm so that the mast doesn't interfere at all! And you get used to reaching aft for the tiller.

Then, little by little, you begin to take advantage of that mizzen mast. If you want the tiller lashed amidships (as when lying to under the mizzen), rather than reach for a piece of line, you just wedge the end of the tiller down against the after side of the mizzen mast. And if you want her to steer herself for a couple of minutes while you go do something else, you just leave the tiller up against the weather side of the mast and go about your business. (If you have a Rozinante and want to astound friends who aren't used to her, just walk away from the helm. The tiller will fetch up against the mizzen mast and the boat will just keep right on going, but your friends, not realizing that this is going to happen, either leap for the tiller or look at each other as if to say, "Why did we come sailing with a crazy person?")

And then, unconsciously, you begin using that mast as a benchmark while steering. You find yourself reaching for it with your thumb and automatically gauging exactly the amount of helm you have on, using your thumb against the mast as a measuring stick. And that thumb quickly becomes an amazingly sensitive rudder angle indicator. By now you're ready to install false mizzen masts in way of all tillers. Such a spar might even triple as a binnacle stand and boom crotch.

The *Arete* had the 10-foot oar that Mr. Herreshoff recommended stowed away below as shown in the construction drawing. Her oarlocks on the cockpit coaming are perhaps 18 inches farther aft than the position shown by Mr. Herreshoff. The rowing position worked fine, however; there was plenty of room to stand up and pull facing aft, of course, and you could also stand up and push, bracing your back against the mizzen mast. You can move her along at 1 or 2 knots, 1 knot being a steady pace for

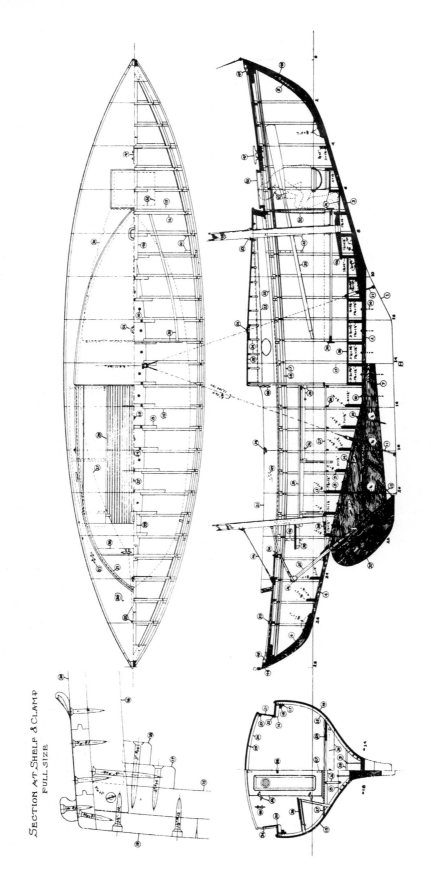

SECTION AT SHELF & CLAMP
FULL SIZE

She is not a roomy vessel, but she has a long waterline for her displacement. (Sensible Cruising Designs by L. Francis Herreshoff, International Marine Publishing Company)

distance and 2 knots being a sprint that most people couldn't maintain for more than a few hundred yards. The tiller arrangement comes in handy for rowing, because once you get her going, you can keep her going at a comfortable cruising speed with the tiller up against the mizzen mast on the opposite side to the oar, and that will keep her going pretty straight. This takes some practice, and it doesn't really work if you're trying to maneuver the boat in close quarters around a harbor, in which case a second person to steer is almost a necessity for good control. For any serious rowing of the Rozinante, though, I think the oar should be the longest possible contraption that will stow below, namely, something like 14 feet. That would mean it ought to have plenty of weight in the handle for balance, but such an oar would be quite superior, I think, to the 10-footer, which is a bit scant for such a big boat.

But the really easy way to move the Rozinante under oars, we discovered, is to tow her. With any kind of a decent pulling boat, you can add a full knot to the Rozinante's speed under oar by using the dinghy as a tug and towing the mothership astern. And with a short towline of about 20 or 25 feet, maneuverability in cramped quarters, such as coming alongside a dock, is excellent, for as master of the towboat, you can pull, twist, and nudge as the occasion demands. Towing a boat with a dinghy, even a boat much bigger than the Rozinante, tells you an awful lot about her: her weight, how she turns, her windage, how she carries her way. Towing the *Arete* certainly demonstrated — even more forcibly than ghosting along in a light air or driving through a big head sea shortened down to jib and mizzen — just how very easily driven is the Rozinante's hull. You can't believe you're towing a 24-foot-waterline boat.

The *Arete* has a 4-h.p. Johnson long-shaft outboard that stows neatly under the port cockpit seat and mounts on a simple bracket that fits into a bronze track, one of which is bolted to the outside of the planking just below the rail amidships on each side. We didn't use the motor much, but the few times we did, it seemed very easy to put on and take off, and it shoved her along easily at about 5 knots. We never discovered how much breeze it would push her in-

to, because if there is any wind at all, you can't resist sailing a Rozinante.

I had the *Arete* underway 30 times during the summer. Francis Herreshoff wrote of the handiness of the Rozinante for evening sailing, and that certainly proved to be true. We had a lot of afternoons of gentle to moderate to fresh southerlies on Penobscot Bay that summer, and it became a most pleasant habit to leave the office a bit after five, having picked up a crew or not, as the case might be, row out to the *Arete* on her mooring in Sherman Cove, tumble aboard, make sail, and be underway in five minutes, feeling her heel over and gather way to just fetch out through the spindles between Sherman Point and the ledges. Once in the Bay, we'd pick out just which hole in the islands would make the best sail full and by on the starboard tack. The late afternoon breezes were so constant in direction that it almost always turned out to be "let her go about so, below East Goose Rock to miss that sunker in there, then sharpen up a bit to weather the end of Lasell Island, and then let's shoot past 10 feet off the lee side of Goose Island and see if we can surprise the seals on the other side. Then we might as well let her go for Pulpit Harbor over on North Haven."

The people in Pulpit Harbor must have thought we were nuts. We'd keep sailing in there at six-thirty or seven in the evening and, instead of anchoring, spin her around and sail right back out again. Coming back across the Bay, we'd generally head up just to weather of Saddle Island and then have a nice reach for Camden. Some of the sunsets behind the Camden Hills were kind of pretty.

I expected the *Arete* to sail very well in light and moderate weather, but I did not realize how very handy, able, and dry she would be in a big breeze and sea.

I would not call her an extremely fast boat, but she is certainly quite fast. Of course we had a few brushes with other boats. She didn't quite hold a Scheel 30 to windward in a light breeze, but she sailed even with her on a reach. She worked away from a Tartan 30 on the wind in a moderate breeze. In a faint breath and perfectly smooth water, she wouldn't quite hold an Oxford 500 on the wind. On all these occasions, the other boats had big genoa jibs.

Sailing with Bill Peterson's 28-foot schooner *Susan* (described in Chapter 9), designed by his father, Murray, the *Arete* was a bit faster going to windward in a fresh breeze but was slower running in the same breeze and much slower running when the breeze eased up. But my excuse for being so badly beaten by the *Susan* running up the Damariscotta River is twofold: I should have had her wing and wing longer, as Bill rightly had his schooner, and we were towing a dinghy that was by then half full of water and had to be snubbed right up under the stern to keep her under control, where she was certainly making more waves than was the *Arete*.

I guess my conclusion as to the Rozinante's speed is that she is faster than most boats of her length, but not faster than all. Somehow that statement doesn't seem very helpful. Let's try another comparison: The fastest boat of the Rozinante's length that I ever sailed in was the *Aria*, my old Buzzards Bay 25-footer designed by Francis Herreshoff's father. (The *Aria* was described in *More Good Boats*.) There is no doubt in my mind that the *Aria* would sail rings around the *Arete*, but the *Aria* was designed as an out-and-out racing boat. I never thought of the *Aria* as being at all hard to handle, but the Rozinante, by comparison, with her three little toy sails, is absurdly easy to handle.

I guess the most instructive sail I had in the *Arete* was the day Dana and Dorothy Sheldon and I went out for a couple of hours in the afternoon when it was blowing a gale out of the north-northwest. It was calm enough in the harbor, but out on the bay you could see little else but good-sized white breaking crests. We gave her the jib and mizzen and ventured forth. She poked her nose out around Sherman Point and began climbing over the steep head seas, still protected by the hills from the full strength of the wind. We laid her up close-hauled on the port tack and slanted out into the worst of it to see what she would do.

Well, she did just amazingly well. A couple of crests broke maybe six inches over the bow, but this foamy stuff washing aft was breakwatered away by the pointed forward end of the house. There was a bit of spray flying back over the cockpit now and then, but that was far more the exception than the rule. In the hardest gusts,

she put her lee rail perhaps just under, but it was clear she wasn't about to be overpowered with that amount of sail in that amount of breeze, and she was never in danger of shipping water into the cockpit to leeward. Best of all, she drove to windward at as much speed as you wanted in that sea, and she had the power to keep accelerating in the hardest gusts of all.

We all agreed it was difficult to estimate the strength of the wind that day, because it wasn't steady. It was what you think of as blowing 35 or perhaps 40 knots, but that really means that it probably never blew less than 15 or 20 and gusted to 35 or 40. Probably some of the short bursts were a bit heavier.

It was grand going, but my agreement with Ted had been one of caretaking, not testing to destruction, so before long we tacked and hightailed it home. Off the wind, she was as docile as a lamb and steered no harder than she ever does.

Another interesting time was beating out past Whitehead Island at the south end of the Mussel Ridge Channel on a sail from Camden to Friendship. It was blowing 25 to 30 knots; we had her under jib and mizzen. We had just picked up a nice fair tide. "Nice" is probably the wrong word, because that current did a good job of heaping up the head seas as it poured out of the Mussel Ridge. The roughest water lasted only 500 yards, and Bob Howard and I were about to congratulate ourselves on getting through it in one piece when a couple of seas must have combined into one and along came a high, steep, freaky-looking thing. The *Arete* climbed it with equanimity, but then her bow fell down into the huge gaping hole on the far side of it and her stern pounded down on the back side of it with a jarring crash. As the stern dropped away from Bob, leaving him hanging onto the coaming six inches above the cockpit seat, he shouted, "Some . . ." And as he caught up with the seat again, out came, " . . . boat!" At the same time, I was thinking, "Some wave!" But Bob was right. The boat certainly was more remarkable than the wave. It took me a little time to realize what had happened. Usually when the bow of a boat dives into the ocean and there's a great crash, it means her bow has pounded. But the *Arete* didn't pound

The Arete *working out of Camden's inner harbor. (Bill Page)*

her bow; she dove into that hole beyond the big sea, finally fetched up on its bottom, pitched back the other way, and whaled the backside of the receding sea with her stern. In the old days, she would have been saying, "Take that! you sunuvabitch," but in this enlightened era, I suppose she was saying something like, "I am very upset with you because you display your power like that and toss me about and I become quite anxious." Either way, old ocean ain't going to do nothin' but just keep on heapin' up and rollin'.

I never had the *Arete* running in a heavy following sea. Her stern is so fine you wonder if it would always lift in time. Ted Sprague says he hasn't run her off in really rough water either, but as an experienced inlet runner, he wonders how she'd do in such conditions. My guess is she'd do just fine, but it's only a guess.

But now we come to the real crunch of thinking about this wonderful Rozinante as a boat for sailing in rough water. Francis Herreshoff wrote, "Best of all a canoe yawl can be about the safest vessel that can be had since her design is based on those most seaworthy open boats ever known — whaleboats. Rozinante is a partly decked-over whaleboat with a ballast keel that will make her non-capsizable." Clearly this statement is made in the context of coastwise cruising and daysailing, not offshore pas-

sagemaking, yet still it may be a bit too strong. After all, the Rozinante is basically an open boat carrying around a big chunk of lead. If a large quantity of water enters her cockpit opening, she will sink like a stone. The question is, of course, what is the risk of that happening on a boat that is to be sailed coastwise, not across oceans? That question leads to the related one, "What is the likelihood of being caught out?" Will the Rozinante ever be caught so far from shelter that she cannot escape the wrath of a rising gale before the seas get really big and dangerous? Well, I for one am willing to take that risk, because if I find myself in that situation, I will have made so many consecutive errors in judgment — not to mention having lost sight of the very purpose of cruising — that I will deserve to lose the vessel and drown.

Keep the Rozinante within striking distance of protected water and she will, I believe, stand as much wind and sea as she will encounter.

Now, through all these words, I hope you haven't lost the feeling of the *Arete's* lovely, pointed stern, slipping away and away through the water. When you leave her to row ashore in the dinghy, examine that stern. Get its shape really in your mind. And then pull up ahead and look at the Rozinante from right forward. Can it be that that little slip of a skinny thing has carried us so far? She has.

2/ The *Ayesha*

> **Length overall: 26 feet 9 inches**
> **Length on waterline: 25 feet**
> **9 inches**
> **Beam: 7 feet 6 inches**
> **Depth: 3 feet 3 inches**
> **Sail area: 379 square feet**

Which of us boat dreamers hasn't dreamed of getting a hold of a nice wooden ship's lifeboat, giving her a keel, putting a rig and some bunks into her, and going cruising?

Many sailors have so dreamed, and many have done it. One who comes to mind is Rockwell Kent, who hoisted a lifeboat off the deck of a steamer in southern Chile, fixed her up for cruising, did considerable sailing in the fascinating channels near the tip of South America, and wrote and illustrated with his woodcuts a nice book about the adventure called, simply, *Voyaging*.

Many designs have been published suggesting how to convert a lifeboat from a craft to provide safety to many people on a stormy sea into a boat in which a mere handful can cruise in some comfort on waters and at a time of their own choosing. None is better, in my opinion, than the plans worked out 70 years ago by Sidney Newlands Graham.

This Scotsman was given a clinker-built ship's lifeboat and decided to convert her into a cruising boat with the help of his good friend, C. G. McGregor. As a matter of fact, Mr. Graham was given his choice of two lifeboats that were being discarded from a liner. He felt

he selected wisely, for when he came to pick up the boat of his choice, "a firewood merchant was busy with the other." He described his windfall as being "in reasonably good condition."

He named the boat aptly the *Ayesha,* after the favorite wife of Mohammed, who was said to have been very astute and always able to make the best of a tricky situation.

The *Ayesha* has the traditional, dignified look of her type, what with her hollow ends, nice sheerline, plumb — though not quite straight — stem, and raked sternpost. The very first thing Messrs. Graham and McGregor did after acquiring the craft was to take off her lines and record her shape on paper. They found she was 26 feet 9 inches long overall, with a waterline length of 25 feet 9 inches, a beam of 7 feet 6 inches, and a depth — not draft — of 3 feet 3 inches.

Next, the two boyish dreamers sketched out plans for rigs, cabin houses, and interior arrangements until they came up with a set they liked. Then they rolled up their sleeves and went to work on the boat, propped up in a shed near the Clyde.

They gutted her but left in the thwarts to hold

her sides together until the deck beams should go in.

They put a keelson inside the boat 9 inches wide and 2¼ inches deep. They fitted 4-inch-by-1¼-inch bilge stringers 20 feet long. They put in deck beams, built the cabin house, and put in carlins. Then they took out the original thwarts.

They made a pattern for a keel and had it cast in iron. While the casting was being done, they built the steering well.

When the iron keel came back, they built a fairly deep wooden keel and deadwood, tied it all on as strongly as possible, and bolted on the iron keel. The *Ayesha's* draft was now 3 feet 11 inches.

In converting a lifeboat, the construction of the fin keel is vital and is all too often the weak point of the vessel. The Graham-McGregor team used heavy, diagonal, ''garboard'' planks backed, ultimately, by long, heavy floors, which would appear to be a sound, strong construction.

All of this work is described in some detail in an article in the *Yachting and Boating Monthly* for April 1908. Unfortunately, the article was written before the *Ayesha* was launched and tried, so nothing is recorded of her performance under sail. Thus, with my usual audacity, I can speculate on her sailing qualities in the knowledge that, while some may argue with my conjectures, it is unlikely that there is anyone who can say with certainty, ''This is what she did.'' More's the pity.

The great feature of this design is the bold, great keel the Scotsmen put on her. She's right up to date in being a fin-keeler that is cut away fore and aft, though she does lack the modern high-aspect-ratio keel profile of modern racing (and thus of all too many modern cruising) boats, much to her advantage as a cruising boat. Though not as ''efficient'' to windward, she'd have a quality of far greater importance to the cruising person: steadiness on the helm. In fact, she has the symmetry of some other well-known double-ended self-steerers, such as, for instance, the *West Island* (see *Good Boats*).

She'd be stiff, for her ballast is fairly low and she has a bit of flare above the waterline throughout her length.

The added acreage of her keel does give her considerable wetted surface, of course, so she might need a main topsail and a balloon jib to do her best in moderate going.

The rig her converters conceived for the *Ayesha* spreads 379 square feet of sail. Her mainsail has 200 square feet; the mizzen, 94; and the jib, 85.

The reefs shown are not exceedingly deep, but there are three in the mainsail and two each in the jib and mizzen. She would balance well under mainsail alone or with jib and reefed main.

The jib is set flying and tacks down to a ring on the bowsprit. You'd want a storm jib cut to set well with the bowsprit traveler in almost against the stem. A lightweight ballooner could be set on the forestay, and with the working jib down out of the way, such a sail could be brought across easily when jibing or for poling out.

All of the running rigging leads aft to the steering well. I'd want more purchase on the mizzen peak halyard than the single part shown. Her topping lifts belay on the booms, but it is much handier to make up the standing part on the boom and lead the running part down the mast. That way it can be reached readily even with the boom broad off.

For newcomers to my prejudices, I'll point out that there ought to be a vang leading from the main gaff through a block at the mizzen masthead and down the mast so the helmsman can easily control the shape of the mainsail, taking the twist out of the sail as if by magic.

I'd set the running backstays a bit farther forward, so they could be left set up when short-tacking.

I suppose experience teaches most of us our pet peeves. Setting up the running backstays on the gaff yawl *Brownie* (another *Good Boat*) was often my job in my growing-up years. The tackle was made up of heavy manila (purchased a bit oversize by my frugal father so it could be relied on for an extra season or two). I can't remember this rope ever being new; in my day, it was always gray and prickly and usually swelled with either spray or rain.

The mainsail bore against the lee backstay a bit if it were left set up, so the stays had to be

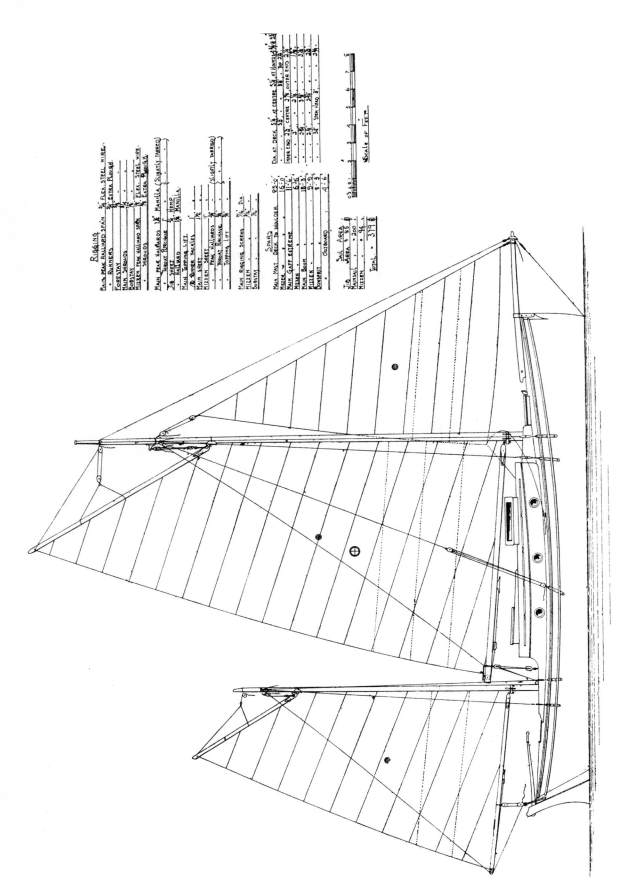

A perfectly good cruising ketch that once merely lay under davits on a ship's boat deck. (The Yachting and Boating Monthly, April 1908)

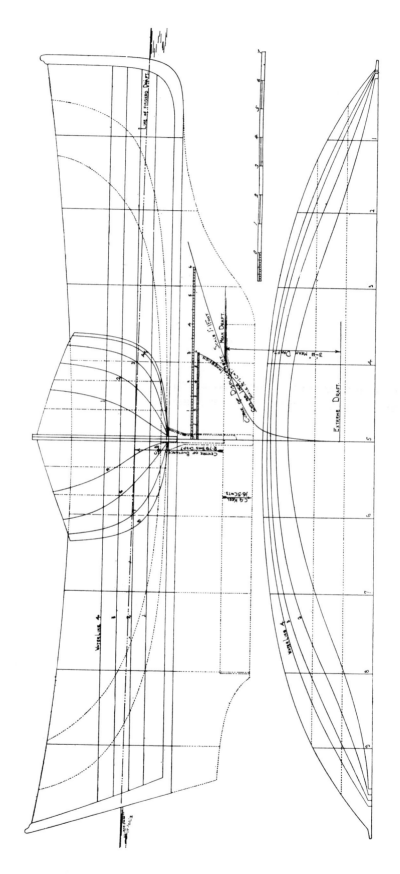

Suspended below her handsome traditional lifeboat lines is a long and fairly deep fin keel. (The Yachting and Boating Monthly, April 1908)

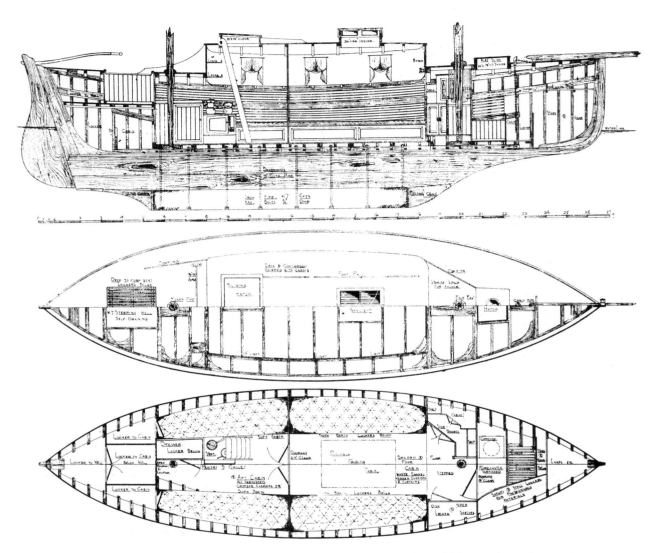

Her companionway has been moved forward just far enough to allow sufficient uncluttered space at the after end of the cabin for the galley. (The Yachting and Boating Monthly, *April 1908*)

slacked and set up on each tack. If Pop let you leave your lee backstay set up for a short hitch, you knew he was feeling unusually generous. Anyway, the job of setting up the new weather backstay was often mine, and rare it was that as the yawl settled onto her new tack Pop would look at the stay and say, "That's the stuff." Mostly, he just made a face, which meant you should have gotten more on it, but he supposed it would have to do. Often enough, he said, "Well, I guess I'll have to give you a luff." Then you'd feel bad because instead of letting her really get going on the new tack, up she'd

have to come again and slow down with everything rattling and banging, while you got in what you should have gotten in the first time.

So, anyway, I vowed the first few thousand times that if ever I had anything to do with it, I'd move running backstays just far enough forward so that even a meticulous master could let his crew leave them both set up when short-tacking. I really think it does make sense. But belay all this. (Yes, I'm afraid it was intentional.)

The *Ayesha* has side decks 14 inches wide, not bad for an ex-lifeboat. There's a breakwater

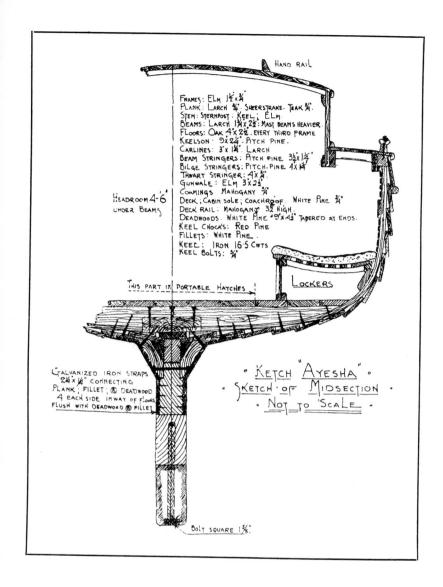

FRAMES: ELM 1½ x ¾.
PLANK: LARCH ¾. SHEERSTRAKE. TEAK ¾.
STEM: STERNPOST. KEEL: ELM.
BEAMS: LARCH 1¾ x 2½ MAST BEAMS HEAVIER.
FLOORS: OAK 4 x 2½. EVERY THIRD FRAME
KEELSON: 9 x 2½. PITCH PINE.
CARLINES: 3 x 1¾. LARCH
BEAM STRINGERS: PITCH PINE 3½ x 1¾
BILGE STRINGERS: PITCH PINE 4 x 1¼
THWART STRINGER: 4 x ¾.
GUNWALE: ELM 3 x 2½
COAMINGS MAHOGANY ¾.
DECK; CABIN SOLE; COACHROOF: WHITE PINE ¾"
DECK RAIL: MAHOGANY 3¾ HIGH.
DEADWOODS. WHITE PINE 9 x 4½ TAPERED AT ENDS.
KEEL CHOCKS: RED PINE
FILLETS: WHITE PINE.
KEEL: IRON 16·5 CWTS
KEEL BOLTS: ¾"

HAND RAIL

HEADROOM 4-6
UNDER BEAMS

THIS PART IN PORTABLE HATCHES !

LOCKERS

GALVANIZED IRON STRAPS
2¼ x ¼" CONNECTING
PLANK; FILLET; (&) DEADWOOD
4 EACH SIDE IN WAY OF FLOORS
FLUSH WITH DEADWOOD (&) FILLET

KETCH "AYESHA"
SKETCH OF MIDSECTION
NOT TO SCALE

BOLT SQUARE 1⅛"

The construction of the keel is of interest. Note the diagonal ''garboard'' planks lending their strength to the structure. (The Yachting and Boating Monthly, April 1908)

between the forward hatch and the house, which makes a handy place to keep stuff from going adrift.

The coaming protecting the steering well ends rather abruptly, it seems to me. The helmsman has nothing to lean back against, and furthermore, any spray coming aboard on the weather side will inevitably give him a wet seat of the pants. I'd want to continue the coaming on aft and let it intersect with the rail. In the stern, she has a locker for life jackets.

The companionway arrangement is unusual. She has a true hatchway down through the top of the cabin house, with the after end of the house left solid. This rig has two advantages and

only the disadvantage that you have to do some stepping up over. If she should be pooped, it would be much harder for the water to get below than with the usual companionway arrangement. Also, this design allows for far more use of the space under the bridge deck, in this case for the galley between the after ends of the after transoms. The stowage space beneath the steering well opens into the galley, so the cooking area is reasonably commodious, and the whole thing has been all but stolen, for in many a boat the comparable space is put to far less vital uses.

Doors separate the forward and after cabins. This arrangement is very British and very sensible. The British are used to living in less space, as a rule, than we Americans. They gain privacy not by sheer distance from each other but by the installation and actual use of doors. Enter an Englishman's living room for a casual conversation and he'll surprise you by shutting the living room door tight behind you. So, doubtless, would Mr. Graham and Mr. Mc-Gregor if you went aboard the *Ayesha* to interview them about their clever conversion. Before you knew it you'd be shut into their snug saloon for a good, uninterrupted look 'round.

You'd find headroom of 4 feet 6 inches, for this fin-keeler started life, after all, as a shoal-bodied lifeboat. The saloon table is portable and can be folded up and stowed away either forward or aft. There's plenty of stowage space in the forward end of the saloon.

Tucked away forward out of the way, as it should be, is the W.C.

It's not often that we know just how a boat is painted without being able to see the vessel herself. Mr. Graham wrote up his painting scheme, however, so here it is: "Outside we propose painting her all white, as a boot-topping would not look very well with clinker.

Construction inside the forecastle and after cabin will be red-leaded, and the bulkheads and sofa fronts varnished; the fore-cabin will be in white enamel, with green matchings, and crimson in the after-cabin. On deck the canvas will be painted cream or pale ochre, the cabin-top white, and the remainder varnished." Now, how many ship's lifeboats do you know with crimson matchings in the after-cabin?

Mr. Graham's conclusion to his article is also worth quoting: "In conclusion, I may say that altering a boat is not so simple as the various fireside discussions make it out to be, yet there is great pleasure and interest in the work. We started with a good outfit of tools, and devoted on an average four nights a week to our workshop, starting at seven and finishing at from ten thirty to eleven o'clock. Now we can look forward to the time when we will be afloat and can still spend our spare time on her, but in her natural element."

So don't throw away your old wooden ship's lifeboats; make them — as did Sidney Graham and C.G. McGregor — into handsome and able cruising ketches.

3/ The *Sans Souci*

> **Length on deck: 32 feet**
> **Length on waterline: 27 feet**
>   **6 inches**
> **Beam: 7 feet 8 inches**
> **Draft: 11 inches**
> **Sail area: 445 square feet**
> **Displacement: 4,450 pounds**
> **Designer: Thomas E. Colvin**

Thomas E. Colvin is one of those smart people who has worked things out so he can live on board a boat all he wants and do plenty of long-range cruising, or not, as the spirit moves him and his family. He has a wonderful junk built to his own design.

Before Tom had his life quite so well organized, he designed a rakish, able sharpie for his own more limited use. He called her the *Sans Souci*, "without a care," and that is, of course, a very good name for a sharpie, for she is far simpler to build, maintain, and sail than any other kind of boat that will do what she will do. Simplicity afloat leads to carefree cruising.

Tom has had a lot of experience with the sharpie type. He wrote me such an interesting letter about the *Sans Souci* that I want to share just about the whole thing with you:

> I am enclosing a rolled lines plan for *Sans Souci.* You will note there are several different vessels shown on this plan. I built the first one with the boards — after two years of sailing she came on the market and I purchased her and converted her to a keel model, and sold her to Florida. In the meantime I also built a centerboard model with the centerboard offset from the centerline of the vessel. She was

sold to South America. Next came *Josepha,* a keel model in steel and a clipper bow, but gaff rigged. These vessels are very smart sailers and it was difficult for me to determine if the centerboard was faster than the keel version. I developed an intense dislike for leeboards, as I dislike the noise associated with them, also the nuisance in short tacking in shoal water.

Since the original hull built in 1962 there have been 60 or so of them built in the U.S. as well as 16 other countries. These vessels have been very popular in Australia and New Zealand, with the British Isles and Europe a close second.

Several have been used for light freighting between islands and for fishing — these vessels were all center boarders but the centerboard was on the centerline in true sharpie fashion and bulkheads at each end of the trunk, thus having a division of the hold area. They could normally carry about two tons, but I did see one in Surinam loaded with goods and 20 or so persons to about 2 inches of freeboard. I commented about this to the captain, who allowed that 'they hadn't loaded her down as they expected some bad weather.'

My sharpie designs are of greater hull depth than the true New Haven sharpie, following the practice of my family, and are therefore drier in a seaway and from family notes much better in general, except for oystering.

Tom Colvin.

While I *do not* recommend the small sharpies for long ocean passages (under 45 feet), this has more to do with the minimum volume, minimum headroom, and the necessity of always having to sail them. In the larger sizes, stability and comfort are almost automatic. I have, however, made several long voyages in small sharpies — Florida to Trinidad and return in a 24-foot hull, with 9-inch draft. My wife and I rode out a hurricane at sea in a 40-foot sharpie — safe enough, but I would rather not repeat the experience.

The *Sans Souci* has been rigged as a jib-headed ketch, gaff ketch, standing lug, Chinese lug, New Haven spritsail, Florida spritsail and Florida gaff. One was temporarily rigged as a Bahamian sloop, but the rig proved too powerful for her.

All in all, the sharpie still offers the most for the money, but only as long as the original simplicity is adhered to. With the addition of auxiliary engines, bronze fittings, standing rigging or exotic woods, the cost soars out of proportion to the end product, and often destroys their inherent fine sailing ability.

That point Tom Colvin makes about having to sail a sharpie all the time is worth noting; the *Sans Souci* is not a boat to be left to her own devices in heavy going. Despite the occasional heroics performed by sharpies offshore in heavy weather, they are not at their best in such conditions. Other types are better for offshore sailing; where the sharpie comes into her own is, of course, in shallow water.

Of the various modifications to the *Sans Souci*

design that Tom mentions, I'd prefer the one with the offset centerboard. (The board goes down alongside the keel, instead of through the middle of it, so that the slot is a bit up out of harm's way when the boat is lying on the bottom, hopefully to foil the efforts of small stones to wedge themselves up between board and trunk.)

Tandem centerboards, one forward and one aft, have great appeal in a boat like this. While the forward trunk might bring unwanted bundling to the double berth, the after one, back in the watertight cockpit, might be kept low enough to make an admirable drain.

A keel sharpie just doesn't make any sense to me. You throw away the great advantage of the type — extremely shoal draft — in return for getting rid of a centerboard or leeboards. If shoal draft is not a requirement, it's better to have a boat designed with a keel in the first place than to hang a keel on a type whose every characteristic was developed so a keel wouldn't be necessary.

Merely as a matter of appearance, I prefer the plumb bow of the *Sans Souci* to the clipper-bowed version, I suppose perhaps subconsciously because the plumb bow is part of her ancestral heritage handed down from the New Haven sharpie.

The *Sans Souci* is 32 feet long on deck, with a waterline length of 27 feet 6 inches, a beam of 7 feet 8 inches, and a draft of 11 inches. Her sail area is 445 square feet, and she displaces 4,450 pounds. She has 1,000 pounds of inside ballast, which, of course, is vital to her general health and well-being. Her ballast is in the form of 60-pound lead pigs boxed in on her bottom along the centerline.

There is just nothing to her under water. My, but wouldn't she fly off the wind! She has a very high waterline-length-to-displacement ratio. She's very narrow, but the flare in her topsides would help her stability considerably, and her generous rig has been kept low.

With her balanced rudder, she'd steer mighty easily and would certainly turn quickly enough. If you were standing forward, you'd want to know the tiller was held by a friend. The shoal rudder shown on the inboard profile drawing would be fine until, on a broad reach in a breeze, a following sea lifted her stern high enough so the thing lost its grip just when you didn't want it to. The old-timers had these rudders rigged on the New Haven sharpies so the whole rudder could be lowered in such conditions. Francis Herreshoff solved the problem on his Meadowlark sharpie design by giving the rudder a pivoting retractable blade.

The round sharpie stern, planked vertically, has always appealed to me greatly as a handsome shape and is so on this design, in my opinion, even with the increased freeboard.

The bottom of the *Sans Souci* is, of course, cross-planked. Her topsides are carvel planked over white oak framing. Her deck is plywood covered with fiberglass. The sides of the cabin house are mahogany.

The rig of the *Sans Souci* certainly looks handy. Her mainsail has 189 square feet; the mizzen, 137; and the jib, 129.

Her only standing rigging is her headstay and her bobstay. The centerboard version of this boat would be a delight to short-tack, with nothing to touch but the tiller.

In a breeze, you'd have to shorten sail; the *Sans Souci* will only live up to her name if you don't try to drive her. You'd want to leave the mizzen clew reef earings all rove off. She'd balance under jib and mizzen, especially with the mizzen reefed. She'd also balance under mainsail alone and would be very handy with just that sail, though you couldn't expect her to do a lot to windward as a catboat.

The outboard end of the jib club is on a slide so you can adjust the curvature of the sail's foot. You'd slide the club all the way forward when lowering the sail so it wouldn't bind on the stay. You'd want a topping lift and downhaul on this sail. And lazy jacks on main and mizzen.

She could have a great sort of fisherman staysail to hang up between the masts, as did some of the Chesapeake Bay bugeyes. The peak would go to the mizzen masthead, the throat would be, say, a little more than halfway up the mainmast, and the sail would sheet to the stern. Such generous light-air stuff makes great good sense on a boat with no engine.

When even that gossamer sail fell limp, you could get out your yuloh, if in deep water, or your quant, if in shoal.

Notice the nice shape of the cabin house on the *Sans Souci*. It's just right, with its round for-

FAIR WINDS FROM KUNG FU-TSE

When you write to Tom Colvin, the reply comes on this postcard from whatever port where the vessel pictured may have called. (Thomas E. Colvin)

ward end raked back perpendicular to the sheerline like the boat's stem, its sheered sides, and its round portholes of just the right size. That house is a fine detail that helps give the boat her handsome good looks.

Below, she has, naturally, just sitting headroom. I'd want to put a hatch in the top of the cabin house on the centerline in front of the stove. That would give you another place besides the companionway to stand up for a stretch. Don't forget the main boom, though! On a rainy day, it could be topped up with a tarp over it.

The after berths make an interesting arrangement. They will sleep three children (one athwartships) or two adults.

There's a 25-gallon water tank under the forward port berth. She has a W.C. under the star-

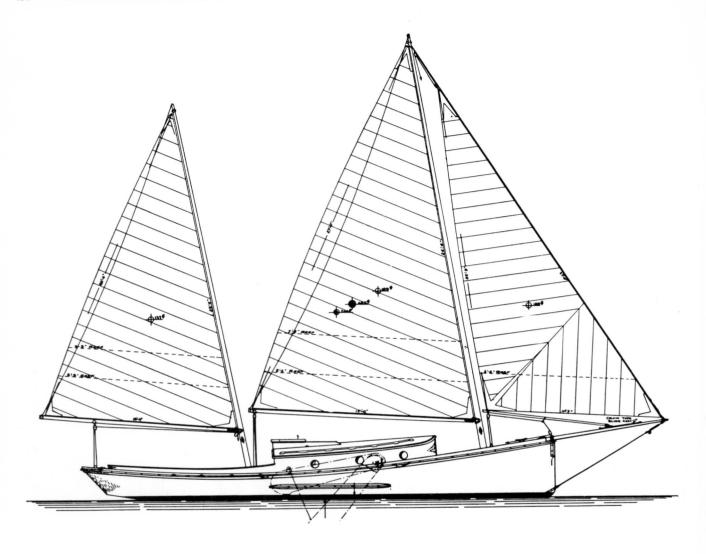

Tom Colvin gave the Sans Souci *a handsome profile.* (Yachting, *February 1964*)

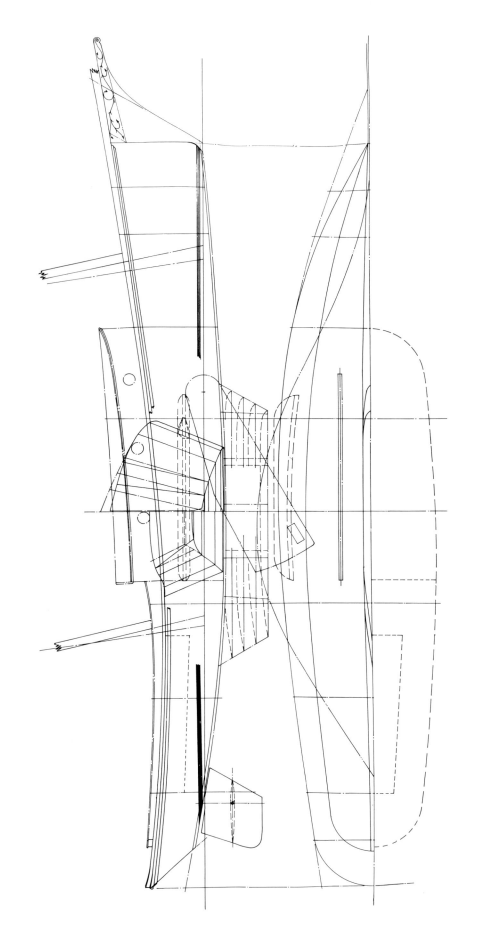

Her underbody is almost nonexistent when she is upright; she'd be some flyer off the wind. (Thomas E. Colvin)

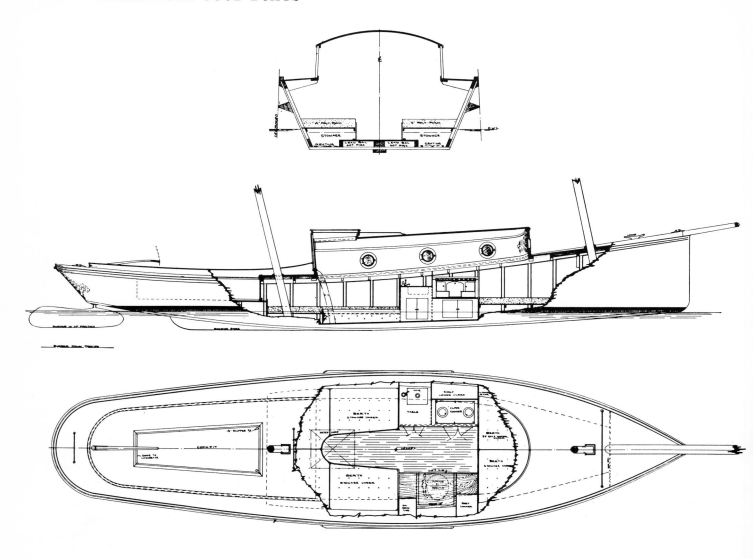

Her snug cabin has all the amenities, including room to sit up straight. You might want another hatch in the cabin house. (Yachting, February 1964)

board seat, but you'd want a bucket, too, for versatility. (I am always amazed when a boat puts to sea without a bucket. No marine head or bilge pump can compete with it at all.)

I think the *Sans Souci* is a fine daysailer and cruising boat for two. She would also make an admirable singlehander. Her flat bottom is great for beaching or drying out, and imaginative people could find a lot of seclusion in her, even on a crowded coast. Yes, she can pound in a seaway, but yes, she can also be put on a trailer fairly readily so as to spend time in distant cruising grounds.

The *Sans Souci* would indeed give carefree cruising if, as her creator Tom Colvin suggests, she is kept simple. She'd also be fast and handy. And she has a wonderful rakish look that is almost piratical.

4/ The *Ingrid*

> **Length on deck: 37 feet 6 inches**
> **Length on waterline: 30 feet**
> **Beam: 11 feet 4 inches**
> **Draft: 5 feet 6 inches**
> **Sail area: 816 square feet**
> **Displacement: 12½ tons**
> **Designer: William W. Atkin**

The readers of the old *Motor Boating* magazine got a good deal. Every month, William W. Atkin would design another fine cruising vessel, just for them.

His monthly articles on boat designs weren't just casual commentaries about somebody else's designs; each one was an article about a boat whose design he had created from scratch himself, and the accompanying plans were all painstakingly drawn by him. They included not only an outboard profile and sail plan, lines, and plan and elevation of the cabin arrangement, but also a detailed construction plan in plan view and elevation with a number of sections thrown in for good measure. And the table of offsets. Month after month. A number of these monthly designs have become classics.

You can recognize them, because Billy Atkin had some trademarks: whatever the hull form, the boat would be ruggedly handsome; the sides of her cabin house would be straight with no curves at all and would be pierced by small, round portholes; and her masts would stand straight up without much rake.

One such classic was the ketch *Ingrid,* a much-refined Colin Archer redningsskoite type.

Enough has been written recently about these Norwegian sailing lifeboats so that it would be repetitious to describe the *Ingrid's* ancestors here. There is John Leather's book *Colin Archer and the Seaworthy Double-Ender.* Three vessels related to the redningsskoite have been described earlier in this *Good Boats* series: Phil Rhodes' *Tidal Wave* in *Good Boats;* and Manuel Campos' *Gaucho* and Billy Atkin's own *Eric* in *More Good Boats.*

The *Ingrid* is 37 feet 6 inches long on deck, with a waterline length of 30 feet, a beam of 11 feet 4 inches, and a draft of 5 feet 6 inches. She displaces 12½ tons and has 6 tons of ballast, 4½ tons in an iron keel and 1½ tons inside. Her sail area is 816 square feet.

I think the *Ingrid* has a beautifully developed set of lines. She has a hollow entry and fairly fine waterlines aft. Note that above the waterline the bow has considerable flare. Her bow and buttock lines are easy.

She has a nice wineglass-shaped midsection, and her sections are all curves, like a boat from the Baltic. She has flare all around just above the waterline curving back to tumblehome at the rail.

Billy Atkin in 1950. (John Atkin)

She is much finer and sharper than her redningsskoite ancestors and would sail the better for the changes, giving up in return the extreme buoyancy that allowed the redningsskoites to live through some frightful experiences on Norway's winter coast.

The *Ingrid* has a gentle sheerline. Would that her house had some sheer. I think a very slight dipping curve in the top edge of her cabin house would change her from a merely handsome boat to a really pretty one. That's one of Billy Atkin's trademarks with which I wish he had dispensed.

Her long, iron keel gives her extremely good protection for taking the ground, either intentionally or unintentionally. It's held on by 10 1¼-inch bolts.

Her wood keel is specified to be of yellow pine or white oak, 10 inches by 16 inches in section. The space between her floors is filled in with cement to a depth of five inches; Mr. Atkin warned that the cement must go directly onto bare wood.

Her frames are of oak, doubled, with one set inside the other to finish 2½ inches square on 12-inch centers. Clamp and shelf are each 1¾ inches by 6 inches, of yellow pine or fir.

Billy Atkin called for planking of 1¼-inch white cedar and ceiling of ⅞-inch white pine.

Her deck beams are of oak, 2 inches by 2½ inches. There's a diagonal brass strap, 6 inches by ⅛ inch, on deck in way of the mainmast to keep the deck from wringing. Her deck is laid in white pine, 1½ inches by 2 inches.

Her house is 1¾-inch white pine, or mahogany if you want to be fancy. The cockpit sole is a complete watertight platform running out to the sides of the vessel and all the way aft to the stern.

The *Ingrid* is rigged with tall, narrow sails, with the mainsail being especially tall and narrow. She has a lot of feet of masts for her sail area. The 816 square feet is broken down as follows: mainsail, 346; mizzen, 185; staysail, 123; and jib, 162.

Note that the mizzen mast steps on the cockpit sole above the engine. She has a wide traveler for the mizzen sheet, so there is room to swing the tiller.

Her mainmast tapers from a maximum of 7 inches, the mizzen from 6 inches. The heftiest part of her bowsprit is 5½ inches in diameter.

Each single-part jib sheet has its own comealong on deck abaft the fairleads. She has enough area in her headsails and mizzen to get her to windward in a strong breeze without the mainsail. On the other hand, she will balance nicely with the mainsail alone when off the wind or for jilling around the harbor.

Think what a huge balloon jib she could carry!

Billy Atkin told his readers what they ought to carry on boats of his design in the way of ground tackle. This was back in the days before the Patent Office was flooded with ideas about featherweight anchors, so he was talking about anchors designed on a pattern seamen developed before the Patent Office bought its first inkwell. For the *Ingrid,* Mr. Atkin said you ought to have an 80-pounder and a 40-pounder, with 300 feet of ⅜-inch chain for the former and 200 feet of ⁵⁄₁₆-inch chain for the latter. Amen.

Billy Atkin really didn't want to get into the business of recommending specific engines, but he did allow as how a Gray 6-40 with a two-bladed, non-feathering wheel would shove the *Ingrid* along at 7½ miles per hour. Note that her propeller shaft is horizontal, another Atkin trademark.

She has a 30-gallon fuel tank under each

The Ingrid Princess, built and owned by Blue Water Boats, smoking along. (Jerry Husted)

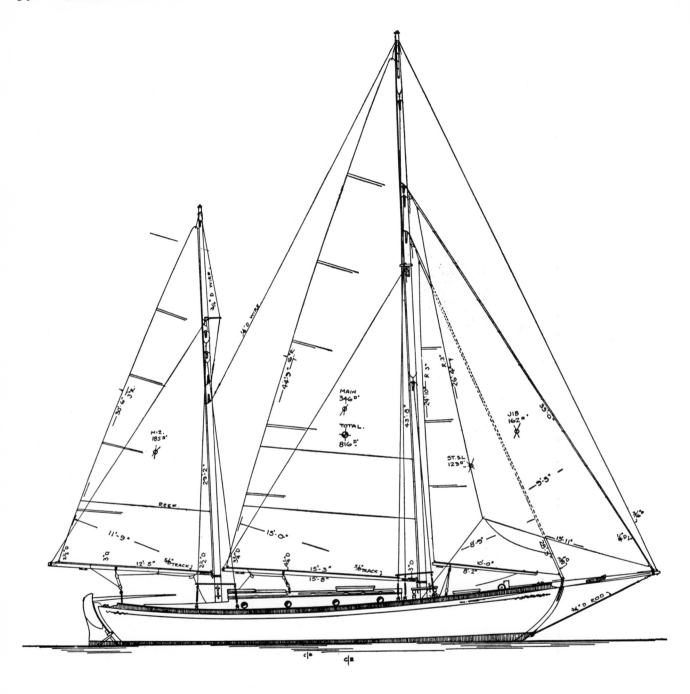

The Ingrid *is one of the best of Billy Atkin's double-ended ketches, designed for the readers of* Motor Boating *magazine a half century or so ago.* (Workable Plans for Practical Boats, *edited by Charles F. Chapman*)

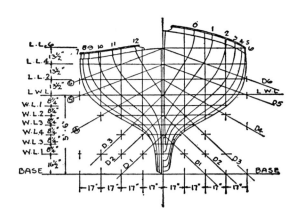

Below and Right: *She shows the influence of her redningsskoite ancestors, but she is a highly refined granddaughter.* (Workable Plans for Practical Boats, *edited by Charles F. Chapman*) **Bottom:** *Mr. Atkin always provided a detailed construction plan of his designs.* (Workable Plans for Practical Boats, *edited by Charles F. Chapman*)

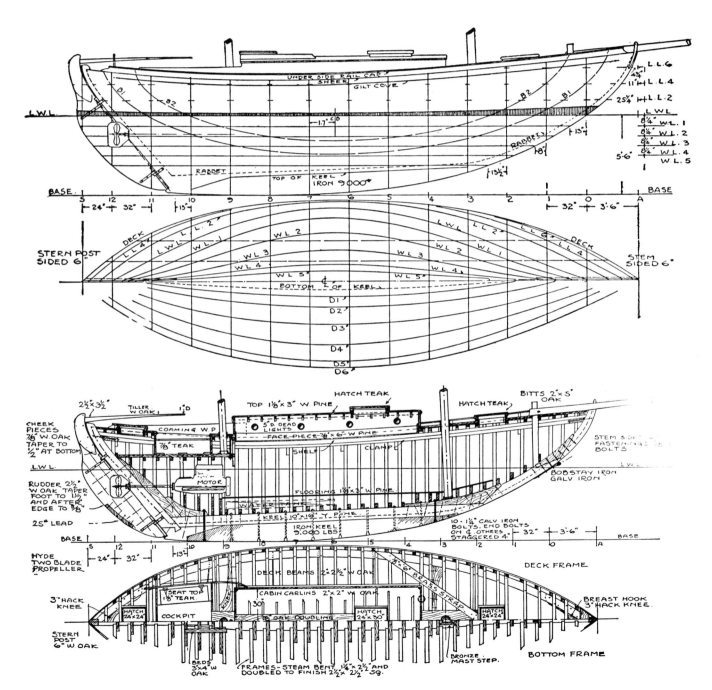

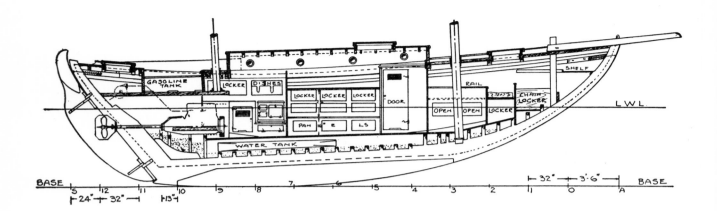

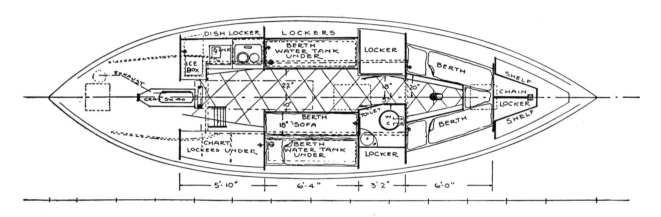

With a waterline of 30 feet, the Ingrid *is big enough so that her tried-and-true cabin arrangement has those nice little extras. (Workable Plans for Practical Boats, edited by Charles F. Chapman)*

cockpit seat. There's a big, long water tank in the bilge, and two more water tanks under the transoms in the saloon.

With her narrow house, the *Ingrid* has something like three feet clearance between the house and the rail. What a pleasure to walk forward on such a boat! Below, she has what might be described as a standard arrangement plan, with a forward stateroom, head, and hanging locker next aft, saloon amidships, and galley and chart table aft.

She has the best of all possible arrangements for the main cabin, with two seats of different widths, and two bunks, one of which is a sea berth that can be left made up.

She has fairly low freeboard and a low house, yet she's big enough to have six feet of headroom. Her chart table is nearly six feet long. In the head, the wash basin drains into the toilet, a sensible arrangement that saves an overboard discharge.

The *Ingrid* has a pretty hull, and her tall rig and fairly long bowsprit give her considerable grace, in my opinion. She would certainly be a seakindly vessel with an easy motion. Her design is a remarkable achievement just taken by itself. That she is, in a sense, merely a monthly product indicates a prolificacy on the part of William W. Atkin that I find mind-boggling.

5/ A Crocker Ketch

> **Length on deck: 40 feet**
> **Length on waterline: 33 feet**
> **10 inches**
> **Beam: 10 feet 11 inches**
> **Draft: 6 feet**
> **Sail area: 968 square feet**
> **Designer: S.S. Crocker, Jr.**

I have been utterly fascinated with the Mystic Seaport in Connecticut for almost as long as I can remember. Growing up 10 miles away from the place, I was often over there to see what was going on and to admire the latest vessel acquired.

I remember the day the *Joseph Conrad* arrived and being allowed to go on board and help sweep down her main deck. She is a perfect little square-rigger, and to a youngster was some kind of a dream ship. It wasn't good enough to be on board her, tied up in the upper reaches of the Mystic River. At the very least, I had to imagine, while taking in views of her deck and complicated rig from every vantage point, some of the passages she made in Alan Villiers' *Cruise of the Conrad,* when he took her around the world in the Thirties. I particularly remember the tediousness of beating her up through the Sulu Sea with its frustrating variable airs and anxious navigation. It was an exhausting mental exercise, even when you had the very vessel herself to help you.

Nowadays, I am more likely to be at the Seaport on some publishing errand or for some committee meeting. Don't worry, I always sneak away to admire the ships and boats. The other thing I always try to do is find some time to spend in the stacks of the Seaport's wonderful library. I head right for the magazine section, where they have bound full runs of *Yachting, The Rudder,* and the rest. That's where you can find plenty of good boats.

Not long ago, I ran into a Sam Crocker design I'd never seen before. She is a handsome and able cruising ketch that he designed in 1922. Her lines show a hull that would be seakindly, and she is fine enough to have a good turn of speed.

When you dust off this design back there in the library stacks, you find that she is 40 feet long on deck, has a waterline length of 33 feet 10 inches, a beam of 10 feet 11 inches, and draft of 6 feet. Her sail area is 968 square feet.

I think she has a well-drawn sheerline, well-balanced ends drawn out visually by her bowsprit and boomkin, a pretty curve to her stem, a nice rake to her curved transom, and, all in all, a very handsome profile.

She has plenty of lateral plane. She has a good run. And she has a fine, hollow entrance, but with considerable buoyancy in the bow

Sam Crocker.
(S. Sturgis Crocker)

above the waterline. Her sections are quite shapely.

That big, deep rudder — hung outdoors for simplicity — is needed, for it is narrow and its post has considerable rake.

The ketch has plenty of working sail area; there is no need for light stuff unless you want to bother with it just for fun. Her mainsail has 436 square feet; the mizzen, 303; the fore staysail, 100; and the jib, 129. I like those three reefs in the mainsail, so you can shorten her right down. The sail cries out, of course, for a vang on the gaff led to the mizzen masthead and down to the cockpit.

You'd want to leave your mizzen reefing gear all rove off, so you wouldn't have to take a leave of absence to pull the clew out, and if she's really jumping, never mind those last two reef points.

Note that she has both topping lifts and lazy jacks; she's big enough to deserve them.

Of course there are plenty of places to hang up light sails if you want to show somebody your heels on a light day. She'd love a balloon fore staysail, a high-cut overlapping jib, and a main topsail with its jackyard extending 15 feet above the masthead. (If you're going to crowd on sail, you might as well go ahead and do it.)

Note that the jumper stay on the mizzen mast apparently runs to the cockpit floor. That may be an error in the plan; you'd think it would return to the mast just below the gooseneck to be less obstructive.

The ketch has plenty of deck space. Her house is only moderately long and is quite narrow.

Her boomkin looks long enough, but if it were even 2½ feet longer, you could use it as a cradle for a nine-foot dinghy to be hoisted out using the mizzen boom as a derrick.

The mizzen mast in the middle of the cockpit is an obstruction, to be sure, but it does have its advantages. Nobody's going to fall across the cockpit of this boat, lurch though she may, and it makes a wonderful place to stand leaning and watch her go.

She has no fewer than three hatches down into the engine room from the bridge deck. There is a big flush one right over the engine itself, flanked by smaller square ones with coamings. Miraculously, none of the three is in way of the companion hatch, so that even if all three were left open and someone rushed on deck from below, he'd still have a chance of surviving. If you had Ralph Wiley's companion ladder arrangement of two vertical ladders — one on

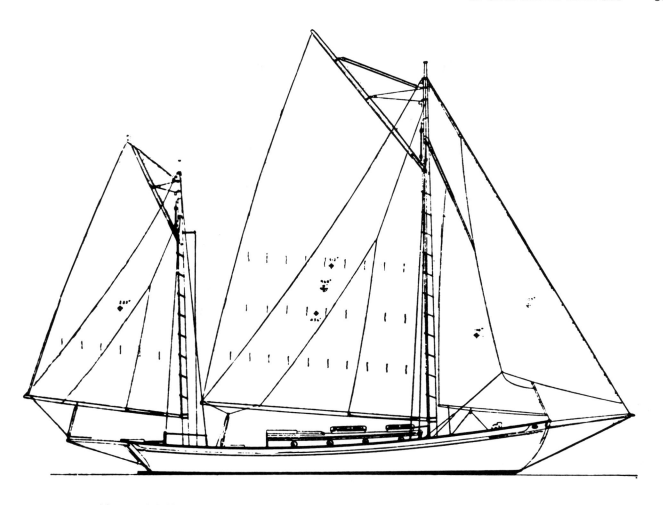

Above: *A half century ago, cruising boats carried quite a lot of working sail area. Not a bad idea.* (Yachting, *December 1922*). **Below:** *The lines of the Crocker ketch show a vessel with a nice combination of seaworthiness and reasonable speed.* (Yachting, *December 1922*)

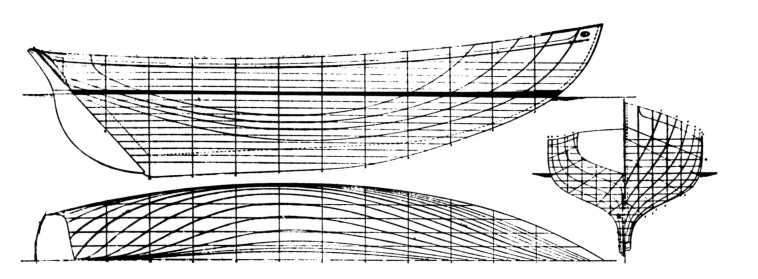

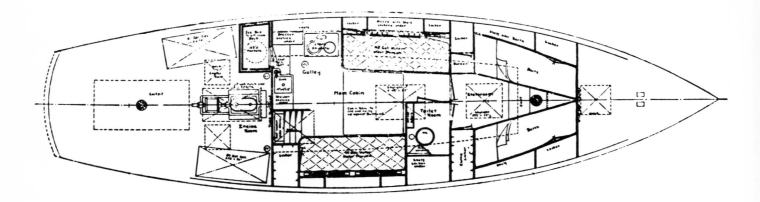

She is nicely laid out with plenty of room for up to four people for cruising, or two people for living on board. (Yachting, *December 1922*)

either side of the companionway — then you could have a door between them leading into the engine room so you could go back and forth on a rainy day without moving any ladders or getting wet.

Her tanks are big. In the engine room are two 80-gallon fuel tanks, which would certainly give her considerable range under power. Under the saloon transoms are two 45-gallon water tanks.

Her L-shaped galley is an admirable arrangement. She has a big icebox, which fills from the deck, and in front of it is a thwartships seat. That's a great idea. What a fine place in which to chock yourself off while waiting for the water to boil or while peeling the spuds.

How do you like her asymmetrical main cabin? I think the staggered arrangement of the transoms with galley and head in diagonally opposite corners makes sense. It gives a bit more

of a sense of privacy to the place, with somewhat separate corners for different activities. Her big skylights would let in plenty of light and air. The cabin table folds and swings up against the bulkhead, thus opening up plenty of floor space when wanted.

She has lots of shelves and lockers. There are two big hanging lockers, one aft by the companionway and one in the forward stateroom.

Her forward bunks are a bit farther aft than is often the case, which would help out if you were trying to sleep up there in a head sea.

Her separate little fo'c's'le would make a really fine bosun's locker.

Taken all in all, I think this Crocker ketch is an admirable cruising vessel for two to four people. She'd also be a fine boat for living aboard for two.

She's gathered more dust than she deserves.

6/ The *Yale*

> Length on deck: 43 feet
> Length on waterline: 33 feet
>   4 inches
> Beam: 11 feet 8 inches
> Draft: 6 feet 6 inches
> Sail area: 874 square feet
> Designer: Charles D. Mower

Sir Wilfred Grenfell began his illustrious career with five years of ministering — in both the medical and the religious sense — to British fishermen working the North Sea. Then in 1892, he established a similar service for the fishermen of Labrador.

Grenfell soon became interested in trying to improve the living conditions of the permanent inhabitants of that cold, rugged stretch of coast, and in 1912 he founded the International Grenfell Association, usually referred to simply as the Grenfell Mission.

When Sir Wilfred retired in 1932 there existed in Labrador, largely because of his efforts, the following facilities: six hospitals; four hospital ships; seven nursing stations; two orphanages; two schools; 14 industrial centers; and a cooperative lumber mill.

The construction, maintenance, and supply of all these outfits naturally required much transport of goods and people. There was no thought of building roads on such a mountainous coast; the obvious way to move stuff was by water.

The Labrador coast was — and is — a tough

place to navigate. Local knowledge is more important than the chart; unmarked dangers abound; and the weather, even during the summer and fall navigation season, is quick to change, usually from bad to atrocious. The vessels sailing in such an environment must be able indeed.

Such a vessel, the ketch *Yale,* was designed for service in Labrador in 1910 by Charles D. Mower. Mr. Mower is probably best remembered for his long, low, fast yachts, but he demonstrated his versatility with the design of the *Yale;* she's no Long Island Sound racer.

It is interesting, though, to compare the design of the *Yale* with that of a pure yacht, another double-ended, gaff-rigged ketch of about the same size designed 20 years earlier in Scotland by William Fife: the *Maud,* which was described in *Good Boats.* The *Maud* is a little narrower, a little deeper, has finer waterlines and more sail area. She's probably just as able as the *Yale,* but she couldn't have carried nearly so much.

The *Yale* is certainly a big, husky boat. She has full waterlines, deep buttock lines forward,

Charles D. Mower.
(The Rudder, *March 1927*)

and a full run. She is deep-bodied and has a rather deep plank keel.

The ketch is 43 feet long on deck, with a waterline length of 33 feet 4 inches, a beam of 11 feet 8 inches, and a draft of 6 feet 6 inches. Her sail area is 874 square feet. She has two tons of outside ballast in the form of an iron keel — just the thing for Labrador — and three tons of inside ballast consisting of iron laid in cement. Her scantlings are unusually heavy because of what she was asked to do.

According to Dr. Tom Paddon of North West River, Labrador, who used to sail in the *Yale* and knows her well:

> She had oak frames and planking — and had an inner shell of oak planks on the inside of her timbers, which was not, of course, a true watertight double hull but certainly helped make her extremely strong.
>
> In 1914 or 1915 she went on a rock still called 'Yale Rock' some 8-10 miles west of Indian Harbour. I was aboard but for some reason don't remember the affair at all, perhaps because I was born in 1914. She was left to her own devices while passengers and crew rowed back to Indian Harbour in a dory and men and materials were rounded up for salvage. The weather remained moderate, but she did bump and bang on the rocks continually for the next nine days except at low water, and local people could hardly believe their eyes to see her survive this. She had only some planking bruised and badly chafed to show for her ordeal and was still tight.

The *Yale's* rig is certainly moderate. Her mainsail has 390 square feet; the mizzen, 251; the staysail, 122; and the jib, 111.

Her mizzen is unusually big in proportion to the other sails, primarily to keep the mainsail small and relatively easy to handle. Look at the extremely deep reefs drawn in on the mainsail and mizzen, and note that the second reef in the mizzen cocks the boom up a bit extra to keep it out of a rough sea.

Her spars are heavy enough and the main shrouds lead far enough aft so that she doesn't need backstays. They probably didn't even bother with a vang from the end of the main gaff to the deck via a block at the mizzen truck.

Dr. Paddon wrote:

> The fact was that when sailing in company with other schooners, of which there were thousands in the fishery — most people weighed and put out at first light so that you often saw the entire schooner population of last night's harbour sailing in a group — she was about the last to reef anything. Her spars were too heavy to carry away, and as her canvas was always very good and her stays were galvanized wire rope, and she was simply too stiff to knock down, she could just carry everything until things got really wild, and she made some very fast runs — some of them really beyond the theoretical maximum imposed on her by ordinary naval architecture. I have heard various people claim that she simply *couldn't* have covered a certain distance in a reported time without being blown right out of the water, but my father reported departure and arrival times, point to point, very precisely because he was very interested in what she *could* do. He also could get very impressive performance to windward, tacking, and again she could carry enough sail in a good blow so only the size of the head sea she had to cope with could hold her back, and though she looks rather bluff, the fact is that she was very heavy for her size and a very nice shape, and the little ship would really get through the seas. Only cutting into a head sea from dead ahead, under power, was she really uncomfortable. Lively — yes — I couldn't gloss that over. Last two lines of a bit of verse he wrote for his family:

> She made them sick, she made them green
> She made them reek of kerosene
> But of all ships in steam or sail
> There's none to be compared to Yale.

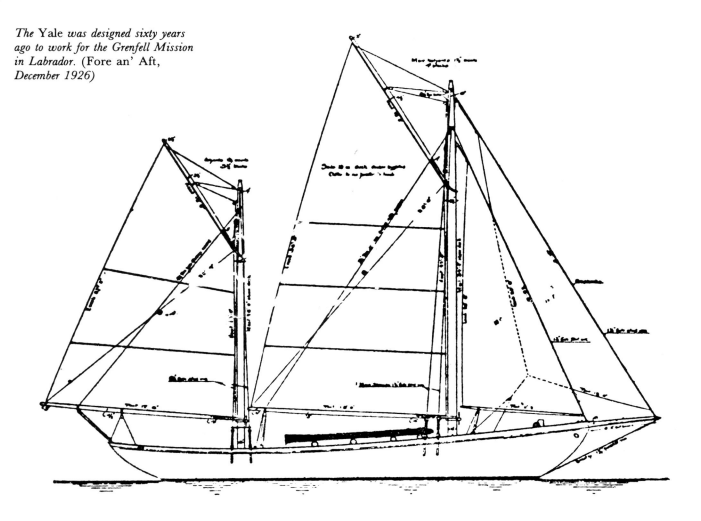

This is also a reference to engines. The first engine was a Remington Hothead, possibly the most efficient, economical, and reliable engine of its time and very tolerant of what grade of fuel it used (usually kerosene and whatever you chose to throw in), but it had one serious defect. Ignition was by a red-hot steel bulb, though there was probably a diesel effect as these engines could idle well — when the bulb should have cooled — but once the engine stopped for more than minutes you had to unscrew the bulb and heat it red-hot with a blow torch. If the glow-plug used in many of the early diesels (battery heated electrically) had been available, the Remington would have started easily anytime — and would have swept the market. I have been in a number of situations where any delay in starting would have caused the loss of the *Yale* . . . So around 1920 she got a 10 h.p., 2-cycle, 1-cylinder Mianus — no frills — jump spark and 'ignitor.' No muffler could long survive

this engine, so we did without. Each stroke was about like a 20-bore shotgun and could be heard over miles of still water and at night announced her arrival well in advance. Below was the only quiet place for miles. It gave her 6¼ knots, which speaks well for her hull design. Around 1926, she got a 4-cylinder, 20 h.p. Kermath — surely one of the most reliable and businesslike marine engines ever. Quiet, easily started by hand, economical, it didn't increase her speed much but was a joy to maintain, and she *would* tow much harder and faster than with the old one-lunger.

She has a very low, narrow house, for she often carried a deck load in her work. The cockpit is just a small footwell.

Below, the *Yale* has a very straightforward layout for flexibility of use. Her big, versatile main cabin can sleep four in pipe berths or

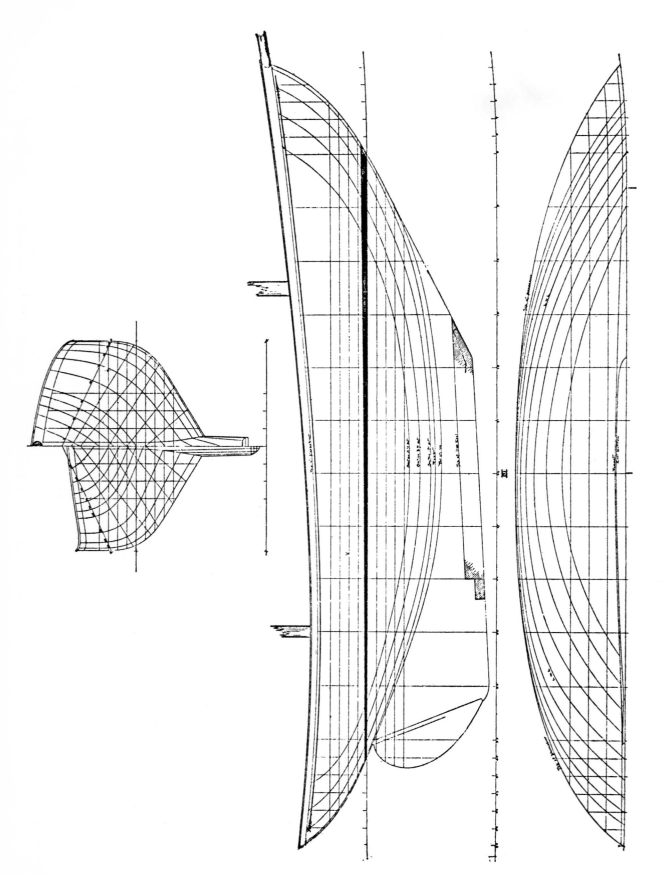

Her lines show a big, husky hull that could and did carry considerable vital cargo along one of the world's most dangerous coastlines. (Fore an' Aft, December 1926)

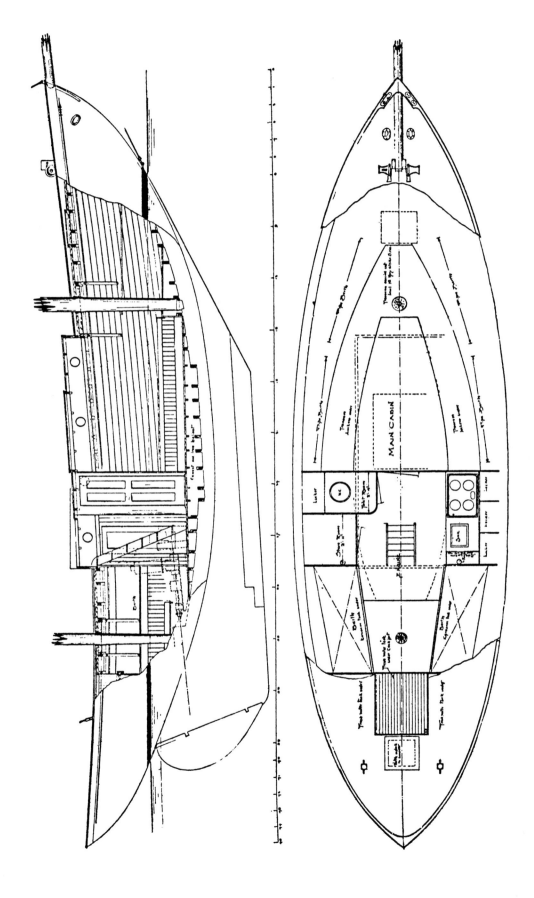

Her layout is the essence of simplicity and versatility. (Fore an' Aft, *December 1926*)

The Yale *on an unusually calm, clear day in Labrador.* (Yachting)

crowd in more on the settees and sole if necessary, or can be crammed with cargo. There is a good-sized storeroom just to port of the companionway.

The common sense of the *Yale's* strong, simple design will become apparent as we join her now for a typical sort of chore she was asked to accomplish.

It's mid-November 1927, and word has come into the Grenfell Mission's northernmost station that important winter supplies have just arrived at a port 80 miles away. It's very late in the season, but there's nothing for it but that the *Yale* leave North West River near the head of Lake Melville, right in the middle of Labrador where the ocean cuts its way through the coastal mountains into the interior, proceed the length of the lake, go to Rigolet, where the lake meets the sea, load the stuff, and return, 160 miles round trip.

The supplies will be more than she can carry alone, so she'll have to escort back the only vessel available to help at Rigolet, the ancient, 25-ton schooner *Thistle,* a craft already condemned to be scrapped. There will be seven on board the *Yale* on the outward trip, four of

whom will man the *Thistle* on the return run. Not all are experienced seamen.

The *Yale* gets underway and makes her passage down to Rigolet at eight knots under power and sail combined, close-hauled in a strong breeze and freezing conditions. So far so good. The crews spend the night loading the cargo aboard the *Yale* and the poor old *Thistle.*

Early next morning they get underway in a dead calm, and the *Yale* tows the *Thistle* under power 30 miles to St. John Island, where they seek shelter for the night.

The *Thistle* anchors and the *Yale* ties up alongside her. It breezes up in the night and the *Thistle's* anchor starts to drag. By the time the *Thistle's* tired old windlass can bring the anchor to the hawse, both vessels have been blown out of the harbor, anchor and all, in a moderate gale. The *Yale* again takes the *Thistle* in tow. They can only go to leeward. They find a bit of shelter for the *Thistle,* anchor her again, take off her crew, and then, under sail and power in the gale, get the *Yale* into Caravalla Cove. The gale changes direction and increases, making Caravalla a lee shore. They clear out and move her to another cove where there is better protection.

They see that the *Thistle* has apparently dragged ashore.

It is three days before the gales let them get back to the *Thistle*. They fear that her deck cargo has been lost, but it is intact, frozen to the deck.

With the help of some Eskimos, they transfer as much cargo as they dare from the *Thistle* to the *Yale*, jamming it into the saloon and engine room. The rest they cache ashore. Then the *Yale* gets underway again and drives through another rising gale with snow, around and among shoals, finally making it back to North West River with her huge, valuable load. It is probably just as well the *Thistle* was blown ashore. Had she attempted this last passage, she almost certainly would have been lost with her cargo and people.

This was the kind of operation the *Yale* was designed and built for and the kind of sailing she did almost routinely. A person seeking an ex-pedition vessel, perhaps to take in harm's way, could do a lot worse than look to this design.

Dr. Paddon tells what happened to the *Yale:*

Sold about 1930 to a local fisherman and trapper, *Yale* never deteriorated a jot, but was too much for him and his needs, so he sold her to a Jewish independent trader, a very likeable man who proved to be a skillful sailor and on occasion could handle her singlehanded. He loved *Yale* passionately. Years later he was washed overboard off of her when alone — somewhere off Bonavista — and *Yale* was found floating disconsolately alone. Sold to a fisherman, she fished for years, and, if my memory serves me, she was last seen at anchor sometime in the 1950s with her great iron keel crosswise — about to fall off. The hull was said to be tight and strong, but she was apparently considered not economically worth repair, and I don't believe she sailed again . . .
It took 40 years to make her tired, and white oak and bronze fastenings and a very heavy pitch-pine deck probably explain her prolonged youthfulness.

7/ A Ketch by William Garden

> **Length on deck: 48 feet 6 inches**
> **Length on waterline: 41 feet**
> ** 7 inches**
> **Beam: 13 feet 2 inches**
> **Draft: 5 feet 11 inches**
> **Sail area: 968 square feet**
> **Displacement: 52,500 pounds**
> **Designer: William Garden**

Many sailors, when they dream of chucking the shoreside life and putting to sea for a long cruise in their own vessel, conjure up images of the South Seas.

Little wonder! The South Seas have a plethora of islands, those most intriguing of all ports of call; vast stretches of ocean supplied with not only tropical weather, but also ample quantities of a cruising sailor's best friend, the trade wind; a heritage of beautiful people with an amazing maritime tradition of voyaging in small craft; and a later heritage of interesting people fleeing the industrial, commercial, and technical age to eke out a modest living, usually with a trading schooner.

If the images need any reinforcement, the sailor has only to turn to his bookshelf and pull down the likes of Nordhoff and Hall, Harry Pidgeon, Somerset Maugham, Melville, Richard Maury, Fanning, Slocum, or Irving Johnson.

A real dreamer may even be able to picture himself becoming something of a South Seas fixture: the storyteller holding his circle of listeners entranced long into the night on the wide veranda, his white linen suit barely visible in the tropical darkness, his craggy face outlined briefly in the glow of a long cheroot.

All that is needed to make these dreams come true is a suitable vessel and the will to go.

Twenty-five years ago Ken Dixon and Burt Buffington, two merchant marine officers, decided to do it. They asked William Garden to design them a boat to go to the South Seas. Bill Garden turned out the plans for a double-ended ketch that is moderate and easy in all respects.

When her plans appeared in *Yachting* magazine in January 1956, she was labeled, "a South Seas ketch." That headline certainly caught my eye, and the design has set me to dreaming many a time, but I like to think I am attracted to this Garden ketch more for her inherent fine qualities than for her romantic associations.

She is, at any rate, a boat whose short overhangs and rig give her a husky appearance, yet whose displacement is moderate and whose lines are quite fine. She should be easily driven.

The sheer is strong, yet is in no way extreme. Her draft has been kept very moderate. Being rather shoal-bodied, she has easy bow and buttock lines. There's a bit of flare way up in the

Bill Garden.

bow. She has a slightly hollow entrance and quite a bit of hollow in the stern.

The ketch is 48 feet 6 inches long on deck, with a waterline length of 41 feet 7 inches, a beam of 13 feet 2 inches, and a draft of 5 feet 11 inches. Her sail area is 968 square feet, and her displacement is 52,500 pounds at the load waterline. She has 11,600 pounds of outside lead ballast, with another 2,000 pounds of lead inside.

I think this boat has a most handsome rig, thanks to the rake of her masts and the angles made by her headstays and main gaff. And another reason Bill Garden's rigs always look so good is that he is no miser when it comes to drawing mastheads. He always gives you that little extra that makes all the difference.

The moderate ketch rig means that no sail on this boat is very big. Her mainsail has 411 square feet; the mizzen, 188; the staysail, 204; and the jib, 165.

The mainsail would set very well with its relatively short, high-peaked gaff. Of course, a vang to the mizzen masthead would ensure perfection.

She would balance well under mainsail and staysail or under mizzen and staysail, either of which rig would, of course, be self-tending when tacking. She'd be a very easy boat to sail

in heavy weather. I'd want single reefs in staysail and mizzen as well as the two reefs shown in the mainsail.

A big balloon staysail would make a fine light-weather sail for cruising. The lazy jacks on main and staysail make sense; I'd want them on the mizzen, too.

Her short bowsprit would help a lot with anchor work. The jib would be easy to handle if rigged with a downhaul and if you had a pulpit on the bowsprit with lifelines coming back to the main rigging. I went through a period when I was most intrigued with the roller jib, but I have come to believe it is a snare and a delusion and now wouldn't take one to sea. I think the likelihood of gear failure is enough greater with the roller jib compared to a hanked-on jib with halyard and downhaul to warrant leaving the roller gear ashore.

Permanent lifelines from a bowsprit pulpit to the main rigging would be the only ones I'd want on this boat. I'd rig heavy rope lifelines between main and mizzen shrouds when underway. Aft, I'd hang a short-tethered harness in the starboard mizzen rigging to wear whenever I had to reach anything on the stern. There's also the tender lashed down on deck to hold onto, and the absence of lifelines aft would let you launch the small boat quickly off whichever quarter was heeled down to leeward. The mizzen boom would make a fine boat derrick.

The double-ender shown as a tender is 13 feet 8 inches long. She does obstruct the after hatch to the lazarette; you'd want to hinge the starboard side of the hatch so you could still get below readily with the small boat stowed on deck, for the access to the engine room under the cockpit is from the lazarette through a watertight door in the engine room's after bulkhead.

The lazarette is a huge place for all kinds of sea stores, spare parts, tools, and bosun's paraphernalia.

The engine room has plenty of space, though not much headroom. It contains a three-cylinder diesel. She carries 450 gallons of fuel in galvanized iron tanks.

The ketch's cockpit well is nicely protected by the tender and the deckhouse. She has two

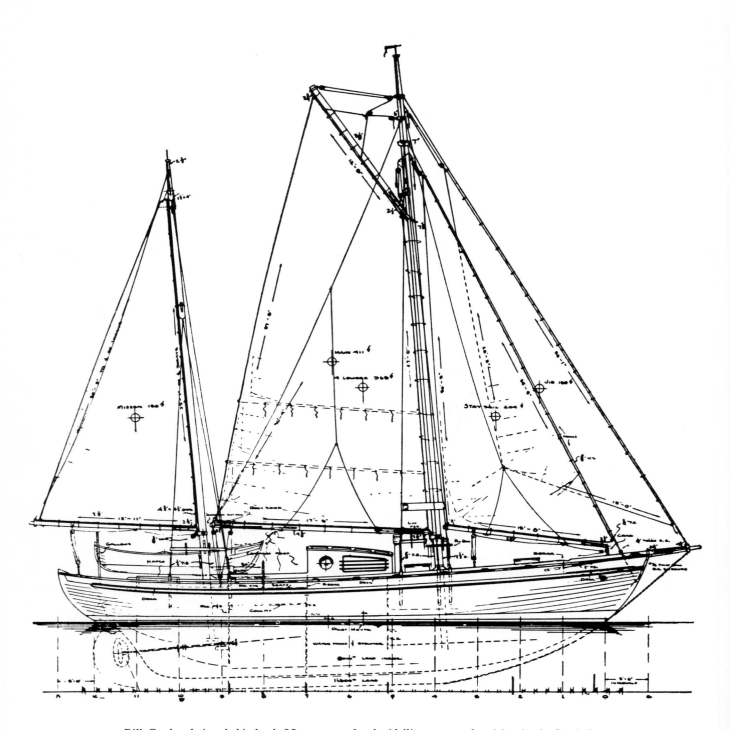

Bill Garden designed this ketch 25 years ago for the idyllic purpose of cruising in the South Sea islands. (Yachting, *January 1956*)

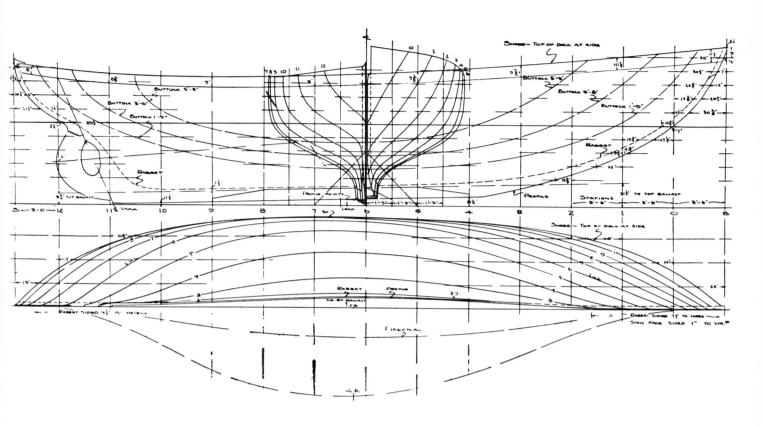

Above: *Her hull looks plenty able, yet she is quite fine and easily driven.* (Yachting, *January 1956*). Below: *Her unusual layout has some strong advantages and a few apparent problems.* (Yachting, *January 1956*)

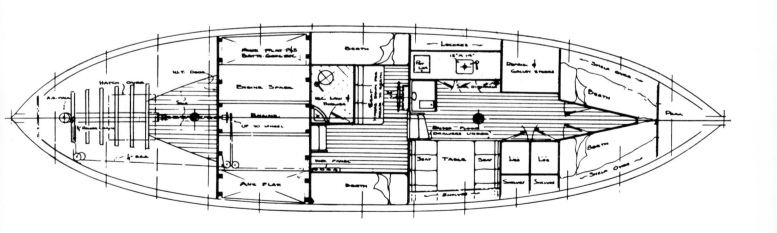

steering wheels, one in the cockpit and one in the deckhouse. Having the choice relieves a lot of the tedium of steering (for those poor souls for whom steering is tedious), though there is not a great deal of visibility from the wheel in the deckhouse. You'd use it only when you had plenty of searoom, and even then would want to pop up on deck for a good look-around every quarter of an hour.

Her deckhouse makes a very comfortable place at sea, even in the tropics. The big side windows on this one are protected by bars; for safety and looks, I'd prefer three ports each side.

The deckhouse sole is just at the waterline. There's a solid watertight bulkhead between the deckhouse and the engine room, and it might make sense to have a watertight door to seal off the deckhouse from the cabin forward — a door that would be kept shut only in heavy weather. If the house were smashed in by an ultimate wave, then the flooding would be limited.

The bunks in the deckhouse are out under the deck and could be curtained off for reasonable privacy, though they are not in a really secluded place for off-watch sleeping when the vessel is underway. The head and washroom taking up a valuable corner of the deckhouse strikes me as being a bit unusual; I'd want to live with it a while, but I suspect I'd eventually want to move all that plumbing to the lazarette, give up the shower, and replace the lot with a nice, big chart table.

Under the deckhouse are tanks for 270 gallons of water and more stowage space. The stowage space in this vessel is remarkable and would be a great asset for her intended purpose.

Although the ketch was laid out for two people, I think her accommodation plan is really better suited for a singlehander. As mentioned, there is really no good place for the off-watch to sleep, for the deckhouse bunks are in Grand Central Station, what with the watch-stander tramping up and down in and out of the deckhouse or muttering over his charts, and the forward bunks wouldn't be much use at sea. On the other hand, the deckhouse bunks would give the singlehander a good place to cork off handy to wheel, compass, chart, and deck.

The arrangement of the forward accommodation has the shortcoming that it doesn't provide a place to sit to leeward when the boat is on the starboard tack. Maybe you could work in a seat at the front of the top-opening icebox to port and hinge a table leaf off the locker front opposite to starboard? Also, I'd prefer an L-shaped settee around the saloon table to the dinette shown so as to provide a more comfortable seat with the boat heeled down to starboard.

She has an oil-fired galley stove; the hatch over the galley just abaft the mainmast makes a good arrangement.

All in all, I think Bill Garden has produced a design for a fine seagoing cruising vessel in this double-ended ketch. It's a design that can set you to dreaming. You'd start out for the South Seas with that big lazarette crammed with sea stores, but as the cruise went on, of course, that mundane stuff would be traded for a cargo of sandalwood, edible birds' nests, and mother-of-pearl.

8/ Bror Tamm

It's all very well for boat designers to draw the plans for good boats on large sheets of paper; you don't have a vessel in which to put to sea until a builder fashions and fastens materials according to the ideas presented by the designer. A good boat results when a designer's good theory is transformed into good practice by a builder.

The ways in which designer and builder work together are as many as are the combinations of designers and builders. Some designers, like Bill Garden, for instance, have considerable practical building experience and design boats that are "easy to build." The problems of the builder are taken into account from the first, details of construction are indicated clearly on the plans, and a good builder should not have too much difficulty making the designer/builder combination work.

Some designs for good boats are concocted with little regard for the problems to be faced by the builder. The builder is left to work things out for himself. If this sort of designer/builder combination is to produce a good boat, the builder has to have plenty of imagination and experience.

In some cases designer and builder are one. This "combination" can range all the way from an "amateur" designing and building his own dream ship to Nathanael Greene Herreshoff designing boats to be built under his own direct supervision at the Herreshoff Manufacturing Company in Bristol, Rhode Island. At least in this situation, it's no mystery who gets the credit for a good boat or who takes the blame for a lousy one.

Sometimes the roles of designer and builder get intermingled. The designer may suggest specific construction techniques to the builder and the builder may suggest design modifications to the designer.

A great many good boats were designed and built by the George F. Lawley Company at Neponset, Massachusetts, in the years prior to World War II, but their construction was supervised more by the various foremen in the yard than by the Lawleys themselves. The yard also built boats to the plans of many of the leading designers of the day. Again, it was the yard foremen who took the prime responsibility for transforming what was on paper into something that would float.

Bror Tamm.

If the vessel that went down the Lawley ways turned out to be a good boat, the front office all too often forgot all about the foremen — not to mention the carpenters, joiners, riggers, sailmakers, and painters — who were an essential part of the designer/builder combination; but if the boat turned out to be lousy, there was usually enough blame to be shared by all.

Bror Tamm was a veteran foreman at the Lawley yard, transforming the ideas of the Lawleys and other designers into a long parade of mostly good boats and, I suppose, the inevitable few lousy ones. Tammy is a prince of a man. Nearing 90 now, he lives in Quincy, Massachusetts. Tammy's eyes and ears are letting him down a bit these days, but his grip is powerful, his memory retentive, and his sense of the great fun of life and boats is undiminished. Make a dumb statement about a boat and he'll land on you with a great roar like a ton of bricks. He is totally delightful. He imparts much lore and wisdom about boats.

Tammy had good schooling in both designing and building boats in his native Sweden. As a boy, he sailed a lot with his father. He loved boats and wanted to work with nothing else. His first job was with a yard in Denmark where he designed 45 vessels, mostly fishing craft.

Tammy came to the United States as a young man and before long had a job at Lawley's laying deck. He proved his worth, stayed on, and did great work for the Lawleys for 40 years.

He started at Lawley's in 1912. By 1916, he was running the mold loft. By 1920 he was also put in charge of the spar and rigging lofts. In 1930, he became superintendent of the yard. During World War II, Lawley's expanded to become a group of 3,000 people building vessels for the Navy. Bror Tamm was the assistant general manager.

So during four decades at the great yard, Tammy did about everything there was to be done to make a good boat. His great forte was spars and rigging.

In 1930, the America's Cup was challenged for and defended by — for the first time — J boats. They had towering, jib-headed rigs in which each designer sought lightness. Two of the boats, the *Yankee* designed by Frank C. Paine and the *Whirlwind* designed by L. Francis Herreshoff, were built at Lawley's. Messrs. Paine and Herreshoff each specified that the 170-foot masts for their boats be hollow wooden spars. At that time, not many hollow wooden spars of any size had been built, but the idea of gluing up 1,100 pieces of wood weighing 4,500 pounds to make a 170-foot stick that would support over 7,500 square feet of sail (plus giant spinnakers) was daunting. Bror Tamm and his men did it.

When designers had rigging problems, they learned to go to Tammy. He would design a fitting to solve the problem, thus creating a good many firsts.

And all the time, Tammy was dreaming of boats, looking at boats, making models of boats, and drawing boats. He came from a place with an ancient maritime tradition that he fully appreciates. Many of his models and drawings reflect that heritage. But Tammy is also a free thinker who can create new concepts in boat design.

Tammy has a lovely wooden box he made about a yard square by six inches deep. It weighs plenty, because it's filled with his boat drawings — everything from rough sketches of

Tammy's design for a 46-foot ketch showing the "split mainsail" that he invented in 1930. (Bror Tamm)

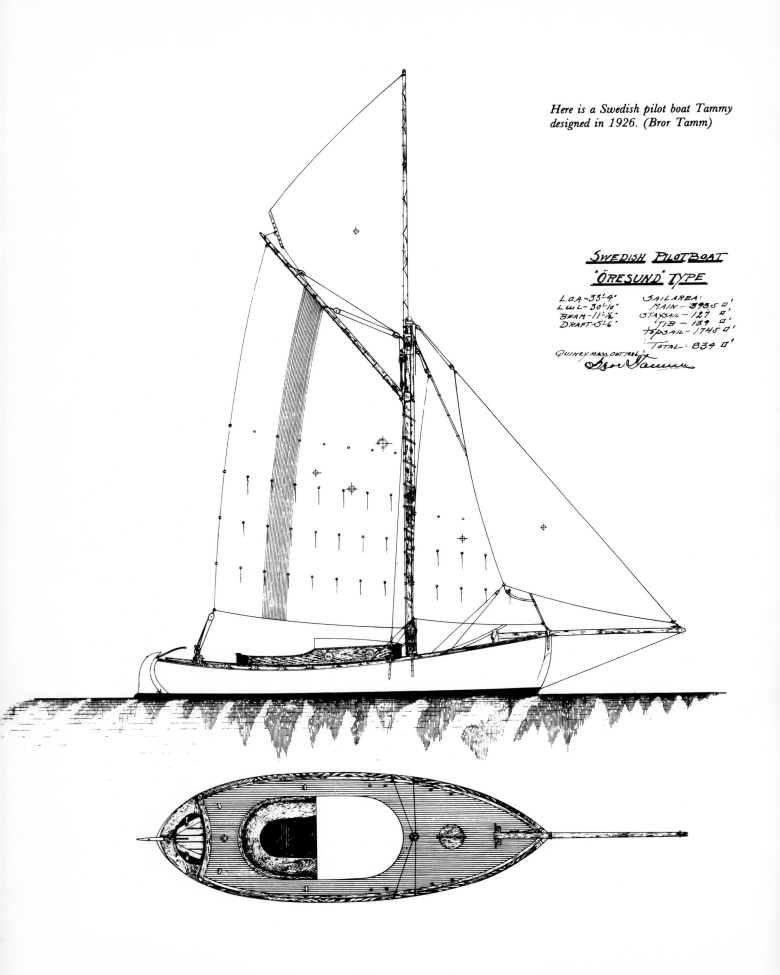

Here is a Swedish pilot boat Tammy designed in 1926. (Bror Tamm)

SWEDISH PILOTBOAT
'ÖRESUND' TYPE

LOA-33'-4"   SAIL AREA:
LWL-30'-10"   MAIN-393.5 ☐'
BEAM-11'-3/4"   STAXSAIL-127 ☐'
DRAFT-5'-6"   JIB-139 ☐'
                     TOPSAIL-174.5 ☐'
                     TOTAL: 834 ☐'

QUINCY, MASS. OCT.1926
Bror Tamm

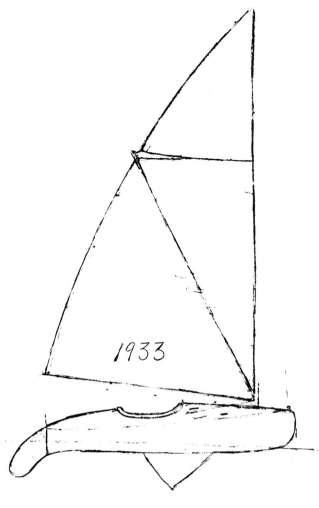

1933

Tammy's idea of a sailing "roadster," complete with three-piece mainsail, all quite stylish for 1933. (Bror Tamm)

an idea for a boat to finished plans of a concept worked out. When Tammy takes his summer vacation at his lake cottage in Norway, Maine, the box travels with him. A guided tour through its contents is a rare privilege; there is a bewildering array of great boat stuff in there. Through Tammy's kindness, let me show you just three of the items to be seen in his magic box, selected to give some representative idea of the collection.

The first item is Tammy's "split mainsail," here seen on a husky ketch he dreamed up. This is a beamy vessel and certainly would be sea-kindly. She is 46 feet long on deck, with a waterline length of 40 feet 6 inches, a beam of 15 feet, and a draft of 6 feet 6 inches.

She has either a trunk cabin that joins a short raised deck forward together with a turtleback aft, or a raised deck throughout with walkways and a cockpit cut out of it. Whichever way you look at the arrangement, it's intriguing. And look at those nice stern windows.

But it is the rig that is to me the most fascinating part of this drawing. Tammy invented the split mainsail in 1930; this particular drawing of it was made in 1934.

The space between the masts is filled in with a mainsail that is two separate sails. While in overall shape this split mainsail may remind you of Fred Fenger's trysail ketch rig, it is really far closer to gaff rig. In Fenger's rig, the lower sail sets on a stay to the mizzen masthead, but on Tammy's rig the lower sail sets on a long spar or gaff. In both rigs, it is the lower sail that is the basic working sail and the upper one that is the light sail. This corresponds, of course, to the gaff mainsail with topsail set above it, and, in fact, Tammy calls the upper of his two sails a topsail.

Tammy's gaff is held up by two topping lifts running to the mainmast, one on each side of the topsail. Only the weather one would be set up, the lee one being left slack so as not to foul the topsail. When tacking, the lee lift would be set up before the tack was made, and the new lee lift would be slacked off after the tack was completed.

When shortening down, you would take in the topsail and reset a smaller one that is both shorter on the hoist and narrower from luff to leech. Then to close the gap between the foot of the smaller topsail and the luff of the mainsail, you would top the gaff up to bring the head of the mainsail close to the clew of the topsail.

To shorten down further, take in the smaller topsail and top the gaff of the mainsail right up against the mainmast. You now have a very secure main trysail. There is no reefing. It's kind of interesting, isn't it?

Item Number Two from Tammy's big box is his drawing of a Swedish pilot boat of the Oresund type, Oresund being the strait that connects the Kattegat with the Baltic Sea. Tammy drew up this boat in 1926.

She is 33 feet 4 inches long on deck, with a waterline length of 30 feet 10 inches, a beam of 11 feet ½ inch, and a draft of 5 feet 6 inches.

She looks much smaller than she is, primarily, I think, because of her cabin house and cockpit arrangement. She has a big, well-protected cockpit opening into a good-sized house. Note the steering well in her stern.

The pilot boat's jib and topsail are her light sails. With them set, she has 834 square feet of sail area. Once they are taken in, she has just over 500 square feet of sail, and, as you can see, her mainsail and staysail can be reefed right down to almost nothing as the weather dictates.

She might make a good daysailing party boat today.

The third drawing is a sketch Tammy made in 1933 of a small sailing "roadster" or "sportabout." Now there's a boat that must have been right up to date in 1933!

She has plenty of sail area with a huge, tall mainsail divided into three parts, like Tammy's split mainsail but with the topsail divided again for greater versatility. That rig might be a handful, but I say she'd be some boat! How would you like to sit in her driver's seat tooling down the bay on a gentle Sunday afternoon?

Knowing Bror Tamm, you have to wonder if "they make 'em like that" anymore. I guess we'll have to wait a few decades to see.

9/ The *Susan*

Length on deck: 28 feet 6 inches
Length on waterline: 22 feet
10 inches
Beam: 9 feet
Draft: 4 feet 1 inch
Sail area: 460 square feet
Displacement: 6½ tons
Designer: Murray G. Peterson

The coast of Maine is as elegant and complicated a piece of geography as anyone could want. Some folks wax enthusiastic over its islands, some over its big, protected bays, and some over its long, beautiful rivers. There are a lot of fine places for people who are addicted to boats.

There is one really great spot that I have been lucky enough to be introduced to. It reminds me a lot of the cove on the Pawcatuck River in Rhode Island where I fooled around in little boats a "few" years ago. This Maine place is a cove just far enough up a river to be quiet from the sea. There's even a ledge that goes just under at high tide to protect the cove from the river. The ledge discourages strangers, but behind it is just enough swinging room for a few boats.

Ashore on the point is, first of all, a big stone dock with a nice old boathouse on it. It used to be a fish shack in bygone years.

Up the grassy slope from the boathouse is a lovely, sprawling house-and-barn, the first part of which was built before the Civil War. All around are woods, except for that big grassy slope.

Tucked away upstairs under the eaves of the fine old house is a paneled room reached by its own narrow, twisting staircase. Small windows look out onto the cove. There are big drawing tables, plenty of drawer space for boat plans, shelves of the best books about boats, interesting guns, paintings of handsome vessels, a rigged model of Slocum's *Spray*.

This is the home of the Peterson family. This is the room where Murray G. Peterson designed his schooners. Here William Peterson, Murray's son, carries on his late father's work, making available his father's plans and providing expert advice and assistance in the construction of Peterson-designed vessels.

This is where I recently saw some handsome bronze fittings for a 28-foot schooner designed by Murray Peterson and being built in British Columbia by a good friend of mine, Nelson Bevard. Bill sold Nels a full set of working drawings for the handsome little vessel and will provide construction advice and help. What a good thing for Murray Peterson's son to be doing.

And what a fine vessel is this schooner, the *Susan*. Mr. Peterson designed her a dozen years ago when he was 60 years old. Wrapped up in

Murray Peterson.

the design for this schooner is a lifetime of experience and thinking relating to just this type of boat. Mr. Peterson's specific idea for the design was a boat that would be easily driven in a light breeze and that would also be very seaworthy.

The *Susan* was beautifully built in Camden, Maine, by Malcolm H. Brewer. Her planking is 1-inch cedar on 1½-inch-square oak frames 9 inches apart. She is 12 years old and hasn't leaked yet.

Murray Peterson sailed the *Susan* a lot and got more pleasure out of her than from any of the dozen other boats he had owned during his lifetime. She is still moored for six months of each year in that cove behind the ledge, and Bill and his wife and mother, for whom the boat is named, often sail in her, standing down the river, and letting her feel the ocean swell. She's well cared for and well sailed.

The *Susan* is 28 feet 6 inches long on deck, with a waterline length of 22 feet 10 inches, a beam of 9 feet, and a draft of 4 feet 1 inch. Her schooner rig has 460 square feet of sail. Her displacement is 6½ tons.

She's the biggest 28-foot boat I ever saw. Approaching her in a dinghy, you notice a certain slab-sided look amidships that makes her seem rugged rather than clumsy. From right astern, her transom looks absolutely massive. You'd swear you were looking at a 60-foot schooner rather than at a 28-foot one. If anything, the illusion is heightened when you step on board. Because of her high freeboard, heavy displacement, and the wide deck space allowed by her small houses and protected by her 7-inch bulwarks, she gives you the feel of a much bigger vessel than she really is.

The *Susan* has short ends and high sides; she's very dry for a 28-foot boat. Murray Peterson gave her a rugged spoon bow rather than his usual clipper bow, because he felt that the form of the clipper bow would be too restricted on a boat less than 30 feet long.

She certainly has a perky sheer. Her draft has been kept moderate. She has very easy bow and buttock lines for such a short boat and a well-formed run.

Her sections are easy from the turn of the bilge to the bottom of the keel. She has a

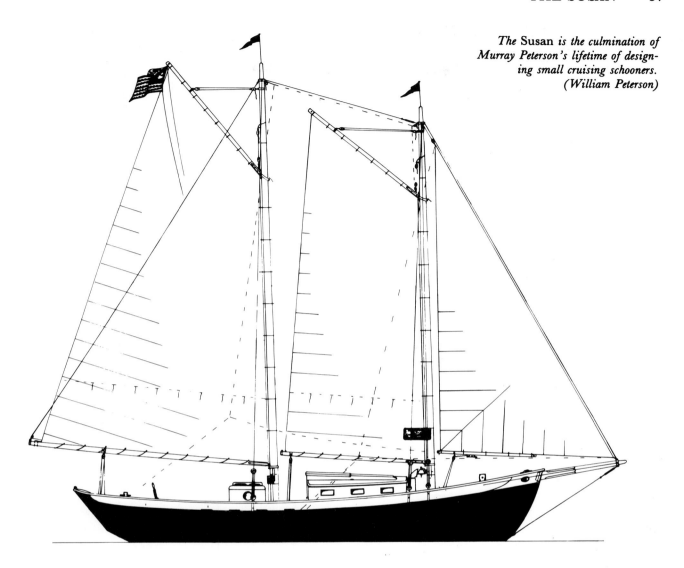

The Susan *is the culmination of Murray Peterson's lifetime of designing small cruising schooners.*
(William Peterson)

reasonably fine, straight entrance. There is lots of bearing aft. Her rudder is well aft and nearly vertical.

Henry Bohndell of Rockport, Maine, made her sails and rigged her. Bill Peterson says that not even a serving has let go in 12 years.

The single headsail makes good sense in such a small schooner. The *Susan* has a good-sized overlapping jib to set in light and moderate weather. Her tall, narrow foresail with its rather long gaff needs, of course, a vang.

Murray Peterson drew up a number of different rigs for this design, of which I show a jib-headed cutter and a gaff-rigged knockabout with a topmast. Partial as I am to two-masted rigs with their great versatility, and partial as I am to bowsprits with their utility and grace, I

really like the looks of that gaff-rigged knockabout sloop. It's the fastest of the three rigs shown. And see how the absence of a bowsprit emphasizes the husky, able look of the *Susan's* hull.

That topsail would be more fun to play with than a barrel of parrots and would really help her along in a light air. Think of the huge balloon jib you could set sheeting to the end of the main boom! Naturally you'd need, to go with it, a topmast preventer backstay set up to the weather quarter to hold things together.

I'd want a third deep reef in the mainsail.

I can hear all three of these rigs crying out for nicely curved gallows frames for their main booms.

Mr. Peterson designed a 6½-foot pram for

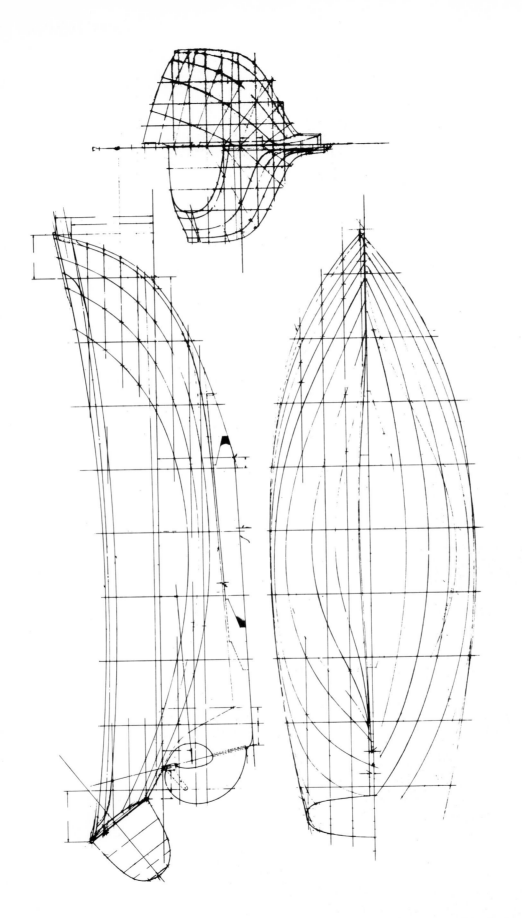

She has a husky, rugged hull and seems like a much bigger boat than she really is. Mr. Peterson said she sailed better than he had any right to expect. (William Peterson)

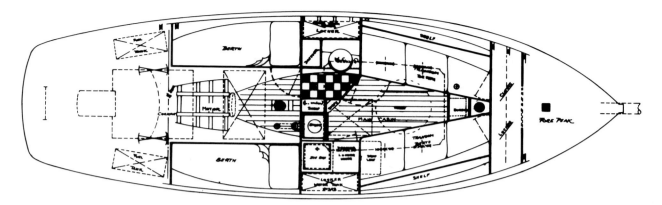

Above: *Her snug forward and after cabins give unusual privacy in such a small boat. (William Peterson)*

Left: *Her galley, with the companionway steps tucked away in the corner. (William Peterson)*

Below: *On deck, she seems like a big vessel. (William Peterson)*

The Susan *takes a handsome picture, whether at anchor* . . .

or with a big bone in her teeth. (William Peterson)

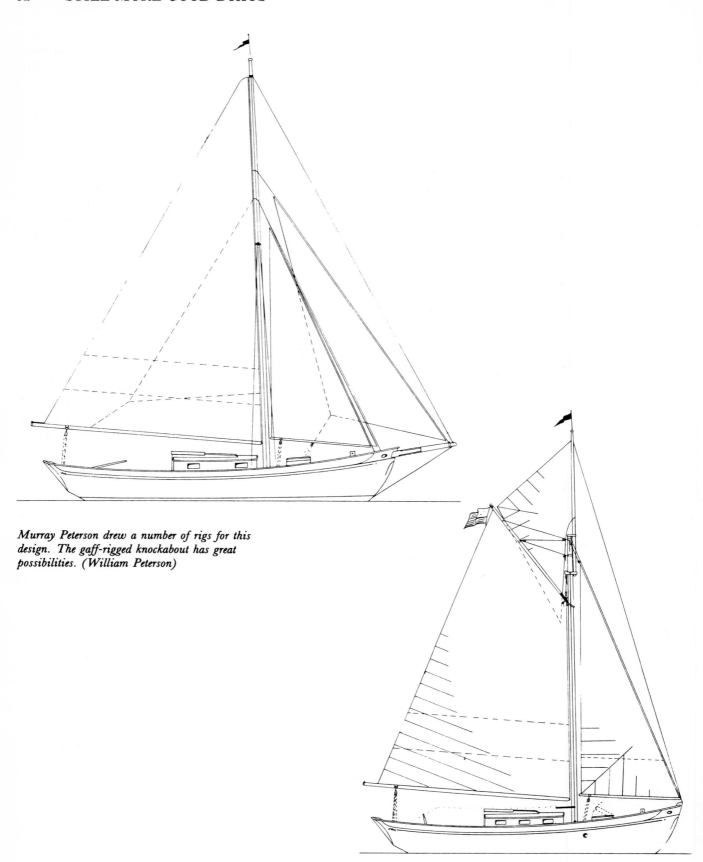

*Murray Peterson drew a number of rigs for this
design. The gaff-rigged knockabout has great
possibilities. (William Peterson)*

the *Susan.* She stows upside down on deck, leaning up against the forward house.

The pram is a shapely and burdensome little vessel. In the barn attached to the old house up beside that ledge-protected cove, Bill Peterson recently built a pair of these nice prams.

The *Susan* has no coaming around her cockpit well. I think I'd want one.

You go down the companionway at the after end of the forward house on a most ingenious ladder. The corner between the galley and the head has simply been filled in with triangular steps. They take up very little space yet are quite handy.

Murray Peterson loved engines and knew how to work on them. In his designs, he gave you plenty of room to get at the engine. While the engines in his boats were always ready to run, it was hard to persuade him to spoil a quiet sail by starting her up.

The *Susan's* engine, a 15-h.p. Volvo Penta diesel swinging a two-bladed propeller, sits right out in the middle of the after stateroom, which therefore must double as an engine room. Some folks would object to such an arrangement and would quickly box in the engine so as to pretend it wasn't there. But a nice engine is not a bad thing to look at, and if it's right in the middle of your bedroom you'll probably take good care of it. On the other hand, with such a handy little sailing vessel as the *Susan,* you could just leave the engine out altogether, given a small measure of patience in the crew.

You get to the after stateroom by ducking through the head. It's the kind of arrangement that seems cramped at first but that you quickly get used to.

The schooner has a pair of fuel tanks aft in way of the cockpit well and a pair of water tanks amidships outboard of the galley on the starboard side and outboard of the head on the port side. The latter tanks would seem to take up rather valuable space, and the design has been modified to put tanks under the after berths.

The forward cabin is a snug little nest. Its small house lets you stand up in the right places and gives six feet of headroom.

The cabin table has leaves that make it a perfect circle, and it can be unscrewed from its base and stowed away when not wanted.

There are lots of lockers in this little vessel, including a big hanging locker going right across the boat just forward of the foremast.

Murray Peterson said the *Susan* was a "lucky" combination of design factors and said that she sailed better than he had any right to expect. Well, there certainly may be some luck in this design, but there certainly is also in it the culmination of the work of a man who devoted a considerable portion of his great talents to designing small schooners.

I think the *Susan* is an ideal cruising boat, no matter which rig you choose. Nels, you are going to have some kind of a good time building and sailing this little vessel.

10/ A Crowninshield Schooner

> Length on deck: 36 feet 3 inches
> Length on waterline: 28 feet
> Beam: 7 feet 10 inches
> Draft: 5 feet 3 inches
> Sail area: 661 square feet
> Displacement: 12,000 pounds
> Designer: B.B. Crowninshield

B.B. Crowninshield designed a lot of schooners, some big, some small. Most of them were long, low, flat, and fast-looking. Some, to my eye, were too flat.

The one shown here, designed by Mr. Crowninshield for his own use as a singlehander 70 and more years ago, has, in my opinion, just barely enough sheer to keep her from deserving wisecracks about being "plain." There is no question she's a flapper, but she has her charm.

Mr. Crowninshield wrote, "I wanted the biggest and fastest boat that I could comfortably handle alone." She would certainly be fast, for she is narrow and fine and is not very heavy. She has a relatively high ratio of sail area to displacement and of waterline length to displacement. And she would be reasonably weatherly, for she has ample lateral plane; of course the emphasis would be on footing, not pointing.

Yes, she has a lot of wetted surface and wouldn't be good at planing and surfing, yet her average speed in all conditions would be quite high.

Mr. Crowninshield's schooner is 36 feet 3 inches long on deck, with a waterline length of 28 feet, a beam of only 7 feet 10 inches, and draft of 5 feet 3 inches. She displaces 12,000 pounds and has a sail area of 661 square feet without light sails.

She carries 6,000 pounds of ballast, with 1,200 pounds outside and 4,800 pounds inside. It's not clear to me where you would put 4,800 pounds of inside ballast in this boat, for her sections are quite shallow, but in any case most of it could go outside, resulting in a stiffer boat, but one with a quicker roll.

She certainly has the Crowninshield trademark of being low-sided. Her least freeboard is but 1 foot 9 inches.

She has moderate overhangs and very easy bow and buttock lines. Her forward sections are Vee'd enough so that she wouldn't do much pounding. She has a little hollow to her garboards. Being narrow, she has quite fine waterlines.

The schooner has an oak backbone with oak floors. Her frames are of oak also, being 1¼ inches by 1¼ inches, spaced on centers varying from 8 inches to 12 inches. Her clamp is of Georgia pine, 3 inches by 3 inches, tapered to 1½ inches by 1½ inches. She has a pair of

B.B. Crowninshield. (Traditions and Memories of American Yachting, Complete Edition, *by W.P. Stephens, International Marine Publishing Company)*

Georgia pine bilge stringers 1¼ inches by 4 inches, tapered to 1¼ inches by 1¾ inches. Her deck beams are 1¼ inches by 1¾ inches, of spruce. Her plank keel is of Georgia pine. Her outside ballast is held on by five ⅝-inch keelbolts, specified to be of brass (!). She is planked with ⅞-inch "country pine," and her deck is ¾-inch tongue-and-groove boards of the same stuff. Her deck is covered with canvas. Her rails and coaming are oak.

So, as you can see, her construction is adequate; she is neither over-built nor gussied up.

Mr. Crowninshield's singlehanded schooner rig is straightforward. The foremast has just a single pair of shrouds; there are double shrouds on the mainmast. They are made up with deadeyes and lanyards. No backstays. Nothing fancy.

Last summer I sailed a smaller schooner than this one with a very similar rig, except that on my boat the mainsail is relatively smaller and the jib and foresail relatively bigger, compared with those on the Crowninshield schooner. The latter's areas are: mainsail, 376 square feet; foresail, 191; and jib, 94.

I found this rig to be very easy to handle singlehanded and also quite versatile under a variety of conditions. One of the nice things about it is that when pressed in a fresh breeze, you can ease her by starting the fore sheet a bit to let the foresail luff. You're not changing the balance of the boat much and you still have the full drive of the big mainsail. Then when it eases up a bit, you trim the foresail back in again. Thus, by juggling the fore sheet, you can keep the boat doing her best while the wind makes up its mind whether or not it's really going to blow hard. If it decides not to, you haven't wasted time reefing, and if it decides it is going to blow and you find yourself carrying a big luff in the foresail all the time, then you can just take it down and be done with it. This boat, with her big mainsail, will carry a bit of weather helm, of course, without the foresail.

The overlapping foresail is not the headache you might think it is, though I suppose it could give you one if you insisted on treating it with a complete lack of respect. The sail really pulls for its size and also helps the mainsail. Yes, the club bangs the mast twice as you tack, though you can prevent this by tacking without touching the fore sheet, and then easing the thing across after she is around onto the new tack. Of course having the foresail aback a moment does slow down the process of gathering way on the new tack.

You always think of a schooner in a gale jogging comfortably under foresail alone. I haven't done that yet in mine, and I wonder what the loose-footed foresail will be like in such conditions. I suspect it will be fairly hard to handle compared with a boomed foresail, because of the necessity for shifting the sheet and because

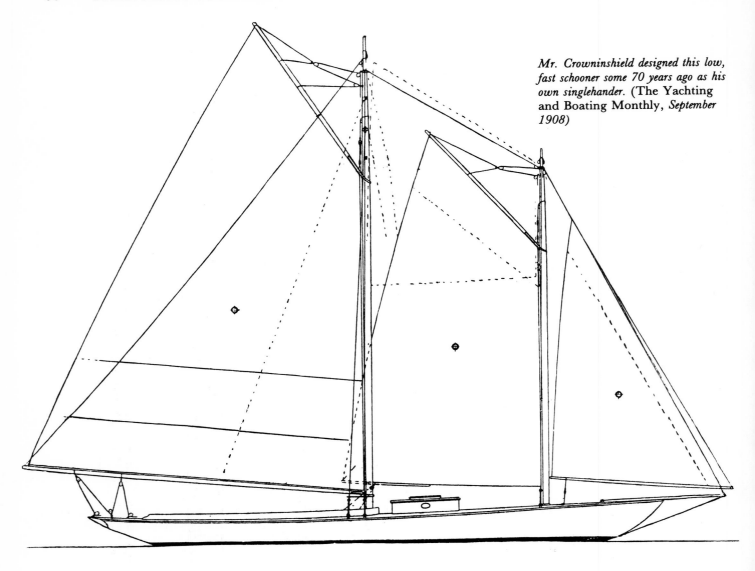

Mr. Crowninshield designed this low, fast schooner some 70 years ago as his own singlehander. (The Yachting and Boating Monthly, September 1908)

the sheet has fewer parts than you'd have on a boomed sail.

Mr. Crowninshield's loose-footed foresail reefs at the top. It would certainly be easier to tie in a reef to the gaff (with the sail lowered all the way, of course) than along the loose foot with the longish club in the way, yet I'm not sure I'd want the bunt of the reef aloft. It would sure make people look twice, though.

The single headsail on this rig works fine. Off the wind she seems to like the sail sheeted in quite flat to hold her head off with less rudder. I've gotten so I hardly touch my jib sheet any more.

Mr. Crowninshield's jib reefs along the luff,

like a sharpie's sails, and apparently its boom slides forward past the headstay in the process. Having the bunt of a reefed sail snugged up to a sharpie's mast seems to make sense, but I'm afraid that hauling the bunt of a reefed headsail up to its stay would hurt the sail's performance quite a lot when working to windward.

The fisherman staysail makes a fine light-weather sail from full-and-by off to a broad reach. Very satisfying to have it pulling away up there.

The worst part of this rig is, of course, that the two gaff sails, with their relatively long feet, don't twist much, and thus there's really no reason to put vangs on the gaffs. Still, next sum-

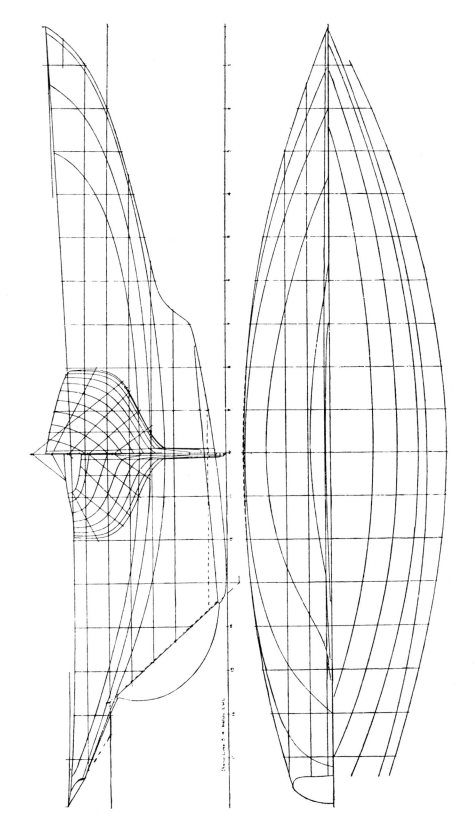

With her deep draft, moderate displacement, fine lines, and generous sail area, she'd turn in a high average speed. (The Yachting and Boating Monthly, September 1908)

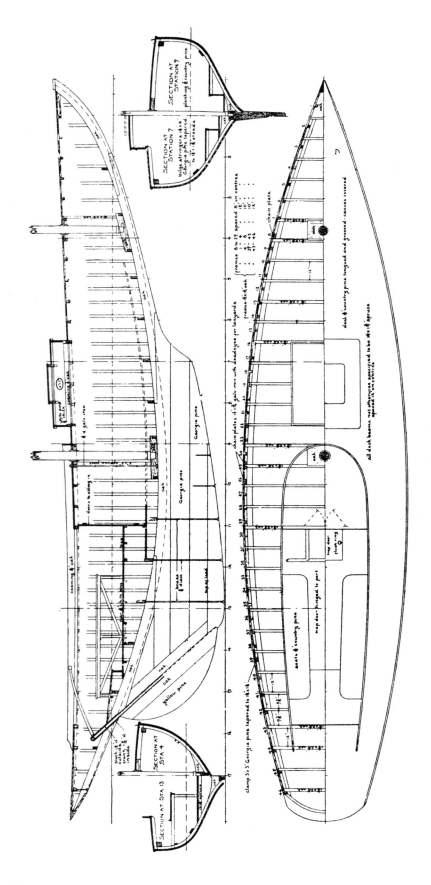

The schooner's construction is straightforward and adequate. Look at all the deck space she has! (The Yachting and Boating Monthly, *September 1908*)

mer I am going to have a main topsail, and I look forward, when running off before it, to leading the bitter end of its sheet aft as a sort of vang to keep the gaff off the lee shroud whenever the topsail isn't set. You could have exactly the same sort of foolish paraphernalia on Mr. Crowninshield's schooner.

There is room on deck on this little vessel to work her and enjoy her. Note that the foredeck comes way back abaft the foremast. What a great place to keep a bunch of anchors!

The schooner's cockpit is not self-draining. The boat is not designed to go "offshore." Her cockpit has plenty of room, though; it's 12½ feet from her mainmast to its after end, and the seats are 6 feet long and still have plenty of room around them.

There's a flush trap door to the bilge at the forward end of the cockpit sole. You'd want a big tent to rig over the main boom to cover this whole place when it rains.

There are doors in the bulkhead between the cockpit and the cabin beneath the after end of the bridge deck. You could slither in through them to go below, or use the hatch up forward.

There is no arrangement plan for this boat. I'd have a transom each side in way of the mainmast, put the galley under the little trunk house, and have a bunk on each side forward. Of course she'd be right up to date pollution-regs-wise with a cedar bucket.

I don't know whether or not B.B. Crowninshield ever had this boat built and had the fun of sailing her. She was apparently built for someone, for a photograph of her appears — and I'm indebted to Charles Storrow of Stonington, Connecticut, for this information — in B.B. Crowninshield's *The Marine Directory and Annual Catalogue of Yachts for Sale and Charter* for 1911. I do know she would be fun to sail, being low to the water, fast, and — well — just plain exciting.

11/ A Hand Double-Ended Schooner

Length on deck: 35 feet 3 inches
Length on waterline: 31 feet
Beam: 10 feet 2 inches
Draft: 4 feet 6 inches
Sail area: 528 square feet
Designer: William H. Hand, Jr.

William H. Hand, Jr., of New Bedford, Massachusetts, was perhaps best known for his designs of fine motorsailers — big, husky ketches like the *Bluebell* and the *Seer*.

But here's a Hand motorsailer that may have been overlooked. This little double-ended schooner was designed and built as an auxiliary fishing boat, I believe about a half century ago.

Her owner was one F.C. Wederkinch, and he used his vessel on the coast of Texas.

(The coast of Texas? One stares at the words in disbelief. Clearly the states of Maine and Oregon have coasts, but Texas? One envisions cowboys warning their herds away from some alien liquid lapping the edge of a ranch. You have to open the atlas to prove to yourself that — yes — Texas really does have a coast. But I digress.)

The schooner would make a fine motorsailer with her midships fish well closed up and her machinery moved up into it out of the after cabin. She has an easily driven hull but would need her power in light weather, for she is short-rigged.

In any case, she is an able little vessel. She might well be named the *Simplicity*.

Bill Hand was in that minority of naval architects who always draw their boats going to the left. I suppose somebody ought to make a study of the correlation of this group with left-handedness. Funny how it's hard to compare a boat design heading to the left against one that is heading to the right. It just seems harder to catch her shape, somehow, force of habit being what it is.

This left-handed business notwithstanding, however, it can be said with safety that Mr. Hand could draw the best-looking short spoon bows (if that's not a contradiction) of anyone. To my eye, he put just the right rugged, handsome curves in the bows of his boats. Alden was good at it, but Hand was the master.

Whether or not you agree with that statement, this schooner does have a nice, high bow that leads into a most pleasing sheerline. Of course it is hard to judge the sheerline on paper. You really need to see it in three dimensions to be sure, for there are other factors at play in the overall appearance of the boat. The British writer Colin Mudie reminds us that a boat, when seen in the flesh, appears to have less sheer than is shown in her profile drawing — he

William H. Hand, Jr. (The Rudder, *March 1927*)

Mr. Hand's little auxiliary fishing schooner would also make a fine motorsailer or freighter. (The Rudder)

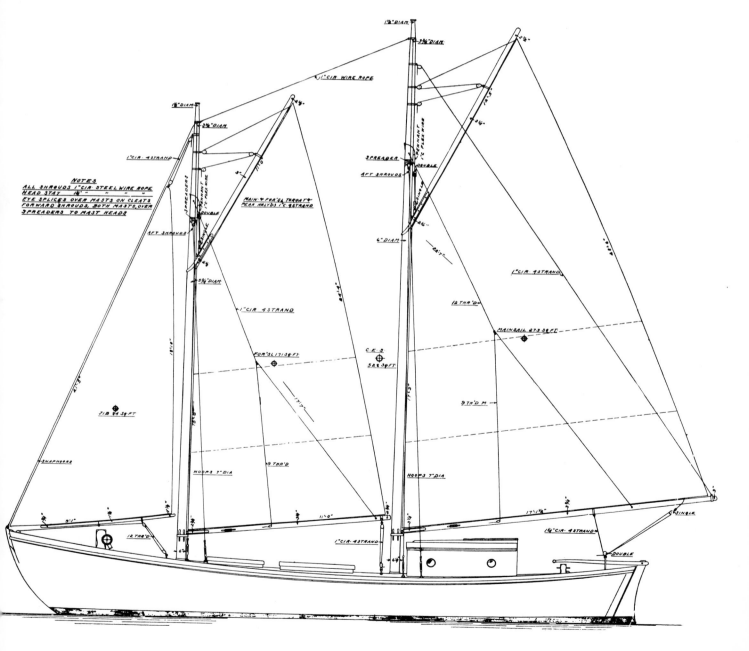

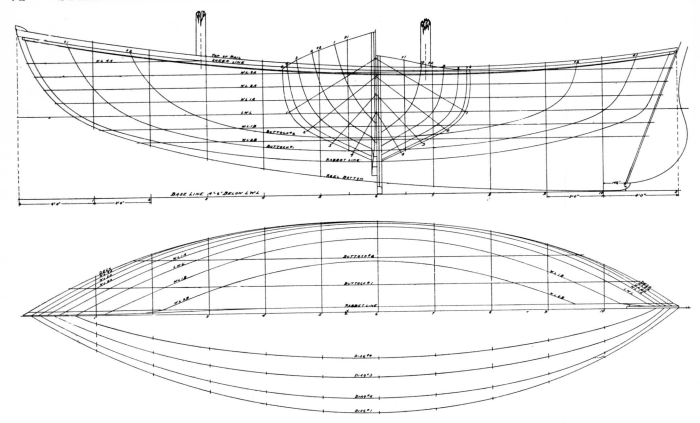

Everything about her lines is easy and moderate. She'd well deserve that word, "seakindly." (The Rudder)

says by three inches for 40 feet of length. When looking at the real boat, the sheer appears to be less pronounced than in the profile drawing, for the curvature of the deck edge takes the sheer-line farther away from your eye near the ends of the boat, Mudie says. I think he's right.

The schooner is 35 feet 3 inches long on deck, with a waterline length of 31 feet, a beam of 10 feet 2 inches, and a moderate draft of 4 feet 6 inches. Her sail area is a modest 528 square feet.

Her bow and buttock lines are extremely easy; she has a long, flat run for a double-ender.

Her sections show that she has a bit of flare all around the hull at the waterline that makes a boat look and be light on her feet and that gives her stiffness as she heels.

Her waterlines and diagonals show a hull that is quite symmetrical and that would stay well balanced when heeled. With her moderate draft and easy lines, her motion should hardly be violent or erratic. Of course, her moderate draft

would keep her from hanging on really well when going to windward.

Her rudder is certainly a simple installation and, being positioned way aft, would make her relatively easy to keep from broaching when reaching in a big breeze and sea, at the expense (as L. Francis Herreshoff reminds us) of the quicker turning that a rudder farther forward would provide.

Her sails are small, there being but 273 square feet in the mainsail, 171 in the foresail, and 84 in the jib. Her deep reefs look businesslike; she can be snugged right down when it breezes on hard. With her narrow stern and overhanging boom, you'd want to leave the reef earings all rove off on the leech of the mainsail.

Her jib is self-tending on a club that is not quite full length. This arrangement lets the sail set better than does a full-length club. You can still rig lazy jacks on such a club — which, as a matter of fact, is a fine idea.

Her high-peaked gaffs look right and give her

sails a good shape. The foresail, with its leech leading aft rather than being vertical as on most schooner foresails, would set particularly well.

She'd balance under foresail alone for jogging along, or under jib and close-reefed mainsail, if preferred.

For running off, you'd want to rig preventers on the booms to keep the sails from jibing over when the person on the tiller forgets for a moment precisely which way the wind is blowing. Ah, but can't you see yourself as that person, chasing away before a fresh breeze, foresail hauled out on one side and mainsail on the other, jib strapped down tight to dampen the roll? The Old-Timer called it "readin' both pages."

She could easily take a 10-foot boat lashed upside down over the hatches between the masts. There is nothing like having a really good small boat with you.

In the house aft could be a couple of quarter berths, their forward ends doubling as settees, and then a galley in the forward end of the house. You could call such quarters cramped or snug, depending on your viewpoint.

All in all, I think this little vessel would make a fine singlehander or two-handed cruiser for long trips. She'd carry plenty of stores, water, and fuel, all amidships where the weight belongs.

Or you could live with the engine back aft and have yourself a nice little freighter.

12/ The *Mary Jeanne II*

> **Length on deck: 36 feet 1 inch**
> **Length on waterline: 29 feet**
>   **2 inches**
> **Beam: 11 feet 1 inch**
> **Draft: 5 feet 6 inches**
> **Sail area: 800 square feet**
> **Displacement: 12 tons**
> **Designer: Philip L. Rhodes**

One of the diverting elements of the history of boating magazines is the way the various editors have handled the matter of sail and power.

I am tempted to say "sail versus power," because there has always been a lot of feigned — and, I suppose, a small bit of real — prejudice about, requiring various editors and writers to denounce power as being inferior to sail, or vice versa.

It's been fun to watch *Motor Boating* magazine add the words *"and Sailing"* to its cover, at first in small, apologetic-sized type, and, currently, in the same size as the original *Motor Boating*. Whatever it has said on the cover, though, no editor of *Motor Boating* has ever been able to resist totally the inclusion of sailing boats within his covers.

Sail magazine appeared in all its pristine glory — soon to be followed, from under the same roof, by *Motor Boating* magazine, in all *its* pristine glory.

Boating magazine has dropped sail for the time being and tells you that it is the "world's largest powerboat magazine."

At any rate, I was hardly surprised to discover a handsome, gaff-rigged schooner design printed on the pages of an ancient issue of Bill Nutting's long-defunct but once wonderful, bilious green, twice-monthly *Motor Boat* magazine.

She is the *Mary Jeanne II,* designed by Philip L. Rhodes more than half a century ago for Julian Cendoya, Jr., of Santiago de Cuba.

She is a fine-looking vessel in her own right, but I am particularly interested in her because of her resemblance to Murray Peterson's schooner, the *Coaster* (see *Good Boats*). The design of the *Mary Jeanne II* predates that of the *Coaster* by about nine years. The *Coaster* is a coasting schooner made to look like a yacht, while the *Mary Jeanne II* is a yacht made to look like a coasting schooner.

The Rhodes schooner yacht is 36 feet 1 inch long on deck, with a waterline length of 29 feet 2 inches, a beam of 11 feet 1 inch, and a draft of 5 feet 6 inches.

She displaces 12 tons and has nearly five tons of ballast, 6,600 pounds in an iron keel and 3,000 pounds of concrete poured inside.

Her sail area is 800 square feet in the three lowers.

She has a handsome set of lines. She'd cer-

Philip L. Rhodes. (Photo by Morris Rosenfeld, courtesy of Philip H. Rhodes)

cedar, and above the waterline with yellow pine, all finished to 1¼ inches.

Note in the construction drawing the size of her knees and the way they are placed to overlap each other in way of the masts.

Not the least important feature of her construction, as regards strength, is her long iron keel running from beneath the foremast all the way to the rudderpost. The great value of an iron keel was brought home to me recently as I looked at a Concordia yawl that had pounded painfully on a Maine ledge. She was hauled for repairs in a nearby yard. Her planking had been chewed right through in a couple of places, stem badly chewed away, deadwood all chewed up, and rudder hanging on by Lord-knows-what. Her iron keel had protected the heart of her, though, and had suffered no damage itself. A lead keel might or might not have held her together, but it certainly would have been mangled in the process. A boat with inside ballast and a wooden keel, even with a stout, protective shoe, might not have been salvageable.

None of us likes to think of his vessel ashore in rough water, but one of the few comforting factors in such a situation would be a long, stout, iron keel like the one on the *Mary Jeanne.*

The little schooner has plenty of sail area. The 800 square feet in her working sails are divided as follows: mainsail, 410; foresail, 226; and jib, 164.

For light-weather work, her main topsail adds another 90 square feet, and the little triangular main topmast staysail, 45, for a full-sail area of 935 square feet.

I think the single headsail is more practical than a double-head rig in a little schooner like this, although there is no question that the *Coaster,* for example, looks better with her jib and fore staysail.

The shortening-down sequence for the *Mary Jeanne* as it breezed on while you were working

tainly be a very seaworthy and dry little vessel, though she might be a bit "pitchy." Her bow lines and buttocks are quite rounded.

She has a nice sheerline carried out by the steeve of the bowsprit and complemented by the angles on which her booms and house tops are set.

Her shapely sections are moderate throughout. She has quite a fine entry.

The *Mary Jeanne's* construction plan is worthy of study. Phil Rhodes wrote, "A great deal of care was taken to secure uniform strength. Every boat 'works' in a sea and then the weak spots get it. It's one thing to pile timber in a boat and quite another to put it where it belongs."

Her frames are bent white oak, 2½ inches by 2 inches at the heel, tapering to 2 inches by 2 inches, and placed 9 inches apart. She is planked below the waterline with Port Orford

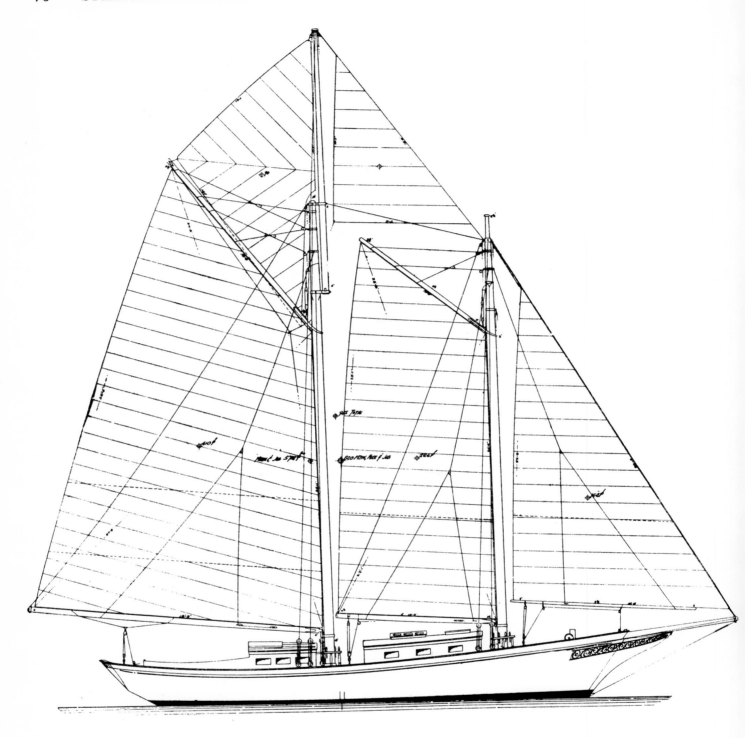

The Mary Jeanne II *is a yacht made to look like a coaster.* (Motor Boat, *August 25, 1922*)

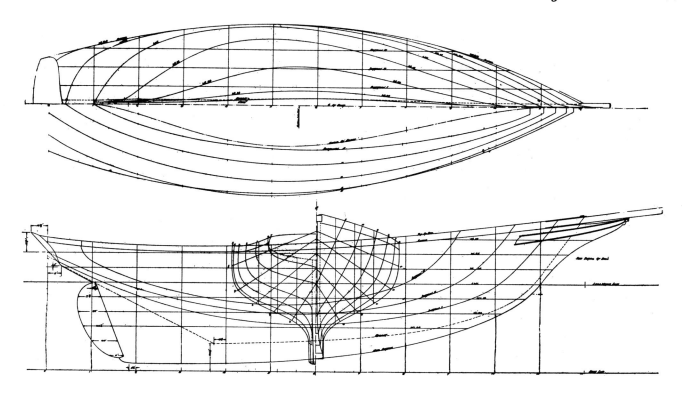

Above: *She is the same size as Murray Peterson's* Coaster, *and quite similar to that later great design, though her lines are finer.* (Motor Boat, *August 25, 1922*) **Below:** *Mr. Rhodes wrote, "It's one thing to pile timber in a boat and quite another to put it where it belongs."* (Motor Boat, *August 25, 1922*)

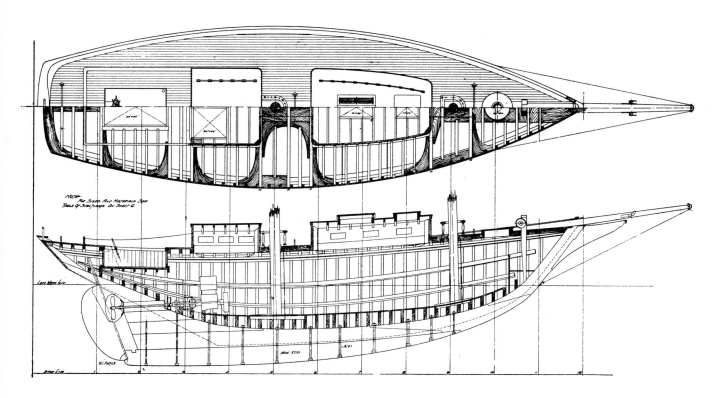

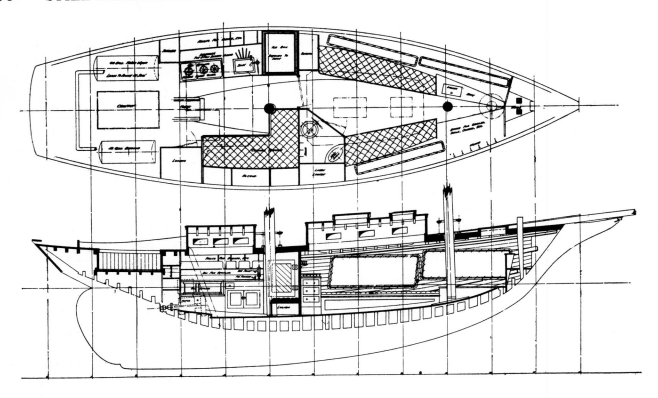

Above: *She is clear and open below, with a beautiful big fo'c's'le.* (Motor Boat, *August 25, 1922*). **Below:** *The sections show an interesting perspective on her hull form and interior arrangement.* (Motor Boat, *August 25, 1922*)

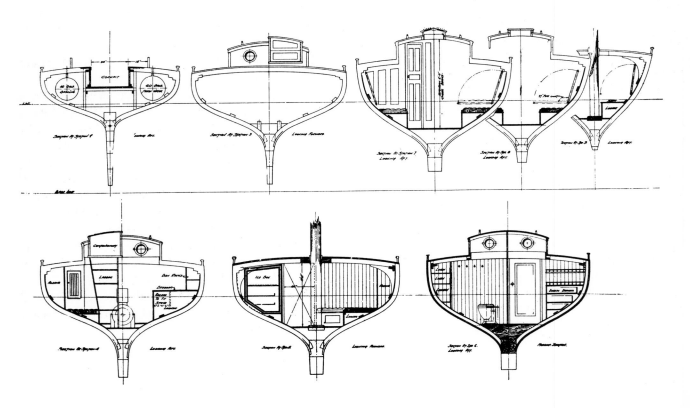

to windward might go something like this: single reef the mainsail; double reef the mainsail; reef the foresail; reef the jib; take in the foresail; and, finally, reset the reefed foresail and take in jib and mainsail.

A lot of reefing? Sure, but the modern racing boys will tell you that with jiffy reefing or slab reefing, it's no job at all. And since jiffy reefing and slab reefing are simply the rediscovery of just plain old reefing, why should we worry in our old coasting schooner? We can't help it if the go-fast guys are just discovering that you can reef a sail with great speed if you leave the reefing gear all rove off and ready to heave on.

A vessel at anchor on a quiet day with her after sail standing always looks seamanlike to me. It's nice to see a yawl or ketch leave her mizzen up after she comes to anchor, unless it's blowing hard, for it will keep her from sailing around in her berth. The same is true of a schooner's mainsail, and on a big coaster, the aftermost sail was often left standing in settled weather just to save the work of hoisting it again to get underway.

When her sails are lowered, the *Mary Jeanne* has lazy jacks all 'round to keep them out of the water, off the deck, and under control until you want to furl them.

Her jib is self-tending and will set well, with its three-quarter-length club. The topmast is rigged so it can be lowered through the cross trees.

Her baby main topmast staysail has the advantage that if rigged with double sheets, it can be left set when tacking and shifted over like any double-sheeted headsail. This sail came to be known as a Queen staysail on schooner yachts, for Nathanael G. Herreshoff tried one on a hundred-and-some-foot racing schooner called the *Queen* that he designed in 1908. It's a nice little sail, but you'd probably want a big fisherman staysail to replace it on a reach in a light breeze. Might as well have a big balloon jib, too. There's just nothing like being able to put up all kinds of big light stuff when there's not much wind.

Of course that whole way of making the boat

go can be deep-sixed by starting up the good old stone crusher — in the case of the *Mary Jeanne*, a 10-h.p. Frisbie that intrudes its way into the after cabin. Her tanks are tucked aft outboard of the cockpit well, a 60-gallon one for water to port and a 40-gallon one for gas to starboard.

Her houses are small in area, leaving plenty of worthwhile deck space. To my eye, the after house should have had two windows per side instead of three. The closely spaced windows aft and broadly spaced ones forward look strange to me.

An 8-foot pram could stow across the after corner of the forward house (if she had a removable midships thwart), for there is no companionway amidships. You expect a hatch there, but in such a small vessel it's not really needed; there is a hatch in the foredeck in case the main companionway aft is full of people or if the Frisbie should catch on fire or something.

She is quite open below with a clear passageway from the companionway to the foremast. There is six-foot headroom under the beams in the houses.

All but her forwardmost berth are far enough aft to be reasonably comfortable in a head sea, and her pipe berths in that wonderful, big fo'c's'le would be a joy to use compared with built-in bunks or transom seats that are supposed to double as bunks.

Mr. Rhodes left a nice lot of storage space forward to starboard.

I'd be tempted to do a bit of rearranging back aft so as to get a place to sit on the starboard tack. The icebox could go aft to starboard where there is now a big locker, and that would make space for a good seat for one person, at least, where the icebox is. If she were on the starboard tack for a week or so, you'd get a bit tired of having to chock yourself off against the mainmast to eat breakfast every morning.

The *Mary Jeanne II* is, I think, a fine little schooner yacht. As to her size, Phil Rhodes wrote, "She is, I believe, just about the lower limit of practicability in a real schooner." Well now, I don't know if that statement is always absolutely true.

13/ A 41-Foot Chapelle Schooner

> **Length on deck: 41 feet**
> **Length on waterline: 33 feet**
> ** 4 inches**
> **Beam: 11 feet 6 inches**
> **Draft: 3 feet 11 inches (board up)**
> **Sail area: 1,259 square feet**
> **Displacement: 26,500 pounds**
> **Designer: Howard I. Chapelle**

Many marine books are spoken of or written of using the word "classic," probably more than really deserve to have such language applied to them. One book that does deserve such strong language is *Yacht Designing and Planning* by the late, great Howard I. Chapelle, published by W.W. Norton in 1936 and still selling well.

You don't think of a detailed explanation of a complex process as being particularly exciting reading, but this book, strange to say, is one of the most exciting Chap wrote. The reason is that the example he chose from among his own designs to illustrate points made in the course of guiding the reader from a mental concept of a boat to a finished design on paper ready to be built to is a very nice 41-foot, clipper-bowed, keel-and-centerboard, gaff-rigged schooner.

As you follow Mr. Chapelle along through chapters called "Preliminary Design," "The Lines," "The Construction and Joiner Plans," and "The Sail Plan," you see this grand schooner take shape gradually before your eyes and you are exposed to the considerable amount of thinking and figuring that backs up a set of plans for the design of a good boat.

Mr. Chapelle's schooner is, then, 41 feet long on deck, with a waterline length of 33 feet 4 inches, a beam of 11 feet 6 inches, and a draft, with the board up, of 3 feet 11 inches. She displaces 26,500 pounds and has outside ballast of 1,645 pounds in an iron keel. Her sail area is 1,259 square feet.

The schooner's lines drawings show how little she would disturb the water on her passage; her fine underbody is particularly well shown in the two perspective lines drawings. She has a sharp entrance with plenty of hollow and a long run.

Her stiffness comes from ample beam and the fact that she picks up bearing as she heels, particularly aft. With moderate outside ballast not hung too low, she'd have a very easy roll.

The generous overhang aft, besides adding much to her looks, allows her to pick up considerable effective sailing waterline length once she gets going.

All in all, the schooner has a very pretty set of lines, I think.

Mr. Chapelle gives full details on her construction. A few of them are: her keel is of white oak and makes up to 5½ inches by 6 inches; the frames, also of white oak, are sided 3 inches and moulded 1⅞ inches; the centerboard trunk is

Howard I. Chapelle. (Zayma Chapelle)

1¼-inch pine; clamps are 1½-inch by 5-inch yellow pine; she is planked with 1⅛-inch hard pine and sealed with ⅜-inch pine; the deck is 1½-inch by 4-inch pine; and the house is of 1¾-inch mahogany.

As to rig — well, it is almost enough simply to say that she is a gaff schooner. What more could any sailor want? Oh I know, there are other rigs with their various advantages over the schooner. I think the following snatch of conversation from H. Warington Smyth's *Sea Wake and Jungle Trail* put them in accurate perspective:

" 'But, Skipper, what really is the best all-round rig?'

"I invariably quote Joseph Conrad and say, 'For looks, the schooner; for speed, the cutter; for handiness, the yawl or ketch.' "

Of course the schooner rig, besides being the fairest of them all, has its practical aspects. It's an ideal rig for hard weather once you get the mainsail off. On the Banks, the fishermen used to turn their schooners into snug ketches by replacing the mainsail with a good-sized trysail.

This schooner has a sail area of 942 square feet in her four lowers (mainsail, 437; foresail, 265; fore staysail, 120; and jib, 120). Her topsail has 79 square feet and her fisherman staysail, 247, so with full sail she sets 1,259 square feet.

Notice her long, outside chainplates, the easiest kind to inspect, refasten, or replace.

She has preventer backstays on both masts, a sensible rig. You would set them up as necessary when on long boards, but you wouldn't have to use them when short-tacking.

Her gaffs are low-peaked and would require vangs. I'd even put one — or, rather, a pair — on the mainsail, leading one down each side to be set up on the weather quarter.

I'd want a second reef in the foresail and a reef in the fore staysail.

Her fore staysail is self-tending on a horse. The forward end of the club slides on a track, fishing schooner style, to keep the luff of the sail from binding when the sail is lowered.

It would be fun to send up a jackyard fore topsail when she's on the wind in a light breeze and you wouldn't have to tack for at least a couple of hours.

She has some real anchor gear on deck, a good hand windlass and an anchor davit each side. She's a bit dainty for catheads.

The tackle to lift the board slides on a brass track atop the port side of the house, belaying on its after port corner. The chain pendant would run in a pipe below and in a copper trough to protect the top of the house.

The schooner's deck plan shows brass filler plates around the edge of her deck out against the rail for salting her down. There are four of them forward and no fewer than 21 aft around her quarters and transom.

She has a very big cockpit formed by a coaming set on deck and a large, rather shallow footwell, of a size that will take a couple of folding canvas chairs if there's not a big crowd on board.

Her engine is under the bridge deck. It's offset to starboard with the shaft canted outboard to cancel out the turning moment of the off-center wheel. The water tank is under the bridge deck and there is a fuel tank on each side outboard of the cockpit well.

The house is quite high to give headroom in a rather shoal hull (6 feet at the after end of the house and 5½ feet forward). Mr. Chapelle just managed not to spoil her looks with this house by combining a fairly generous crown with a tiny bit of sheer to the sides of the house. He might have gone just a little bit further with both ideas.

Below, the schooner has lots of space for two or three people, being wisely not arranged to take a big gang cruising. The transoms in the

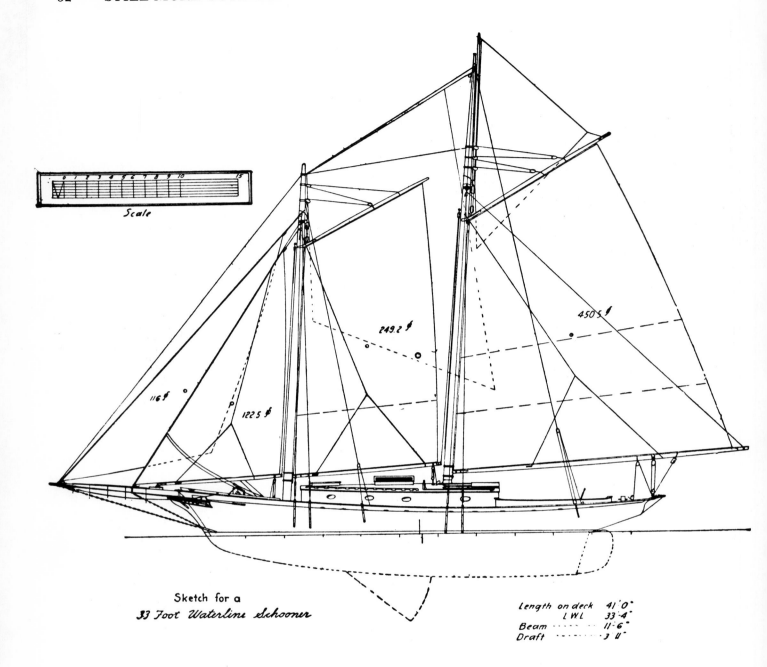

Scale

Sketch for a
33 Foot Waterline Schooner

Length on deck   41'0"
             LWL   33'4"
Beam ------   11'6"
Draft ------   3'11"

Above: *Mr. Chapelle's preliminary drawing of the 41-foot schooner he used as the example in his classic book* Yacht Designing and Planning, *published more than 40 years ago and still a standard text on the subject. The sail areas given are approximate.* (Yacht Designing and Planning *by Howard I. Chapelle, W. W. Norton and Co.*) **Right:** *Her lines show a pretty hull with the moderate draft that makes for an easy motion at sea.* (Yacht Designing and Planning *by Howard I. Chapelle, W. W. Norton and Co.*) **Far right:** *Forward and aft perspectives of the schooner's lines.* (Yacht Designing and Planning *by Howard I. Chapelle, W. W. Norton and Co.*)

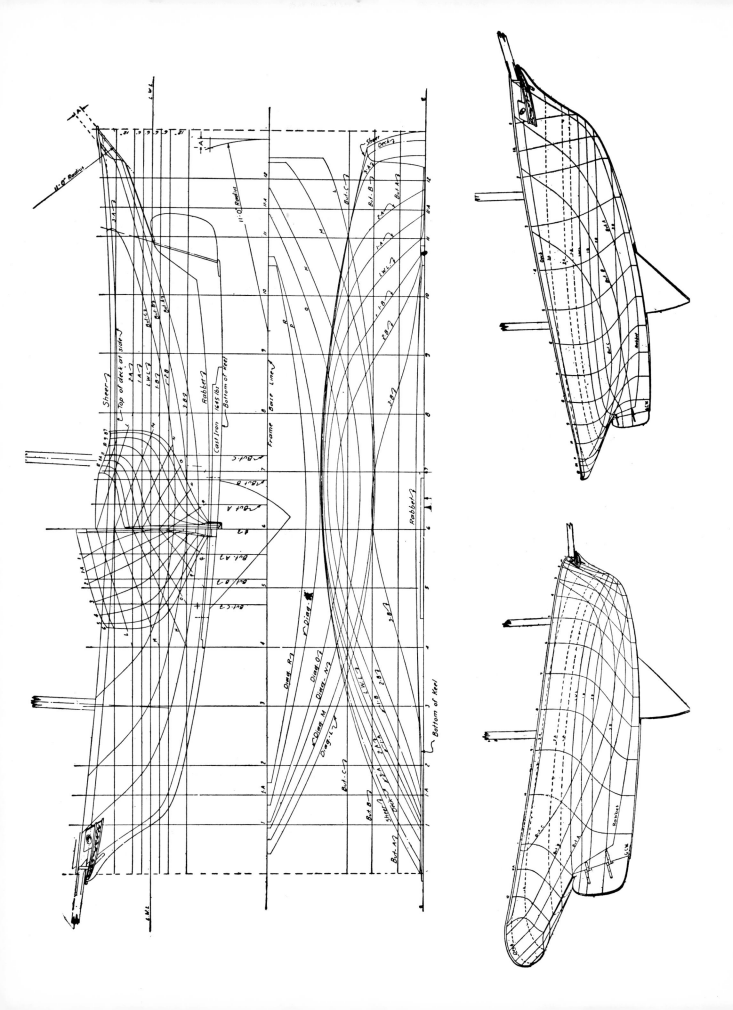

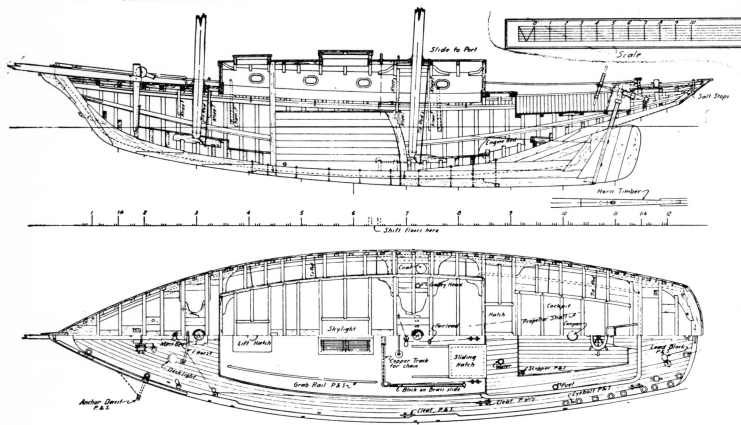

Above: *Mr. Chapelle's construction and deck plans of his schooner. (Yacht Designing and Planning by Howard I. Chapelle, W.W. Norton and Co.)* **Below:** *She is laid out with plenty of space for two or three people. (Yacht Designing and Planning by Howard I. Chapelle, W.W. Norton and Co.)*

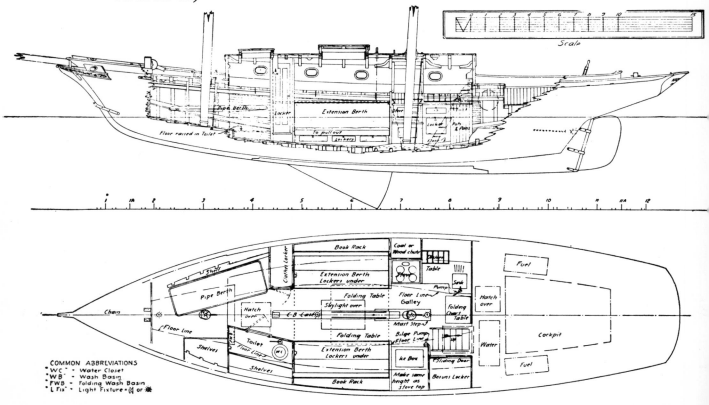

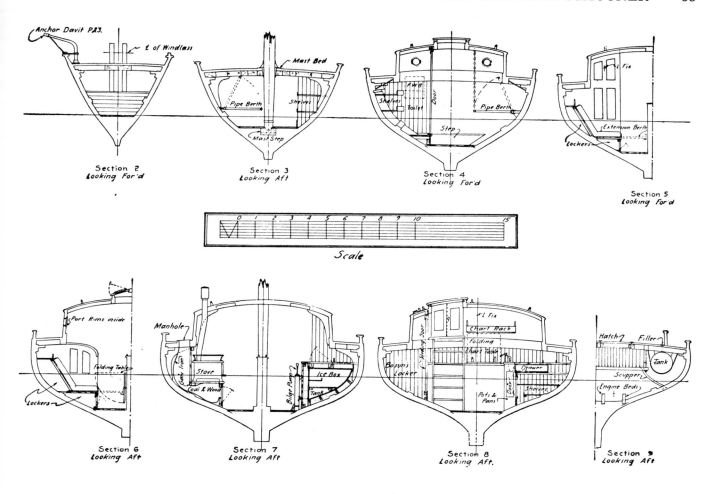

Above: *Sectional drawings help you visualize details of the interior arrangement.* (Yacht Designing and Planning *by Howard I. Chapelle, W. W. Norton and Co.)* **Below:** *Mr. Chapelle shows the reader of* Yacht Designing and Planning *how he makes a rough sketch and notes while the owner tells him his requirements for the design.* (Yacht Designing and Planning *by Howard I. Chapelle, W. W. Norton and Co.)*

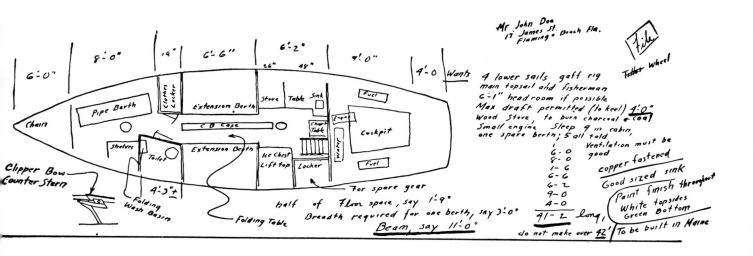

saloon slide out to form berths, and there's a spare pipe berth forward for a third hand. The centerboard trunk supports her cabin table.

In the after port corner of the cabin is a big locker labeled "Bosun's Locker." I would prefer to use this locker for foul weather gear and relegate the bosun's locker to the fo'c's'le, though, of course, there would be the usual ditty bag hanging just inside the engine room hatch in the bridge deck, handy to the watch.

She has a folding chart table at the after end of the cabin on the centerline. When it's folded back, you have full access to the sink.

To my mind this schooner would make a fine coastwise cruising boat. She'd be a lot of fun to sail and would be quite fast, especially once she freed her wind a bit. Don't discount her to windward, though, for she would foot fast six points off the wind with well-cut sails trimmed right, her topsail set, and her vangs in use. Yet, somehow, the way I see her best in my mind's eye is reaching in a fresh breeze with her four lowers set, wind just forward of abeam. A sea comes in under her — feel her lift and give and go down across the trough to the next one. Some fun, I say.

14/ A Starling Burgess Schooner

Length on deck: 51 feet 5 inches
Length on waterline: 38 feet
Beam: 13 feet 1 inch
Draft: 7 feet 7 inches
Sail area: 1,220 square feet
Displacement: 52,760 pounds
Designer: W. Starling Burgess

I wish I knew more about some of the designers of fine cruising vessels who, like William Hand, drew their boats heading west, when the more normal practice is to show boats sailing east on paper. Were Hand, Henry Gruber, Howard Chapelle, and W. Starling Burgess all left-handed?

Starling Burgess, son of the great designer Edward Burgess, drew up a fine cruising schooner in 1931 with her bow to the left, as was his practice. I've long admired this design, but I don't know whether she was ever built. She was to be built at the Herreshoff Manufacturing Company at Bristol, Rhode Island, soon after she was designed, but the list of boats contracted for by Herreshoff's shows no such craft during that era. It may be that she was built at Herreshoff's then but wasn't put on the list because she wasn't designed by N.G. Herreshoff.

The schooner is 51 feet 5 inches long on deck, with a waterline length of 38 feet, a beam of 13 feet 1 inch, and a draft of 7 feet 7 inches. Her displacement is given as 52,760 pounds, and she has 1,220 square feet of sail in her four lowers.

The lines show a moderate and easy vessel that would have both a nice motion and a good turn of speed. Her sections are full of gentle curves. Note how her deadrise continues above the waterline so she will pick up stiffness as she heels. Her ballast is not extremely heavy, but it is hung low for great ultimate stability.

Her moderate overhang forward and fairly long overhang aft give her good looks, in my opinion, and also provide a nice, long platform to take her generous rig and give her people room to handle it. Her bow and buttock lines are fairly deep, but her run is well developed and her waterlines quite fine. Her sheerline is certainly graceful and her freeboard has been kept low enough so as not to detract from her beauty. The diagonals are fair.

This vessel would have no bad habits at sea, save perhaps an occasional slap of her stern when pitching back after diving into a hole on the backside of a steep head sea.

The schooner rig is a versatile rig. In a light air, you can reach along with mainsail, main topsail, balloon main topmast staysail coming nearly to the deck, and big balloon jib. In a hard chance, you can jog along under close-reefed foresail alone and there are lots of sail combinations in between.

Starling Burgess. (Muriel Vaughn)

A fine cruising schooner heading west.
(Yachting, *April 1931*)

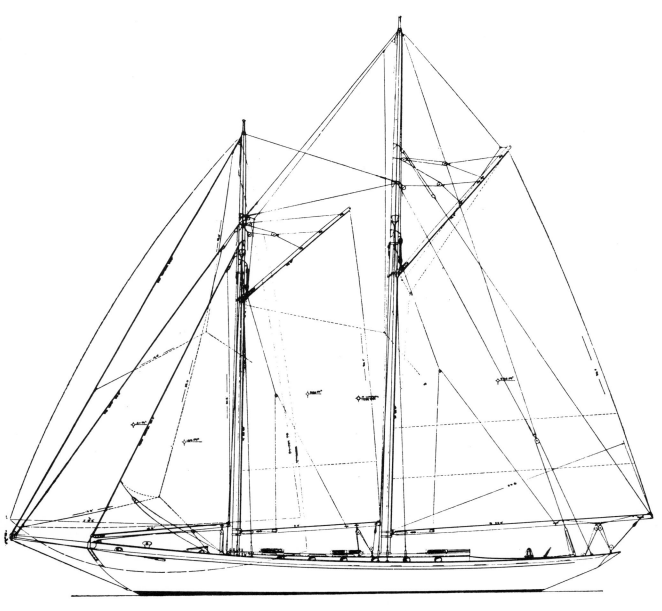

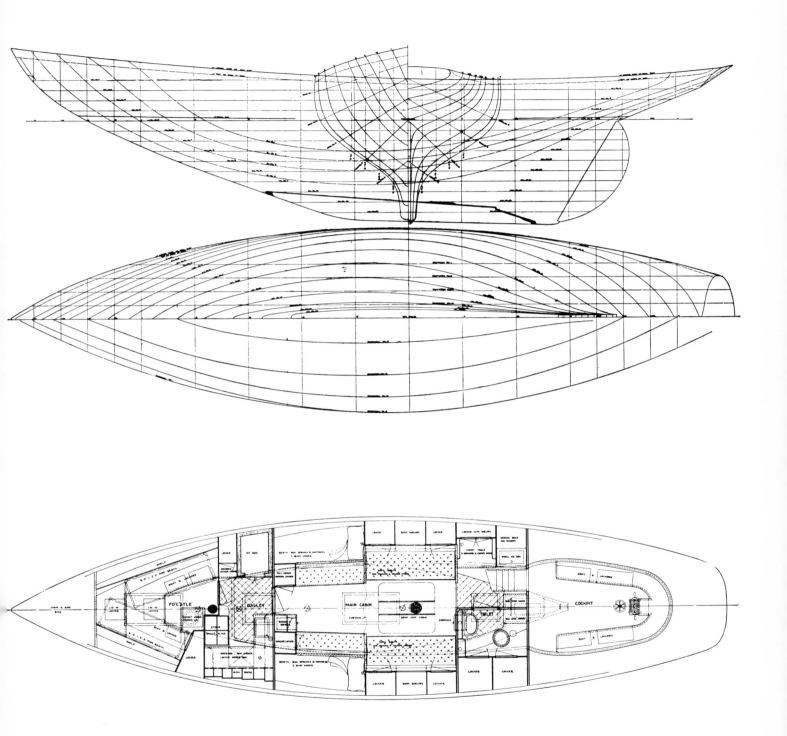

Top: *Her lines are sweet and fair; she is certainly a pretty boat.* (Yachting, *April 1931*). **Bottom:** *The heart of her cabin arrangement is the huge saloon amidships.* (Yachting, *April 1931*)

The pole masts on this vessel give her a modern look. And their nice rake makes all the difference in her appearance. Her gaffs "have some rise to 'em," as my friend Walter Tyler from the Chesapeake Bay would say, which looks well and would keep the sails from twisting too much. Of course she needs a vang on the fore gaff.

I might have given her a slightly taller foremast to make more of her jib topsail and a big balloon jib, which I'd prefer to the single-luff spinnaker shown. A fore topsail probably would not be worth bothering with, but her big fisherman certainly is; it would do wonders for her on a reach in moderate weather.

Note that the lower and upper main running backstays lead to a common tackle for setting up, a sensible rig for most sailing. On a long passage, when you tack infrequently, you might want to set them up separately.

The schooner's house has been kept low and narrow; you could see all around her deck and rails when steering and could thus get a good sense — and enjoyment — of her motion, a vital requisite to good helmsmanship. The low house also makes plenty of secure space on which to work on deck, to say nothing of leaving room to hoist in a good dinghy, either with davits or with tackles on the masts.

She has a nice big cockpit so you could take a gang daysailing. Note that the seats don't go all the way forward, leaving you a place to stand out against the coaming in a comfortable and powerful position for pulling on jib sheets and backstay tails, compared to kneeling on the seat.

She has no bridge deck to climb over, but you'd want heavy boards to go in the companionway, a strong way to hold them there, and enough conscience to use them always in rough or squally weather. You'd want mighty big scuppers in the cockpit.

Her engine is tucked away unobtrusively yet is quite accessible with the removal of some paneling.

The schooner's arrangement is basically like that of the famous staysail schooner *Nina* that Starling Burgess designed three years earlier for the transatlantic race to Spain, the first of many races won by that famous yacht. The *Nina* was a much bigger schooner, being 50 feet on the waterline, but both vessels had a huge saloon amidships, head and chart table aft, and galley forward. The *Nina's* engine was up between the masts, right in the middle of everything. And, like many schooners, she had a second companionway between the masts. This amenity was done away with in Mr. Burgess' later, smaller schooner, I think to advantage, for in this boat the second companionway is not really necessary, since the house is continuous and provides headroom all the way forward and aft. Why break up the main cabin with a source of water from the deck? It's a snugger, quieter place without it.

On the other hand, that big saloon doesn't need always to be a snug and quiet place. As a matter of fact, you could have quite a party in there. Yet this same grand saloon can be divided in two by a curtain to separate the forward half with its outboard bunks from the after half with its wide transoms and good-sized table.

The schooner's galley is fairly far forward, but in this size of vessel the motion shouldn't be too bad up there. The fo'c's'le is good for sail and gear stowage and is okay for sleeping in port, but it is no good for sleeping at sea, except when the vessel is well off the wind.

This fine cruising schooner may be headed the "wrong" way on paper, but it sure would be fun to be the one to set her course at sea or 'longshore.

15/ The *Brilliant*

> **Length on deck: 61 feet 6 inches**
> **Length on waterline: 49 feet**
> **Beam: 14 feet 8 inches**
> **Draft: 8 feet 0 inches**
> **Sail area: 1,715 square feet**
> **Displacement: 38 tons**
> **Designer: Olin Stephens**

It was a great thrill to me to sail with Pop in the yawl *Brownie* to Newport, Rhode Island, from our home mooring 40 miles to the westward in June of 1946 to see the start of the first postwar Bermuda Race. Older siblings used to talk about seeing such stupendous events — even including America's Cup races between the huge J boats — but I was always too young to view these historic occasions. Just when I turned old enough to go, the J boats were replaced by U boats.

So I was very excited when we came rolling in through the East Passage to Narragansett Bay with a boisterous sou'wester on our heels, bore up in smooth water round Fort Adams, and beat up through a big distinguished fleet of ocean racers and spectator boats to find a berth in Brenton's Cove. Busy as I was up forward getting halyards down off their pins ready to run, lashings off the anchor, rode laid out clear, and then jib hauled down and furled, still I saw out of the corner of my eye the wishbone boom of the great ketch *Vamarie*, the long, dark-blue hull of the latest Sparkman & Stephens creation, the *Gesture*, and the handsome white hull of a big, spotless, powerful-looking schooner.

As soon as we were anchored and furled up, I went rowing in the dinghy all through the boats. It was the white schooner that impressed me more than any of them. She was the *Brilliant,* and she just exuded the power of an able vessel, even lying at anchor.

Back on board, Pop told me something about her. He seemed chiefly impressed by her very fancy construction. He spoke of diagonal bronze strapping let flush into planking and deck. He said it was rumored her engine room was a single aluminum casting dropped into the boat up between the masts. No oil, gas, odor, sound, or vibration was supposed to be able to escape from the thing. The *Brilliant* was meant to have all the advantages of an engine with none of the disadvantages. Pop supposed that if the machine blew up, the explosion would merely lift the hatch off the top of the casting and the people having tea back in the cabin wouldn't even have their conversation interrupted. The prospect seemed to amuse him somehow, but I didn't like him poking fun at my glorious schooner.

But he was truly impressed with the *Brilliant.* He asked if I could see her seams, and I

Olin Stephens.

reported that they were certainly nowhere in evidence. I was particularly enamored of the swordfishing-type pulpit at the end of her bowsprit, and, all in all, was really quite jealous of her crew, though I didn't dare let on to Pop about that.

Next day the sou'wester increased, if anything, and we sailed out to see the start under just main and staysail. We were slam-banging along on the starboard tack watching all the big ocean racers come out and enjoying ourselves hugely, when along came the *Brilliant* converging on us from to leeward going dead into the wind under power with her mainsail up and slatting and her foresail being hoisted. Her big crew — apparently including her helmsman — was preoccupied with setting sail from her pitching deck, and on she came oblivious to the fact that a little sailing yawl was about to be splintered against her gleaming topsides. I thought Pop would probably yell to make them bear off, but he must have felt as I did that we were just out fooling around watching while these guys were trying to get ready to go to Bermuda, because all he did was tack when we were 10 feet away from the big plunging schooner. Then, when they all looked over startled at our sudden appearance so close aboard, he fixed her helmsman with an icy stare and said, "Take a look around." I was embarrassed. Imagine treating the *Brilliant* like that.

Walter Barnum wanted a very strong offshore cruiser that could be driven in rough weather without fear of breaking gear or straining the hull. He went to Sparkman & Stephens for a design for such a vessel, and Olin Stephens drew the plans for the *Brilliant* in 1930. The boat was built in 1932 by Henry B. Nevins at City Island, New York, obviously to the very highest specifications. After World War II, she was owned by Briggs S. Cunningham. For the last 24 years she has been owned by the Mystic Seaport and has been used for sail training.

At Mystic, she makes 18 one-week cruises

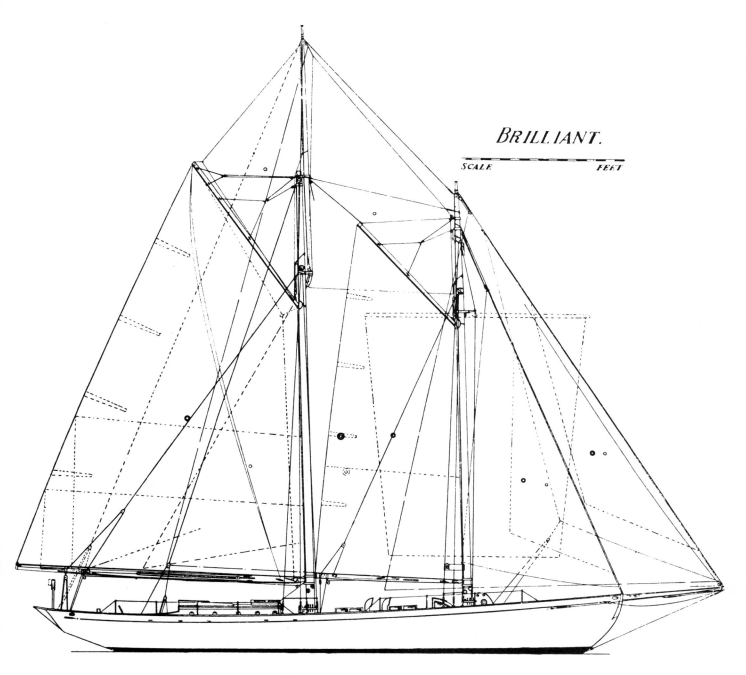

The Brilliant's *original gaff rig.* (Sailing, Seamanship and
Yacht Construction *by Uffa Fox)*

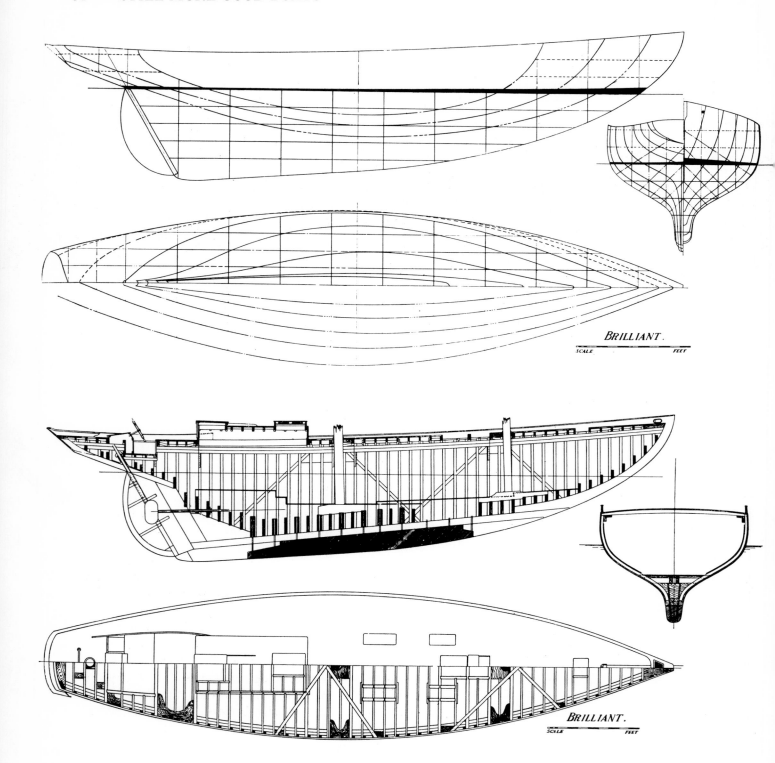

Top: *She has a very powerful hull, yet she is fine enough to be quite fast.* (Sailing, Seamanship and Yacht Construction *by Uffa Fox*) **Bottom:** *Her extremely high-quality construction is the work of Henry B. Nevins and lends awe to just about every conversation about her.* (Sailing, Seamanship and Yacht Construction *by Uffa Fox*)

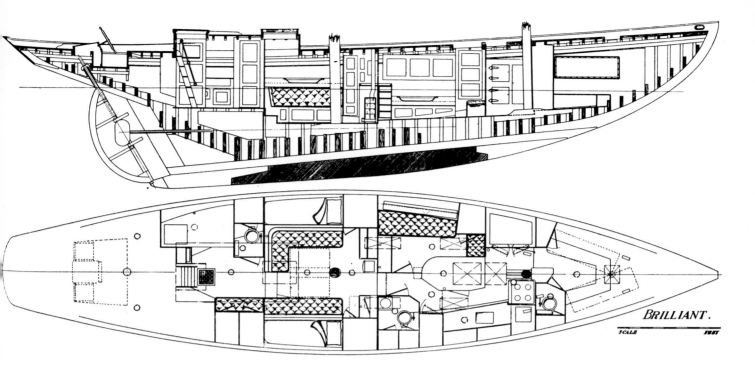

She has an interesting layout. The engine room is up between the masts, and back by the companion-way are all the essentials that need to be handy to the deck. (Sailing, Seamanship and Yacht Construction *by Uffa Fox*)

each summer along the southern New England coast. She has a skipper and mate and takes a group of 10 crew members, nine youngsters with an adult leader. At first her skipper was Adrian Lane, and for the last 19 years her skipper has been Francis E. Bowker, who, having been in coasters, thinks of her as a very small schooner rather than a big one.

Walter Barnum, Briggs Cunningham, and the Mystic Seaport have unstintingly given the *Brilliant* the very best of care, so that although she is approaching the half-century mark, she is in truly excellent condition and always looks very smart. It's still mighty hard to find the seams in her topsides.

Captain Bowker wrote me recently:

> At the present time, the *Brilliant* is hauled out at Mystic Seaport. We have set up on all the keelbolts. It was felt that, after all these years, her bottom should be caulked, but only a few places have been found that indicate any such care. Even the original seam compound remains undisturbed. Except for a piece of

oak in the wheelbox, no piece of original timber has ever been replaced. A man by the name of Murray was Nevins' master carpenter and for many years the *Brilliant* was known as "Murray's Masterpiece."

The *Brilliant* is 61 feet 6 inches long on deck, with a waterline length of 49 feet, a beam of 14 feet 8 inches, and a draft of 8 feet 10 inches. She displaces 38 tons and has 1,715 square feet of sail in her four lowers and 2,082 square feet with her main topsail and fisherman staysail.

Olin Stephens made her fine enough to have an excellent turn of speed; she is not beamy for a cruising schooner of her size. She has a fine entrance with a little hollow at the waterline, easy bow lines, and a long run. The diagonals are extremely fair.

Her rig is very nicely proportioned, her gaffs being well peaked up. She was given a mere Marconi mainsail about 25 years ago.

When shortening down, to get the best out of her you'd want to begin by reefing the mainsail. Beyond that, there are plenty of sail combina-

The Brilliant *on "The Nevins Yacht Elevator."* (Yachting, *June 1933)*

tions to choose from, right down to jogging along under foresail alone. Her main trysail would be a useful sail in hard weather, as would her storm jib and storm fore staysail.

The squaresail was used some in her early years, and it was found that perhaps its best point of sailing was with the wind one point abaft the beam when it wouldn't blanket the headsails.

She would have a big fisherman staysail reaching halfway to the deck for reaching in moderate weather and a huge gollywobbler to catch a light breeze.

Note the vang on the foresail. You'd probably want a club on the fore staysail to make it self-tending. And you might want to pair up the upper and lower backstays on the mainmast, leading them to one tackle.

I like the look of her flush deck with just the trunk cabin abaft the mainmast. She usually carries a boat on a cradle right side up between her masts, which somehow gives her a seagoing look. Some sailors say the drawback to carrying a boat right side up on deck is that it always gets filled with junk, but I say that one of the advantages of carrying a boat right side up on deck is that you immediately have a nice place for a lot of junk where it will stay put, out of the way.

Her cockpit arrangement lets you walk out to the sides of the well, and there is a big protected bridge deck.

Her engine room is, of course, ideal, about its only disadvantage being that a long shaft is required.

The *Brilliant's* arrangement below deck makes a lot of sense. Just inside the companionway, you have everything you need: a big chart table, a small head, and plenty of stowage for foul weather gear.

Next forward is the nice, big saloon with extra headroom under the forward end of the trunk cabin and two berths tucked well back out of the way.

Forward of the saloon is a stateroom with a good-sized head opposite. Then, wrapped around the engine compartment is a big, L-shaped galley with plenty of counter space. There's a fo'c's'le with two pipe berths. Mystic Seaport has added two bunks in the fo'c's'le.

When Walter Barnum got his cruising schooner, he decided first of all to see what she could do at ocean racing. The 1932 Bermuda Race was the last great race of schooner yachts. There were entered a number of John G. Alden's schooners, led by his latest, the *Malabar X.* There was the *Barlovento,* designed for Pierre S.

The Brilliant *driving to windward under full sail. (Mystic Seaport)*

Dupont III by Cox & Stevens. There was the *Mistress*, designed for George E. Roosevelt by Henry J. Gielow. There was the *Brilliant*.

And besides all these great schooners, there were such famous yachts as the *Vamarie, Dorade, Highland Light,* and *Jolie Brise.*

It was an eventful race. The *Brilliant* didn't particularly live up to her name, the *Malabar X* being the winner on corrected time. The *Highland Light,* Frank Paine's big cutter, set a new course record, and the *Jolie Brise* rescued all but one of the crew of the burning schooner *Adriana.*

In 1933, Walter Barnum sailed the *Brilliant* across the Atlantic to go in the Fastnet Race. That year's Fastnet turned out to be a slow, light-weather race that was won by the *Dorade;* the *Brilliant* didn't fare too well.

If the *Brilliant* didn't get the weather she needed to do startling things on the ocean-racing circuit, she certainly was proving herself to be a very lucky and well-sailed cruising boat.

Her transatlantic passage in 1933 from City Island to Plymouth was most remarkable. It was ably described by the *Brilliant's* navigator on the trip, the longtime, sparkling writer for *Yachting* magazine, Alfred F. Loomis. I don't want to tell you what he called his *Yachting* article describing the passage, because that would give away the fun.

Suffice it to say that Alf Loomis and a number of other sailors he described as "old-timers" (he, himself, was an ancient 43 at the time) were lured to sea by Mr. Barnum to help him waft the schooner *Brilliant* across the Atlantic on the wings of the predicted gentle westerlies so she could then be driven hard in the Fastnet Race. Off they went, but instead of gentle westerlies the breeze seemed to hang in the south from one point forward of abeam to one point abaft the beam and vary in strength from moderate to strong.

The breeze held like this for two straight days, and the crew was beginning to grumble to

Mr. Barnum that the cruise was not as advertised. Instead of fanning along upright, her people getting sunburned, the *Brilliant* was well heeled over on the starboard tack, romping along with wet decks, and her people either hunched in the cockpit in oilskins or well chocked off below against the roll.

At the end of the second day, Alf Loomis plotted in his position and remarked that they had sailed over 200 miles in the previous 24 hours. He said he had noticed, as a matter of fact, that they had also sailed over 200 miles the day before. The old-timers, out for a pleasure cruise, looked at each other and looked at Barnum. The latter addressed his ancient crewmen somewhat thusly: "Boys, set the genoa jib and be damned quick about it." And then: "All right, boys," from the depths of the sail bin, "we'll put a couple of topsails on her."

So they drove the *Brilliant* under mainsail, foresail, fore staysail, genoa jib, main topsail, and fisherman staysail.

Mr. Barnum said they ought to take the big jib off her when it got dark, but, strange to relate, it never did get dark on that particular night in the middle of the Atlantic — at least it must have stayed light — because the old men left the big sail right on her.

And the breeze held. The *Brilliant* averaged over 200 miles a day for five days in a row. And one of those days was a paltry 160 miles. On the sixth day she did 214. On the seventh, 202. Now she had done 1,448 miles in seven days, and she had done over 200 miles each day for the last five days — 1,077. She ended up averaging over 200 a day for nine days, and in 10 days did 1,976 miles, for an average speed of 8⅓ knots. Her best day's run was 231 miles, not quite 10 knots.

She had light weather at both ends of the transatlantic passage but still was land to land, Block Island to Bishop Rock, Isles of Scilly, in just short of 16 days, and City Island to Plymouth in 17 days, 18 hours. Some sailing for a heavy cruising schooner!

To put the *Brilliant's* achievement in perspective, it is interesting to look at some other sailing records.

On a whole different scale, the 185-foot, three-masted schooner *Atlantic,* designed by William Gardner, averaged over 10 knots from Sandy Hook to the Lizard, 2,925 miles, in winning the transatlantic race in 1905. In 1980, the 58-foot French trimaran *Paul Ricard* sailed this same course at an average speed of more than 12 knots. The 73-foot ketch *Windward Passage* averaged over 10 knots in 1971 in both the 800-mile race from Miami to Montego Bay, Jamaica, and the 2,225-mile race from Los Angeles to Honolulu. Francis Chichester in the *Gipsy Moth V,* a staysail ketch 41 feet 8 inches long on the waterline, sailed singlehanded 1,081 miles in five consecutive days in the Atlantic in 1970. Alain Colas in the *Manureva* (ex-*Pen Duick IV),* a 69-foot trimaran, sailed singlehanded around the world in 1973 covering 4,500 miles in 22 days on the passage from the Cape of Good Hope to Cape Leeuwin, his best day's run being 326 miles. At any rate, the cruising schooner *Brilliant* is rubbing elbows with some pretty fast company. One of her crewmen in the 1932 Bermuda Race, Graham Bigelow, whom Alf Loomis called "The Old Gray Poet of Norfolk," wrote:

> "Fannies wet all day and night,
>   *Brilliant* sailing like a kite.
> Get that damned club topsail set,
>   Just to make us curse and sweat.
> Set the guinny on the sprit,
>   Sheet her down and watch her split.
> Gulf Stream squalls we drive right through.
>   *Brilliant,* here's to you!"

When Adrian Lane was the *Brilliant's* skipper and Biff Bowker was her mate, they told me the *Brilliant* was about the finest schooner anywhere on the East Coast. I wasn't about to argue with them. She's impressed me with being just that since the first time I saw her.

16/ The *Barlovento*

> Length on deck: 64 feet 5 inches
> Length on waterline: 50 feet
> Beam: 15 feet 6 inches
> Draft: 9 feet 6 inches
> Sail area: 2,419 square feet
> Displacement: 45 tons
> Designer: Henry Gruber

If it looked like settled summer weather with promise of a moderate-to-fresh southwest breeze in the afternoon, Pop would say at breakfast, "This is a good day for an all-day sail." That meant we'd take lunch on the yawl *Brownie* and like as not end up anchoring to eat it in West Harbor on Fishers Island.

One of that harbor's fixtures in the late Thirties was the big schooner *Barlovento*. She always looked like a great ship to me, perhaps because of her hawseholes halfway down the bow. I never remember seeing her off her mooring.

She hadn't always swung to it, though. Her owner, Pierre S. Dupont III, had taken her in the Bermuda Race in 1932. *Barlovento* was the fourth to finish behind the *Highland Light* and two other big schooners, the *Mistress* and the *Malabar X*.

The *Barlovento* had been designed just the year before by Henry Gruber, who worked for the New York City firm of Cox & Stevens. Mr. Gruber later worked for Burgess (Starling) and Donaldson (Boyd). Like Burgess, he always drew his boats going to the left. I think he was an extremely talented designer. As far as I know, Mr. Gruber disappeared from the boat-

ing scene in the late Thirties. I think he may have gone back to his native Germany. Al Mason, also a talented designer, wrote me that Mr. Gruber died about 1970.

The *Barlovento* was built at Pendleton's in Wiscasset, Maine. She is 64 feet 5 inches long on deck, with a waterline length of 50 feet, a beam of 15 feet 6 inches, and a draft of 9 feet 6 inches. She displaces about 45 tons and has a sail area of 2,419 square feet in the Marconi-mainsail rig that was put into her.

The *Barlovento* is what my friend Walter Tyler, the Chesapeake Bay waterman, would call "a deep wader." Her keel goes down and down. She must have a wide range of stability with her low-slung ballast — nor does she lack lateral plane. Her deep, heavy hull will bring her into her own in a big seaway, when she will sail fairly fast yet have a reasonably comfortable, easy motion.

She has a bit of curve and tumblehome in her topsides to give her a graceful, powerful look.

Isn't that bow something? There is more than six feet of freeboard forward. Her overhangs are moderate. She has deep bow lines but a fine entry with a little hollow at the waterline.

Henry Gruber on board the Bluenose. *(Uffa Fox's Second Book by Uffa Fox, International Marine Publishing Co.)*

The schooner was strongly built to a high standard. She has oak frames, yellow pine planking, Everdur screw fastenings, a teak deck, diagonal strapping in hull and deck, and heavy bilge stringers running nearly her full length.

Because in the early Thirties there was great discussion of the ocean-racing rating rule, we have no fewer than four different schooner rigs to look at for this design. Henry Gruber drew her up gaff-rigged with three working topsails and then drew alternate sail plans with a taller Marconi mainsail and shorter foremast, one with a gaff foresail and the other with just staysails between the masts. The gaff rig had 2,315 square feet of sail, while the Marconi and staysail rigs each had 2,250 square feet. Areas and rig allowances were cranked into the rule to see how she'd rate with each rig. For those who are interested in such things, this analysis appears in detail in the May 1931 issue of *Yachting* magazine.

The rig that was decided upon for the *Barlovento* was a fourth one, with a Marconi mainsail and gaff foresail, but with a taller foremast so that a jib topsail could be set and a bigger balloon jib and spinnaker could be carried.

I am glad they didn't put a staysail rig in her. The problem with the rig for cruising is that the boat really needs her main topmast staysail as a working sail most of the time, since the lower staysail is quite a bit smaller than a gaff foresail would be. But the main topmast staysail on a big cruising schooner seems to stay in its locker most of the time, and then you're left with an abortive rig.

The Marconi mainsail is simpler than the gaff mainsail and topsail, and it is a bit more majestic. Majesty could turn to brutishness, though, in a real breeze; the Marconi mainsail has an area of a bit over 1,000 square feet. Its masthead is 72 feet above the deck.

Note, if you will, the vang on the fore gaff, a simple, yet effective piece of rigging sometimes overlooked despite my eight-year crusade to make it famous. A toast, I say, to all good vangs wherever they may be working, quietly and unobtrusively controlling their gaffs and keeping the twist out of their sails.

The light sails available to the master of a schooner are numerous and wonderful. The *Barlovento's* captain could carry a big, high-cut Yankee jib topsail when beating to windward in light or moderate weather, and, on a reach, could break out her huge balloon main topmast staysail, or gollywobbler, lead its sheet through a block on the end of the main boom, and go boiling along.

The *Barlovento* is flush-decked with just a small trunk cabin aft. She has permanent lifelines from the main rigging nearly to her stern; why not run them back to the gallows frame? Her crew would set up high, temporary lifelines from the main rigging running forward.

She is big enough to stow a 12-foot boat on deck between the masts and big enough to carry

(Continued on page 108)

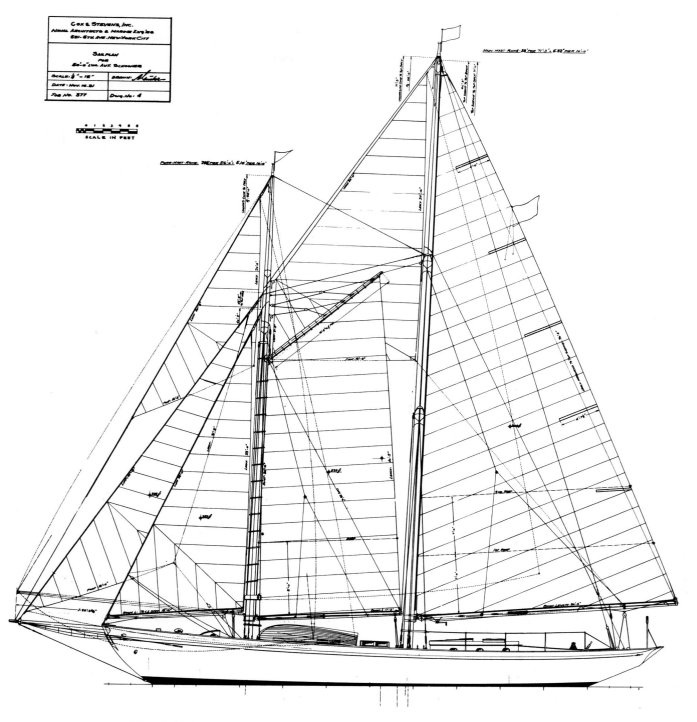

They decided to give her a Marconi mainsail and a tall foremast. (Philip H. Rhodes)

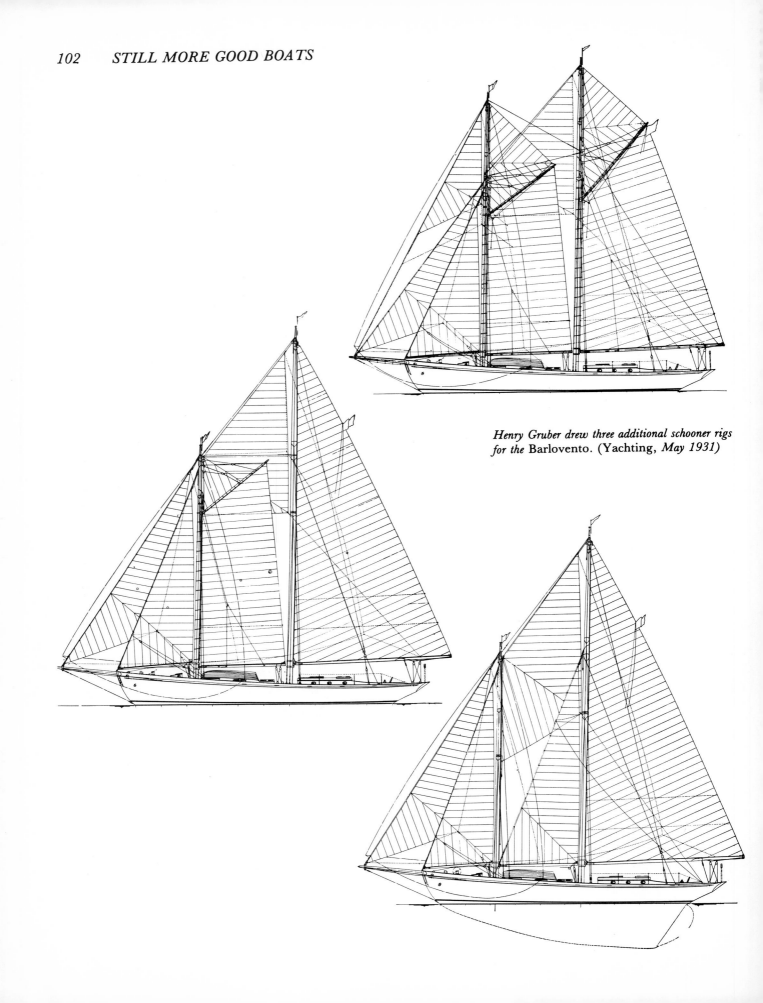

Henry Gruber drew three additional schooner rigs for the Barlovento. *(*Yachting, *May 1931)*

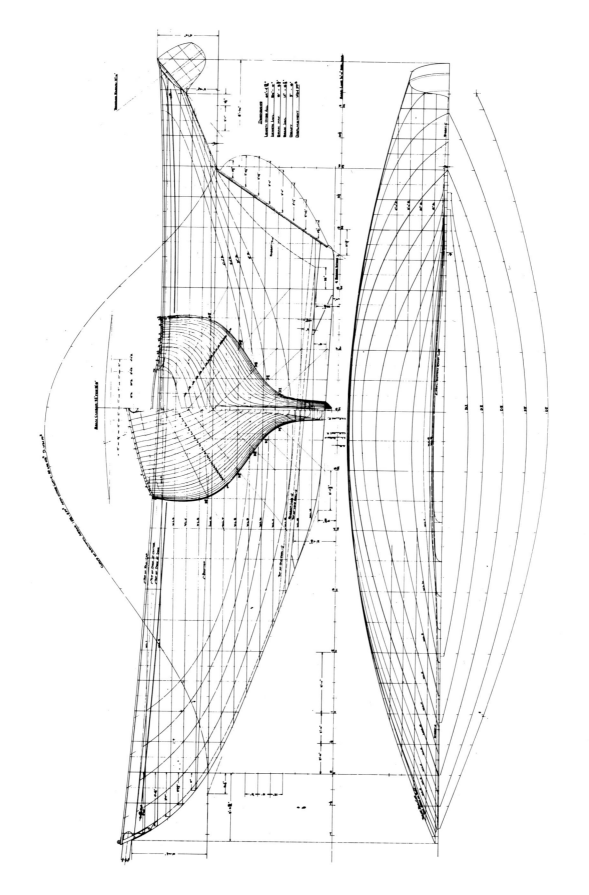

She has a handsome, powerful hull, though she could do with a bit more sheer. (Philip H. Rhodes)

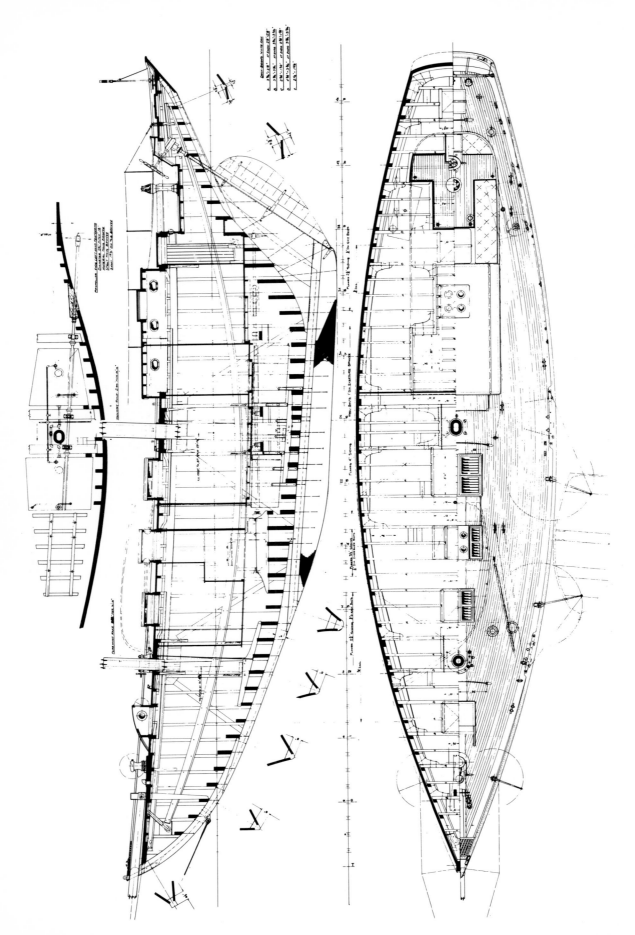

She has metal strapping and long bilge stringers to help her keep her shape. (Philip H. Rhodes)

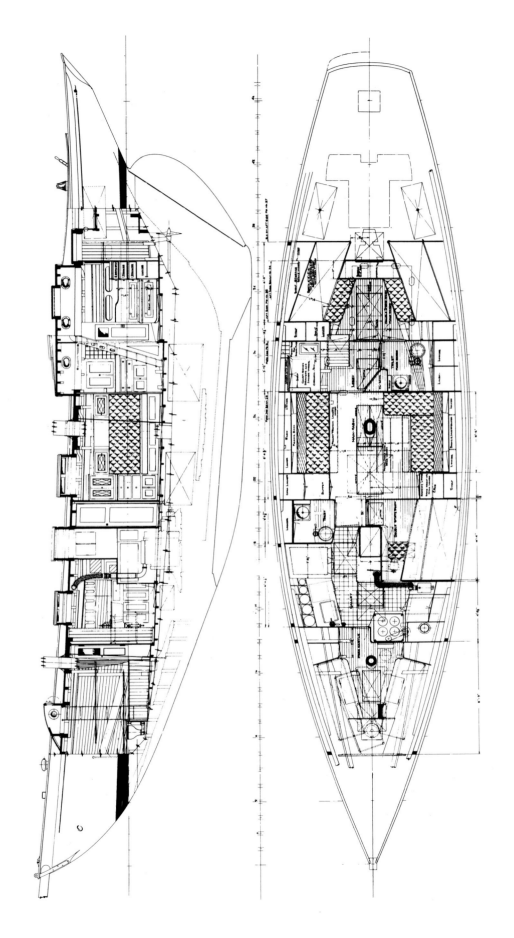

She has bunks and transoms for no fewer than a dozen people. (Philip H. Rhodes)

Some views of the Barlovento. *The below-decks shots show her chart table, handy to the companionway, and the after port corner of her saloon.* (Yachting, *August 1932*)

The Barlovento *is now on the West Coast, where she can enjoy many a fresh breeze. (Diane Beeston)*

(Continued from page 100)

it in davits on the port side most of the time. Sailing with a boat slung out over the side in davits makes you think you're in a big ship.

Her engine is placed well forward, up between the masts. The shaft is off-center to port. The engine compartment has a fidley to the deck for light and air, but considerable woodwork would have to be removed to get at the machine. It's a 4-cylinder Hill diesel developing 40 horsepower and running a 1-kilowatt generator as well as swinging its 24-inch-diameter by 18-inch-pitch feathering propeller. She carries 130 gallons of fuel in wing tanks in way of the cockpit, giving her a range under power of 500 miles. Beneath the cabin sole are tanks for 350 gallons of water.

There is a steerage under the bridge deck and cockpit for the stowage of sails and bosun's stores.

The companionway is in the forward starboard corner of the house. Right at its foot is a chart table. The schooner's staterooms are tucked away where it's quiet. Her fo'c's'le would be all right for sleeping except when punching into a head sea. If there's a crowd on board, four can sleep in the main cabin; upper bunks swing up over the transoms. There is a four-hole Shipmate stove forward in the galley.

I think going in the *Barlovento* would be a fine way to travel. Just think of this great schooner thrashing along on a close reach in rough water under maybe jumbo, reefed foresail, and double-reefed mainsail. Oh, my.

17/ The *Askoy*

```
Length on deck: 55 feet
Length on waterline: 45 feet
    11 inches
Beam: 14 feet 6 inches
Draft: 7 feet 8 inches
Sail area: 1,604 square feet
Displacement: 37 tons
Designer: Hugo Van Kuyck
```

It took me a long time to decide whether the *Askoy* was a good boat or a lousy boat.

There was a time when I thought she had too much hull above the waterline and too little below, that her bow was too stubby and her mainsail too big. I didn't really dare trust how handsome she looks in the portrait taken of her on a nice reach in a smooth sea near the Canary Islands.

Then one late, gray, dismal afternoon, we went into Three Mile Harbor off Gardiner's Bay near the eastern end of Long Island, and there she was. Shorn of her tophamper, her steel hull a bit rusty here and there, she didn't look much like her portrait, but her distinctive features, once observed, left no doubt that this was the Belgian world cruiser, nearly in our own backyard.

Despite the fact that she was obviously not ready for sea, she looked fine, just fine. I was relieved to discover that the *Askoy* is indeed a good boat.

Which goes to show that boat plans — mere inked curves on a flat piece of paper — can be deceptive. They are certainly worth plenty of study, but there are times when there is just no substitute for the real thing in three dimensions. Of course this is just stating something equally as obvious as: Don't marry a girl from her photograph.

The *Askoy* was designed for his own use by Hugo Van Kuyck, an architect, civil engineer, and yacht designer in Antwerp, Belgium.

"His own use" was a cruise around the world. Busy at his professions, Van Kuyck planned to take a long vacation each year, sail his vessel as far around the world as his time allowed, lay her up in a foreign port, and return to work in Antwerp while the *Askoy* awaited his return to continue the voyage.

So Hugo Van Kuyck designed the *Askoy* to be his ideal world cruiser. He wanted a vessel that would be, above all, comfortable; that would have considerable room on board; and that would have an outstanding ability to reach and run. (It is interesting to compare the *Askoy* with the *Varua*, William A. Robinson's ideal world cruiser designed with the same objectives, described in *More Good Boats*.)

The *Askoy* is 55 feet long on deck, with a waterline length of 45 feet 11 inches, a beam of 14 feet 6 inches, and a draft of 7 feet 8 inches.

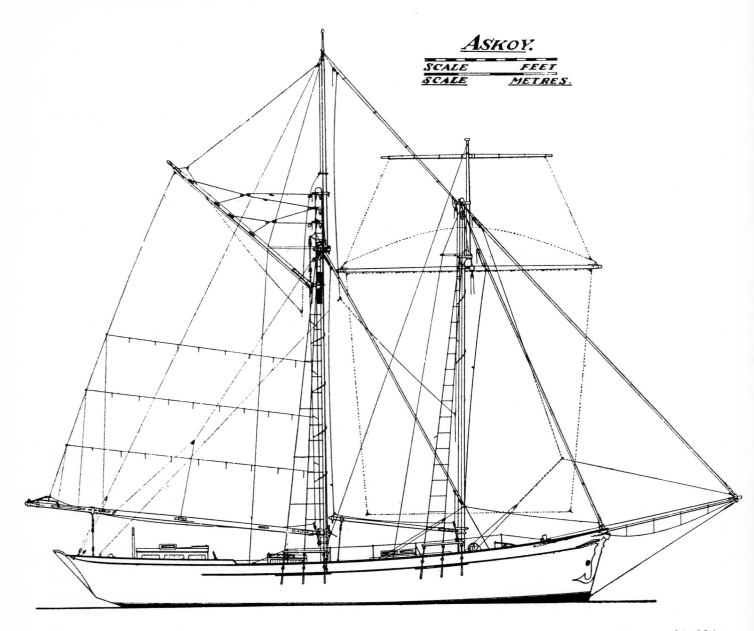

The Askoy *is a topsail staysail schooner designed 40 years ago as an ideal world cruiser by her Belgian owner, Hugo Van Kuyck.* (Thoughts on Yachts and Yachting *by Uffa Fox*)

She displaces 37 tons and has a sail area of 1,604 square feet. She was built by John Cockerill some 45 years ago.

The *Askoy's* lines, I think, show a good combination of seakindliness and speed for an offshore vessel. With her fineness, long waterline, hollow entrance, and long run, she would have a good turn of speed. She ought to have an easy motion, except that in a steep head sea, the end of the bowsprit would be a lively place. Her short clipper bow — if the term can be applied to so abrupt an affair — would help keep her dry, and she needs that fullness up high in her

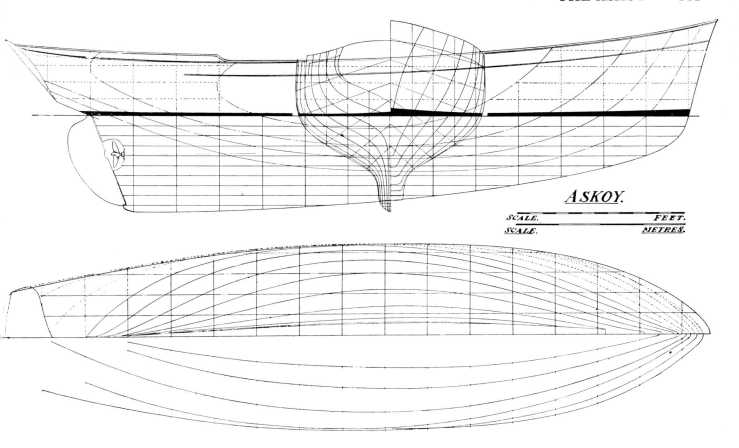

ASKOY.

SCALE.   FEET.
SCALE.   METRES.

Her draft is moderate, her freeboard almost too much, and her surprisingly fine lines indicate a vessel that would make good passages. (Thoughts on Yachts and Yachting by Uffa Fox)

bow to keep it from rooting when pressing down a sea with her squaresails set. The mermaid on her bow is probably the precisely appropriate figurehead, for she might often be up to her waist in the ocean.

The tumblehome in the vessel's upper topsides makes her upper diagonals do funny things, but she would hardly be sailed rail down anyway, and her lower diagonals are sweet and fair.

Uffa Fox, who described the *Askoy* in his book *Thoughts on Yachts and Yachting,* called her a topsail schooner, which is, of course, correct. She is, additionally, a topsail staysail schooner, which you don't see every day. The point is, she is a fore-and-aft rigged vessel and wouldn't carry her squaresails to windward.

The mainmast has been squeezed forward, giving her a big mainsail. As a matter of fact, she is rather reminiscent of an early 19th century English revenue cutter, which had roughly the same assortment of fore-and-aft sails and squaresails set on only one mast.

The fore topsail looks almost like an afterthought. Presumably it would be set only in light or moderate weather, and if you got overenthusiastic with it and it blew away, little would be the harm.

All her sails are loose-footed, including the main staysail and mainsail. Wouldn't that big mainsail drive her, though? Its area is 630 square feet. It has appropriately deep reefs.

The main staysail is quadrilateral, with a very short vertical luff and a short stay from the foremast to the deck at the point of attachment of the mainstay.

Her bowsprit is certainly well steeved, and the jib, with its tack 11 feet above the waterline, would feel little solid water.

Note the running preventer backstays on the main topmast made up to her quarters. With her long gaff, rather low peaked to allow a big

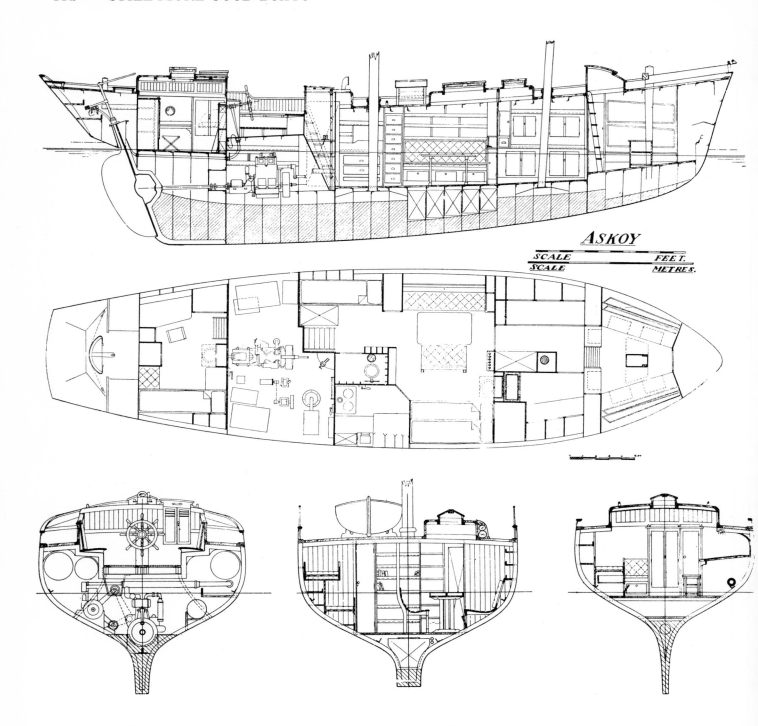

ASKOY

She has an unusual arrangement below, what with her laboratory and darkroom abreast the foremast and her separate captain's cabin in the stern. (Thoughts on Yachts and Yachting by Uffa Fox)

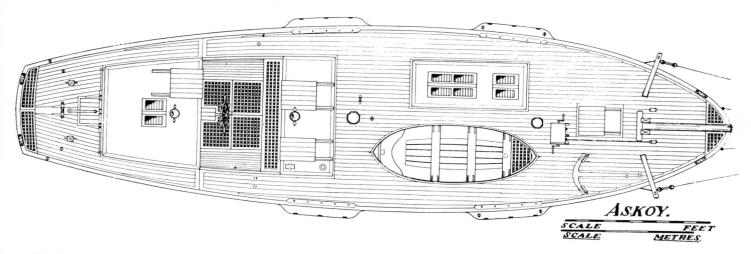

ASKOY.

SCALE   FEET
SCALE   METRES.

Her deck plan shows her to be the kind of vessel in which Long John Silver would feel right at home. (Thoughts on Yachts and Yachting *by Uffa Fox*)

She had a handsome portrait made near the Canary Islands. (Thoughts on Yachts and Yachting *by Uffa Fox*)

topsail, you might be tempted to put a pair of vangs on it. You'd run one each side, starting someplace near the head of the lower mast, hence through a bullseye at the end of the gaff, and then down to belay, with some slack, at the gooseneck. Then when you wanted to take some twist out of the sail or keep the gaff off the lee shrouds with the boom well squared off, all you'd have to do would be to bring the weather vang aft and set it up on the quarter. Pretty nifty, I'd say.

When shortened down to her four lowers, she'd balance better with the mainsail reefed. Would she heave to under lower main staysail alone? My guess is she'd do better with both main and fore staysails and the helm right down.

The *Askoy's* rig is old-fashioned and simple. Yes, there are lots of spars, sails, and strings to pull, but it's all relatively easy to replace — fidded topmasts, deadeyes and lanyards — far from a machine shop.

She has a 35-h.p. diesel engine, and she's big enough to have her propeller well submerged with the shaft nearly level.

The schooner's deck plan is well worked out. She has features reminiscent of a ship, what with her gratings, catheads, channels to take the shrouds, and pinrails for the running gear. There's a lot of room on deck forward thanks to the shape of the bow. The fo'c's'le scuttle is just off-center on one side, the anchor windlass is just off-center on the other. The midship skylight is well off-center to make room for a big double-ender to stow nicely on deck. The boat shown in the deck plan is 13 feet long with a beam of 4½ feet.

Way aft, she has an emergency tiller all fitted and ready.

Could the steering compass, mounted between the hatchways just forward of the cockpit, be easily seen from the wheel? I doubt it. Maybe she ought to have a conventional binnacle; the cockpit is certainly big enough to stand it, and a handsome binnacle would both look well and provide something nice to hang onto or lean against when she takes a roll.

Note the standard compass mounted atop the trunk house abaft the wheel. I assume this one would have a telltale below for the captain.

Her big, deep cockpit is well protected and would certainly give watch standers a feeling of security in bad weather at night. The cockpit sole has enough slant to drain quickly.

The engine room has its own entrance handy to the cockpit. The average headroom down there is five feet.

The *Askoy's* arrangement plan shows some interesting and unusual features. The captain assuages the loneliness of command in his own regal quarters aft. He has bunk, seat, lockers, closet, wash basin, and even a writing desk or chart table with the only porthole in the ship.

At the other end of the vessel is another separate domain, a good-sized fo'c's'le for four with over six feet of headroom allowed by the deep forefoot.

In the main part of the accommodation, up forward in way of the foremast, she has a laboratory to port and a darkroom to starboard. The mere mention of such practical amenities in a seagoing vessel conjures up all sorts of possibilities for purposeful voyages.

The cabin table in the saloon is better separated from the two berths on the starboard side than would be the case in the more conventional arrangement with the table amidships flanked by transoms and the berths all the way outboard, one on each side.

The galley is really set off by itself, a nice feature. I think sea cooks deserve to be able to scoop up their spilled eggs in private; such a capability helps not only their own morale, but also that of the crew.

The head is handy to the deck, as is the sea berth opposite it. It's too bad a tall tank had to go right beside the main companionway; that would have been a great place for a hanging locker for foul weather gear.

The *Askoy* left Antwerp to start around the world on January 16, 1938, with a crew of five. She crossed the Channel to Dover; went down to Falmouth; and then went south to Oporto and Lisbon, Portugal; and Madeira. Then she crossed the Atlantic to Martinique. She was 28 sailing days from Lisbon to Martinique. Mr. Van Kuyck returned home to work, well satisfied with his vessel, and later continued the voyage.

Though he dearly loved his topsail schooner,

The Askoy's unusual rig could almost have been inspired by Gordon Grant's painting of an early Nineteenth Century English revenue cutter. (The Book of Old Ships *by Henry B. Culver)*

Dr. Van Kuyck's second Askoy *is a much simpler vessel than was the first. She's a steel centerboarder 61 feet 4 inches long on deck, with a waterline length of 49 feet 3 inches, a beam of 16 feet 2 inches, and a draft, board up, of 6 feet 3 inches. Her sail area is 1,530 square feet, and she displaces 40 tons.* (The Proper Yacht *by Arthur Beiser)*

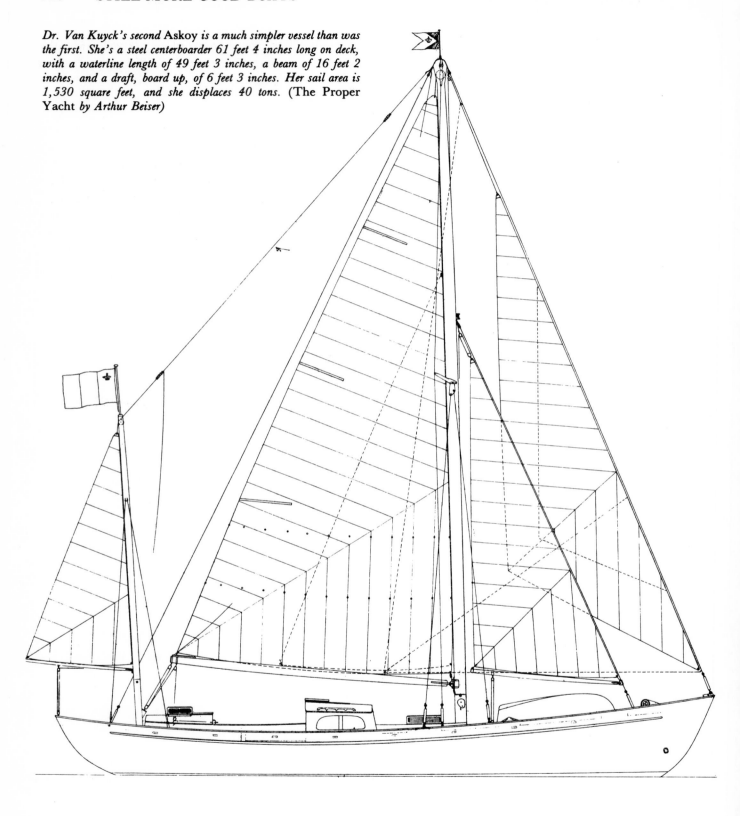

in later years Mr. Van Kuyck designed for himself a far simpler *Askoy II*. She is a 61-foot double-ender with Bermuda rig, technically a ketch but with a yawl-sized mizzen. She has a very moderate draft (6 feet 3 inches) and a centerboard. This interesting boat is described in the first edition of Arthur Beiser's *The Proper Yacht*.

I don't know if the second *Askoy* was to be used for offshore or coastal cruising. True it seems to be, however, that as a sailor advances in years and experience, he tends to progress — like an artist — from the complex to the simple. This is not to say, though, that the complex craft is "bad" or has no place. If you have the temperament and energy, nothing can beat a plethora of spars, sails, and rigging — the more the merrier.

In fact there is considerable truth, I think, in a statement made 70 years ago by one Charles E. Turner in an effort to end a long series of letters in which correspondents beseeched the editor of the *Yachting Monthly* to admit that they, and only they, had found the ideal offshore cruising boat. Turner said there was simply no such thing, all such boats, in his opinion, being too small.

18/ The *Westward*

Length on deck: 100 feet
Length on waterline: 83 feet
Beam: 22 feet
Draft: 11 feet
Sail area: 6,500 square feet
Displacement: 208 tons
Designer: Walter J. McInnis

Drayton Cochran is an experienced seaman who has had some wonderful vessels. His 100-foot motorsailer, the *Vigilant,* designed by Eldredge-McInnis, was described in *More Good Boats.*

Mr. Cochran was very happy with the *Vigilant* and with a smaller version of her that Eldredge-McInnis also designed for him, so when he wanted a full-fledged world cruising vessel in 1962, he went back to Walter J. McInnis.

Mr. Cochran knew what he wanted in his new vessel. He wanted enough stability to recover assuredly from a knockdown, but he didn't want his vessel so stiff that she would have an uncomfortable roll. He wanted a long keel for steadiness running off. He wanted high freeboard for dryness on deck and high bulwarks for security. He wanted a vessel of great strength. He wanted a straightforward rig. He wanted lots of fuel and water capacity.

The *Westward* has all these features. She is about the size of and bears some resemblance to the North Sea pilot schooners of Holland and Germany, though she is fuller in the stern below the waterline and higher-sided than they are.

Mr. Cochran is an admirer of the North Sea pilot schooners and was well aware that Irving M. Johnson had converted two of them, both named *Yankee*, for round-the-world cruising, and that Warwick M. Tompkins had made a successful voyage around Cape Horn in one of them, the *Wander Bird.* Irving Johnson contributed a number of suggestions to the design of the *Westward.*

(Incidentally, the *Westward* is named after the big Herreshoff racing schooner built for Alexander C. Cochran in 1910, a picture of which is still in the saloon of the new *Westward,* I was happy to see on a fairly recent visit to the vessel. There is a fine model of the new *Westward* by Edward B. Freeman in the library at the Mystic Seaport.)

The *Westward* is 100 feet long on deck, with a waterline length of 83 feet, a beam of 22 feet, and a draft of 11 feet. Her sail area is 6,500 square feet and her displacement is 208 tons.

I think she is a most handsome vessel despite her height of rail. Her bow and stern are nicely balanced, and she has a strong sheerline for such a big craft.

I like her nicely curved clipper bow and deep

Walter J. McInnis.

forefoot. She has the rounded stern above the waterline of the North Sea pilot schooner, but it is more drawn out and quite a bit narrower.

She's a deep-bodied vessel for comfort at sea and a big carrying capacity. The curve of her bilge is deep and gentle and her garboard is only slightly hollowed. She has steep bow and buttock lines but a fine entrance.

The *Westward* was built by Abeking and Rasmussen at Bremerhaven, West Germany. Her hull is steel, and her scantlings are in excess of 100-A German Lloyds. She has extra heavy plates at the garboard, at the turn of the bilge, and at the sheer.

Her keel is of an interesting design worked out by Walter McInnis. It's a tube instead of a bar, for Mr. McInnis felt the tube would be less prone to twisting if the vessel should take the ground. The tube has an outside diameter of 7¾ inches and a wall thickness of ⅞ inch. It's filled with cement. The hull plates are welded to it and faired in. Drayton Cochran wrote, "It's a nice job."

The vessel's ballast is cement containing scrap iron. Mr. Cochran likes the combination of cement and steel, saying that the cement protects the steel and needs minimum upkeep. The steel is sand-blasted clean and the cement applied right onto it. The *Westward* also has

cemented waterways on deck and her steel tanks are cemented. The second *Yankee* had cement in her bilge, and when Irving Johnson took off some garboard plating in 1946, the steel was in the same condition as when the *Yankee* was built in 1912.

Another interesting construction feature of the *Westward* is that her cabin sole is made watertight throughout her length.

Her sail areas are as follows: jib topsail, 538 square feet; jib, 508; fore staysail, 457; fore course, 1,292; raffee, 476; main staysail, 651; fisherman staysail, 1,033; and mainsail, 1,538 — for a total of 6,493 square feet.

Her mainmast is set well aft to keep the mainsail from being too huge. Her main truck is 96 feet above the waterline. The mast originally had separate preventer backstays pulling against the lower and upper mainstays. The photograph of her passing an iceberg shows that she was later fitted with a boomkin and permanent main backstay. This was put on by Mr. Cochran in Kowloon to do away with the running backstays.

Because the mainmast is well aft, she has big staysails between the masts. Think how that fisherman of over 1,000 square feet would pull!

Her bowsprit is well steeved and has a nice netting under it. Except in really rough condi-

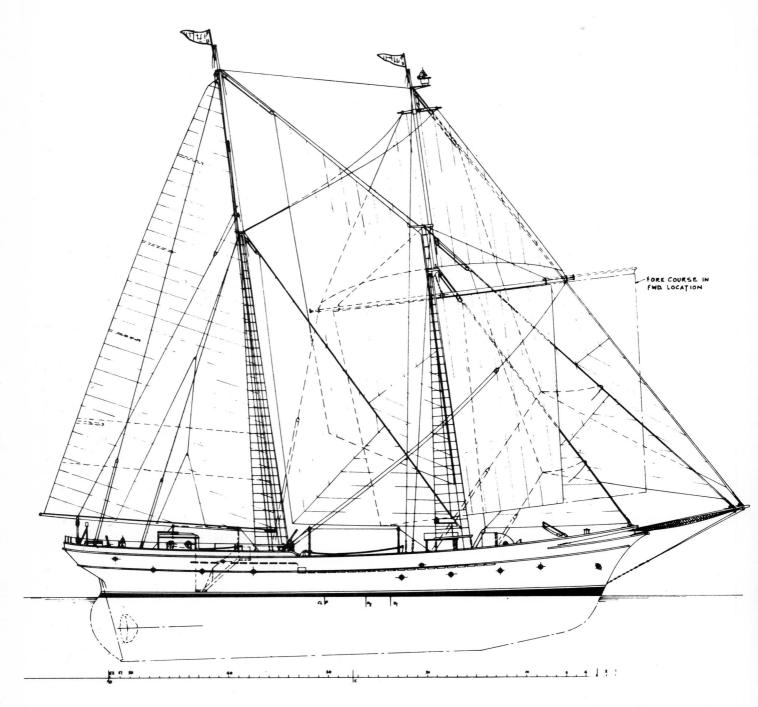

FORE COURSE IN
FWD. LOCATION

The 100-foot schooner Westward, *a fine vessel that has put plenty
of sea miles under her long keel since she was built in 1962.
(Eldredge-McInnis, Inc.)*

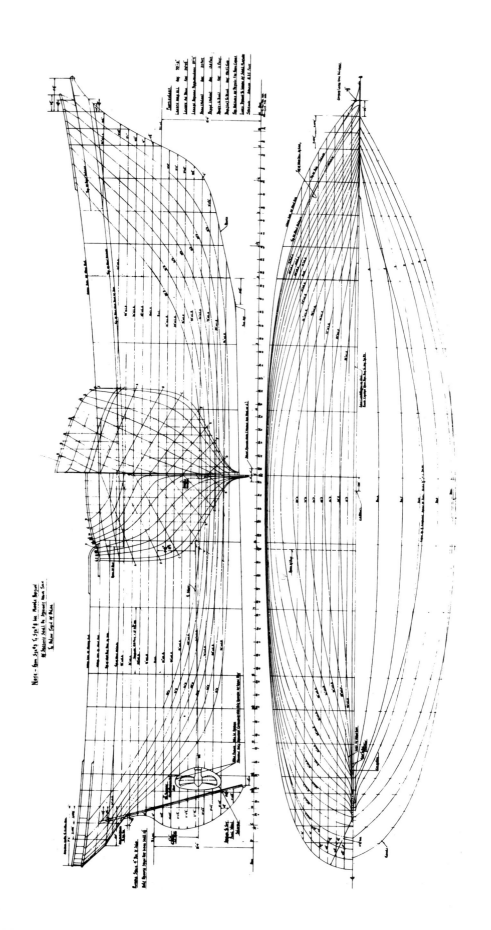

'Deep-bodied but slender, she has proven comfortable and fairly fast at sea. (Eldredge-McInnis, Inc.)

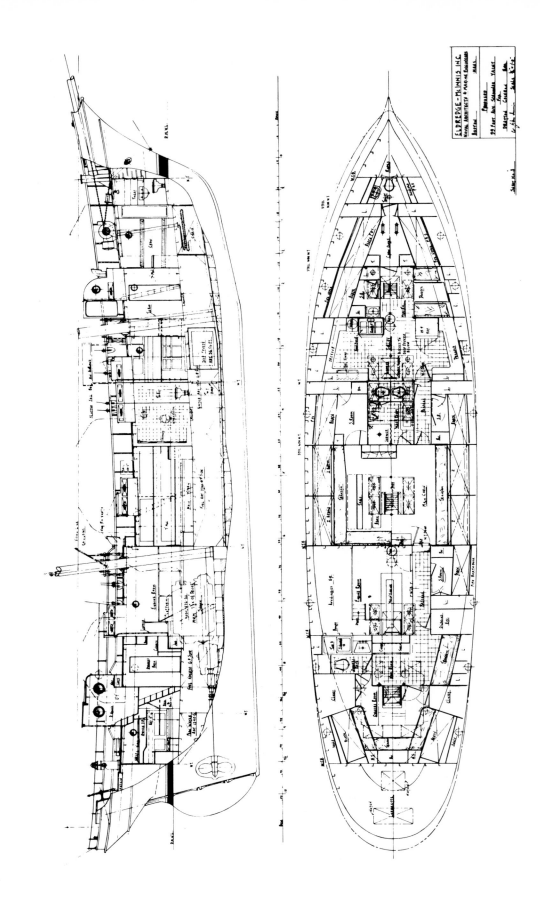

She has plenty of bunks for a big crew and a tremendous capacity for carrying everything necessary to a long voyage. (Eldredge-McInnis, Inc.)

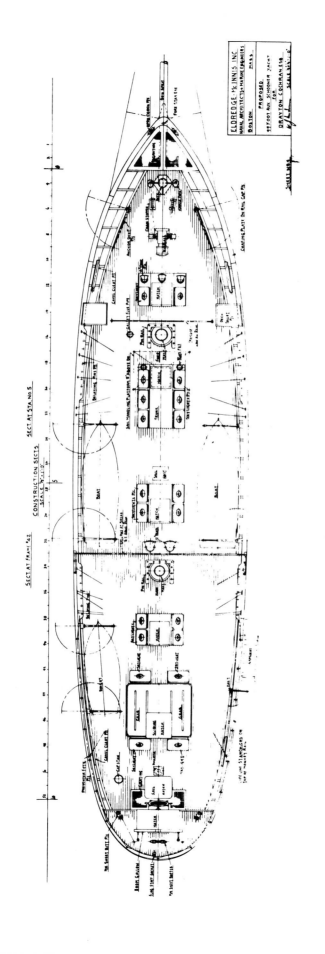

Her deck structures have been kept small and strong, in keeping with her seagoing nature. (Eldredge-McInnis, Inc.)

She is now a school ship and research vessel for the Sea Education Association. (Photo by Peter C. Beamish, courtesy National Fisherman)

tions, this makes a fine, high, dry place for furling headsails or just lying around watching her go.

Her fore course brails in to the mast to furl; the raffee comes down on deck. The braces shown on the stubby raffee yard were never rigged.

The fore yard is about six feet longer than the head of the fore course, and the sail can be shifted along the yard on a track, a trick Mr. Cochran learned from Irving Johnson. This rig lets you shift the foresail out to weather, so it will be blanketed less by the mainsail on a run or a broad reach.

The *Westward* runs with her mainsail, fore course, and raffee, a combination used constantly on a passage she made early in her career from Lisbon to Barbados. By the wind, she generally sails under fore-and-aft sails only.

Shortened down to her four lowers, especially with the mainsail reefed, she would certainly stand some real breeze.

The schooner has a raised quarterdeck, the break coming just forward of the mainmast. There are plenty of freeing ports all along the main deck in case she ships a sea. Her deck structures have been kept small and simple. She has no big glass houses, for she is a seagoing vessel.

Her charthouse is handy to the wheel; there are deck toilets on each side of the vessel in way of the foremast; and she has a tall booby hatch just forward of the foremast.

She carries patent anchors in her hawsepipes. This is certainly a handy arrangement, and I guess she's big enough so that these anchors can be heavy enough to hold her under most conditions. You'd want a huge fisherman anchor lashed down on deck ready to be lifted overboard by her anchor davit, though, for the times when the stockless anchors couldn't hold her.

Her anchor windlass is run by a Farymann

The Westward *lazing along under fore-and-aft sail.* (National Fisherman)

air-cooled, one-cylinder diesel. Mr. Cochran wrote, "You can heave in anything with it."

She has davits and space for a good collection of small boats. Drayton Cochran carried "a very handsome 13-foot, double-ended Nova Scotian 'gunning boat' on the quarterdeck davits, swung out nearly all the time as it was high off the water." He also carried a heavy, sailing yawl boat; a fast outboard runabout; a sailing dinghy; and a Marquesan catamaran, traded for gin.

The *Westward's* quarterdeck rail up by the main rigging is about eight feet above the waterline, so she has an accommodation ladder with a davit to hoist its lower end. This is nice, big-ship stuff and lets you know you're going on board a real vessel.

Down below, the *Westward* has a big engine room with a workbench. The engine is an M.W.M. 340-h.p. diesel. It starts with air and is slow turning. At about 180 h.p., it gives her 8½ to 9 knots.

It's a direct-reversing engine with no clutch. To back down, you shift the cams to reverse the rotation of the engine and give it air to change its mind. The propeller is a variable-pitch wheel made by Hundested in Denmark. The variable-pitch propeller is good for towing, a charitable feature of a vessel with 340 h.p.

She has few sea connections through the hull. There's one saltwater intake for a saltwater system and the saltwater side of the heat exchanger for her engine cooling system. Instead of each head flushing overboard through its own discharge valve, each head drains to a common sump tank that may be flushed at sea through a single overboard discharge. This sump tank vents out through the mainmast. The mainmast also contains the exhaust lines for main and auxiliary engines. The flue for the galley range goes up the foremast. The masts are jacketed inside so that the hot stuff going up them won't heat their outside surfaces too much. It would be nice, working aloft on a cold day, though, to have the mast warm!

Her big fuel and water tanks are in the bilge. She carries 5,500 gallons of water, and there is an awning that can be rigged with a funnel to

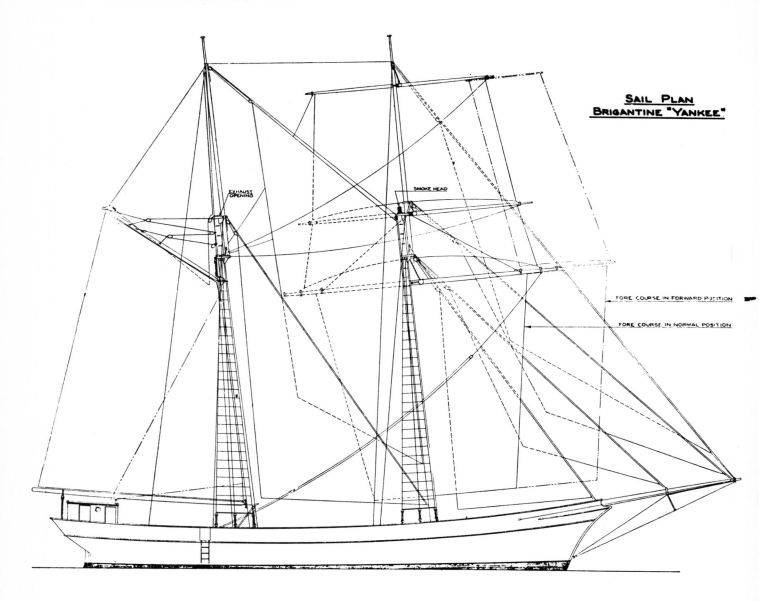

SAIL PLAN
BRIGANTINE "YANKEE"

FORE COURSE IN FORWARD POSITION

FORE COURSE IN NORMAL POSITION

Part of the inspiration for the concept of the Westward *came from the second* Yankee *of Irving Johnson, a seaman who suggested some of the* Westward's *specific design features to her owner, Drayton Cochran. (Yachting, April 1947)*

the tank. There's a good-sized lazarette in the stern and a forepeak up in the eyes of her.

The vessel has central heating.

She's nicely arranged to accommodate a big crew. The saloon has eight bunks. There are a single and a double stateroom aft and two staterooms amidships. Her big galley is forward, and there's a deep-freeze below in the bilge. Farther forward is a dinette and another stateroom. In the bow is a fo'c's'le for four. She has three heads — forward, amidships, and aft. Mr. Cochran wrote, "I wouldn't change her layout at all."

Despite her size, the *Westward* has been kept relatively simple. For instance, she's not loaded down with electronic gear. Drayton Cochran is not enthusiastic about such complexities; he's the kind of sailor who goes where he wants to with sextant and leadline.

Mr. Cochran is generous with his praise for this vessel. She did what he wanted and expected her to do in the way of being seakindly and showed a good turn of speed for such a heavy vessel. He said she would get up to nine knots or so quite readily under sail.

The *Westward* is now used as a school ship by Corwith Cramer's Sea Education Association. Teaching young people about the ocean environment and about what it means to run a ship at sea is a most worthwhile use for this fine vessel. Long may the *Westward* sail.

19/ The *Walrus* and the *Carpenter*

> Length on deck: 50 feet
> Length on waterline: 45 feet
> Beam: 14 feet 6 inches
> Draft: 6 feet
> Sail area: 755 square feet
> Displacement: 26 tons
> Designer: L. Francis Herreshoff

> Length on deck: 18 feet
> Length on waterline: 16 feet
>   3 inches
> Beam: 4 feet 6 inches
> Draft: 5 inches
> Sail area: 69 square feet
> Designer: L. Francis Herreshoff

Lewis Carroll's unlikely poetic pair, the walrus and the carpenter, had some interesting times together. Fifty years ago, L. Francis Herreshoff designed a pair of boats for one of his good customers, Charles A. Welch — boats that at first glance you wouldn't expect to find working together toward a common objective, but that, when you get to know them better, really do seem to team up quite well.

The *Walrus* is a 50-foot motorsailer; the *Carpenter* is an 18-foot surf boat. When you think of these boats working in tandem — the *Walrus* towing the *Carpenter* to some lonely, far-off harbor and then the *Carpenter* coming into her own for coastal and shallow-water exploration — you can conjure up some mighty interesting times indeed!

One interesting time in the *Walrus*, according to Francis Welch, the owner's nephew, was on a snowy Christmas Eve when Skipper Herreshoff, Charles Welch, and others were celebrating the occasion and somebody challenged the rest to sail around the Cape Ann whistle buoy and back. "Off they went around midnight and returned safely the next morning without using any power."

The *Walrus* is a more complicated little vessel than she first appears; she has many unusual design details that have been very well worked out. L. Francis called her an "auxiliary power cruiser," for she is a power vessel with auxiliary sails. It is a combination that makes sense, because those sails, though modest in area, can save you plenty of fuel on a passage.

The *Walrus* is 50 feet long on deck, with a waterline length of 45 feet, a beam of 14 feet 6 inches, and a draft of 6 feet. She displaces 26 tons and has a sail area of 755 square feet.

She has quite fine lines for a powerboat and would be easy to drive under power at moderate speed, say, up to 6 or 7 knots. She has a fairly well-shaped hull for sailing and would sail reasonably well in a breeze, even on the wind. And she would have an easy motion, a necessary characteristic of the successful long-range cruiser or expedition vessel. There is considerable reserve buoyancy in her hull; she'd be a good rough-water boat.

She has a straight entry at the load waterline. The flare in her bow sections keeps her reasonably dry when punching into a head sea under power alone, though the way to make

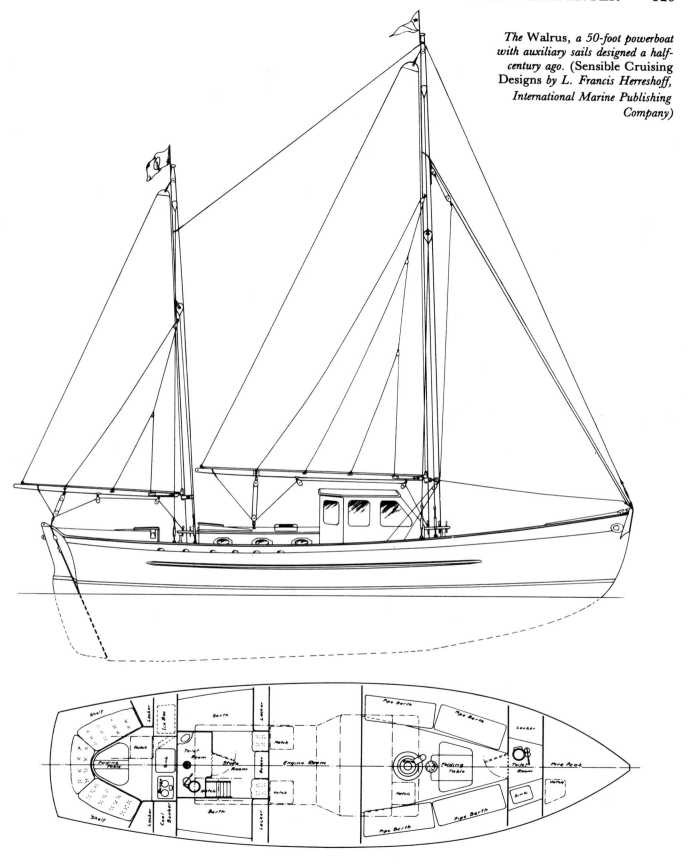

The Walrus, *a 50-foot powerboat with auxiliary sails designed a half-century ago. (Sensible Cruising Designs by L. Francis Herreshoff, International Marine Publishing Company)*

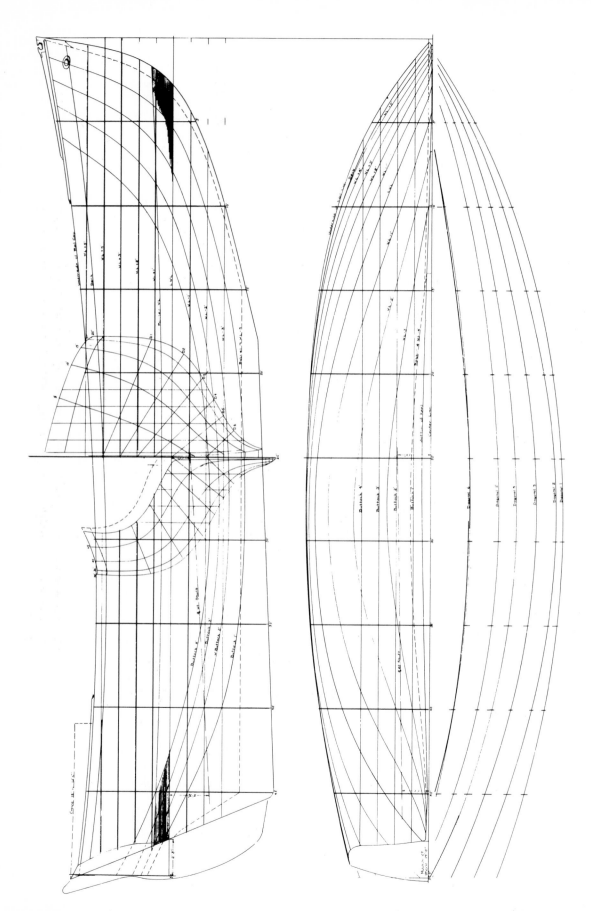

Her lines show a very able and seakindly hull with — above all — an easy motion. (Sensible Cruising Designs by L. Francis Herreshoff, International Marine Publishing Company)

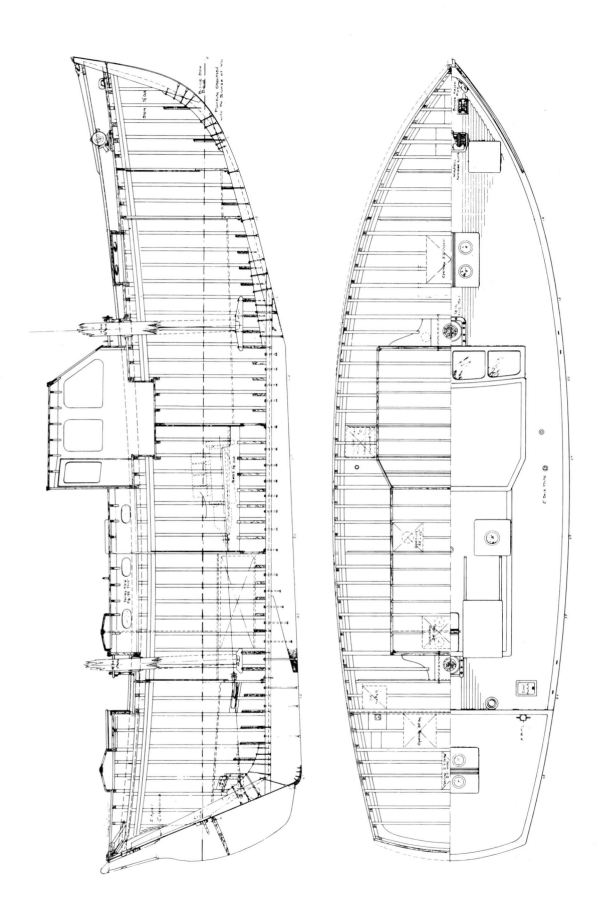

The construction plan and deck layout show the rather extraordinary number of openings she has in her deck. (Sensible Cruising Designs by L. Francis Herreshoff, International Marine Publishing Company)

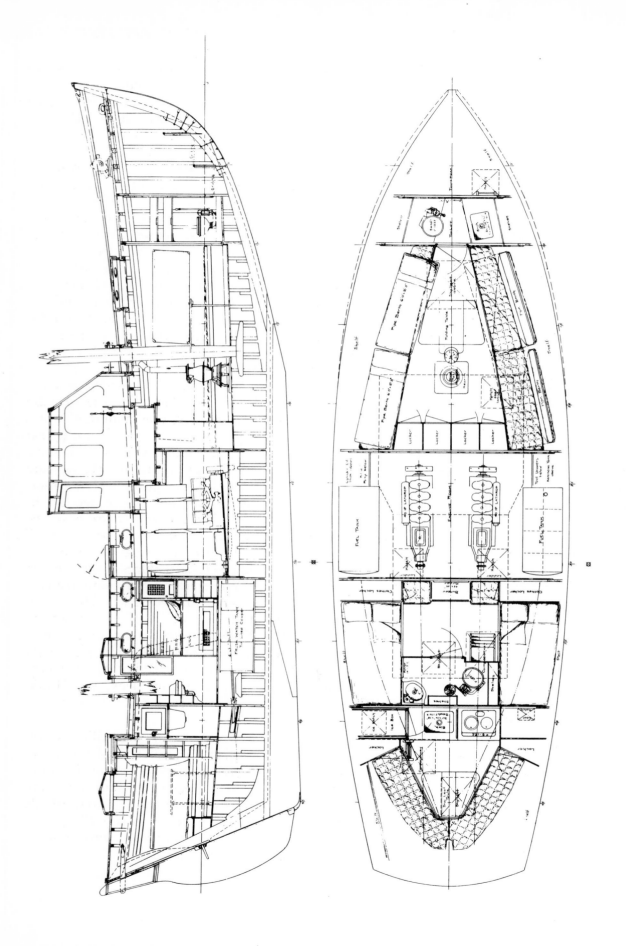

The Walrus has five separate watertight compartments. Her arrangement requires considerable climbing, but on-watch and off-watch functions have been kept well separated. (Sensible Cruising Designs by L. Francis Herreshoff, International Marine Publishing Company)

distance to windward in a boat like this when it's rough is to beat to windward under sail with the lee engine ticking over slowly to help her along.

Her big, heart-shaped transom is curved athwartships to keep it from giving her any hint of clumsiness.

She is sheathed with bronze at the waterline for ice protection. Note that the bottom of her rudder is raised up above the bottom of the keel to keep it out of harm's way.

You'd want heavy sails in the *Walrus* so they would stand up to some real breeze. Note the arrangement of her five-part sheets on main and mizzen, a sensible rig. Note also the useful lazy jacks on these sails. I'd put a club on the jib with a multi-part sheet to make the sail easier to trim and to save coming out of the wheelhouse to tack.

I doubt that I could resist the temptation to put a bowsprit on this boat (with a swordfishing pulpit) and move the headstay out to its end to take a big ballooner for reaching and running (poled out) in gentle and moderate breezes.

The *Walrus* would balance nicely under mainsail alone or under jib and mizzen when it's blowing hard, and would be able to get to windward under the latter combination. Under mizzen alone, sheeted flat, she would hold her head up to wind and sea.

The boat's engines and tanks are right up in the middle of her where they belong. (Her big water tank is under the floor of the stateroom just abaft the engine room.) Francis Herreshoff specified two gasoline engines of 40 to 65 h.p each. Today, they would probably be diesels. Or maybe a producer gas plant!

In any case, the reliability of two engines and two propellers is a great thing to have. And the satisfaction of twisting in place with one screw going ahead and the other astern is wondrous and great when maneuvering in tight places.

I'd want an outside steering station on this boat, probably atop the trunk cabin at the after end of the wheelhouse. You'd have an emergency tiller to go on the rudder head, of course.

She has quarter bitts at the break of her after turtleback. I'd want lifelines on that turtleback leading from the mizzen rigging back to a gallows frame for the mizzen boom.

You could carry a tender on davits to port between the mizzen mast and the wheelhouse, swung out over the rail or in on top of the trunk cabin as the weather might dictate.

The *Walrus* has no fewer than 10 deck openings, not counting the entry into her wheelhouse. There is a hatch in the foredeck leading down into the forepeak; a skylight in the foredeck over the saloon table; two hatches in the top of the trunk cabin for access to the engine room; a companionway and hatch for the stateroom; two small hatches in the deck just abaft the mizzen mast, one for coal and the other for ice; a hatch in the after turtleback for access to the galley and wardroom in the stern; and a skylight in the after turtleback over the wardroom table.

The wheelhouse of the *Walrus* would be a joy. Steering under glass creates a sense of calm well-being as can nothing else. You don't want to get mesmerized, however, into assuming that because you are warm and dry your vessel must be safe. It's worth stepping out into the wet and cold from time to time to get the feel of things. You might find she's starting to ice up or something. Note that the after corners of the wheelhouse on the *Walrus* have been cut off diagonally to make the structure less bulky.

The ketch has vertical ladders leading down into each of her five watertight compartments except for the stateroom, where Mr. Herreshoff has allowed the luxury of a slanted companionway ladder. Those five separate compartments are an excellent safety feature. Most folks want to be able to walk from one end of their vessel to the other without going on deck; the *Walrus* would keep you in shape, and you wouldn't miss much, either!

Her big saloon, with its pot-bellied stove, would be a fine place to be off watch. You could do some really fast sleeping in there, far from the clatter of pots and pans. The four berths are pipe berths so they can be set at a comfortable angle whichever way the vessel is heeling.

She has a fine, big engine room with plenty of headroom and light in its after end.

The bunks in the stateroom are extra wide and there are two little seats either side of the bureau on the forward bulkhead.

The arrangement of the wardroom is like that in British fishing and coasting vessels with V-shaped transoms right in the stern around a little table. If she were pitching into a head sea, there'd be considerable motion in the stern, so it might be good if the cook of the *Walrus* had a stomach slung in gimbals. It would indeed be tempting to put a couple of good-sized ports high in her transom, not only for general enjoyment of the scenery, but also in order that an ungimbaled cook could keep track of what the horizon is up to.

I think the *Walrus* is a handsome boat despite her high topsides, for her bow and stern, sheerline, and sections are all nicely modeled. Her design is all of a piece, as you would expect from the highly artistic L. Francis Herreshoff; her rugged hull, strong, snug rig, wheelhouse, and turtleback all "go" well together, and even her unusual split-up cabin arrangements seem to suit exactly the theme of an able expedition ship.

Al Laytham used the *Walrus* for a commercial swordfisherman after World War II. Jerry and Alva Hefty ran her as a charter boat out of Nassau, renamed *Leilani* and considerably rearranged on deck and below, for many years. I understand she's now owned in Florida.

The *Carpenter* — tender to, or tended by, the *Walrus* — is a fine little seaboat, being a whaleboat type with turtlebacks of her own both fore and aft and a flat bottom for beaching. She would be very able indeed for her size and could carry quite a load of people and gear if required.

She would tow well with her rudder on and lashed amidships and would not ship much water under tow even in rough seas.

She is quite a big boat to row but would move fairly easily, being very narrow. Still, you'd probably want two people on the oars most of the time. Her modest rig would drive her along nicely, except when working to windward in light weather. Then you'd want to start up a lee oar to help her along.

The *Carpenter* is 18 feet long on top, with a waterline length of 16 feet 3 inches, a beam of only 4 feet 6 inches, and a draft, light, of 5 inches. That draft doesn't include the rudder or centerboard, of course.

This boat has been kept fairly light for beaching. Mr. Herreshoff specified $1\frac{3}{8}$-inch white pine or cypress for the bottom; $\frac{3}{8}$-inch cedar lapstrake planking, copper riveted; a spruce clamp $\frac{7}{8}$ inch by $1\frac{1}{4}$ inches; oak frames $\frac{5}{8}$ inch by $\frac{7}{8}$ inch, spaced on $7\frac{1}{2}$-inch centers; and centerboard and rudder to be built up of $\frac{7}{8}$-inch oak. Her flat bottom is sheathed with $\frac{1}{16}$-inch bronze plate for protection when beaching (and a bit of ballast). She has a nicely molded sheer strake a la Herreshoff Manufacturing Company small boats.

The *Carpenter's* turtlebacks add reserve buoyancy and provide big, watertight compartments for dry storage and flotation. Her narrow deck along the rail between the turtlebacks helps keep water from coming in over the lee rail.

The boat has very fine lines indeed. Her waterline is hollow both fore and aft. She has considerable flare above the waterline to give her stability and a fairly high, flaring bow kept to seaward when beaching or launching, to keep her reasonably dry in small breakers.

Did you ever watch an experienced surfman direct the launching of a boat out through the breakers? I had the chance once in Barbados. A fishing boat was going off the beach early in the morning, and an elderly gentleman, directing the operation, stood with his bare feet planted deep in the sand where the tag ends of the waves washed 'round his ankles. He watched the breakers intently for half an hour, and I have never seen more alert concentration applied to anything. During that time there were, of course, trains of big waves with longer periods of smaller waves in between. A couple of times a fairly smooth interval at the end of a series of smaller waves tempted him, and he began to raise his hand in a signal that the young fishermen should try it, but each time he saw something he didn't like and changed the "go" signal to a "wait" signal. To my inexperienced

The Walrus *hustling along with a full crew alow and aloft. Her harpoon and big gin pole are at the ready.(Muriel Vaughn)*

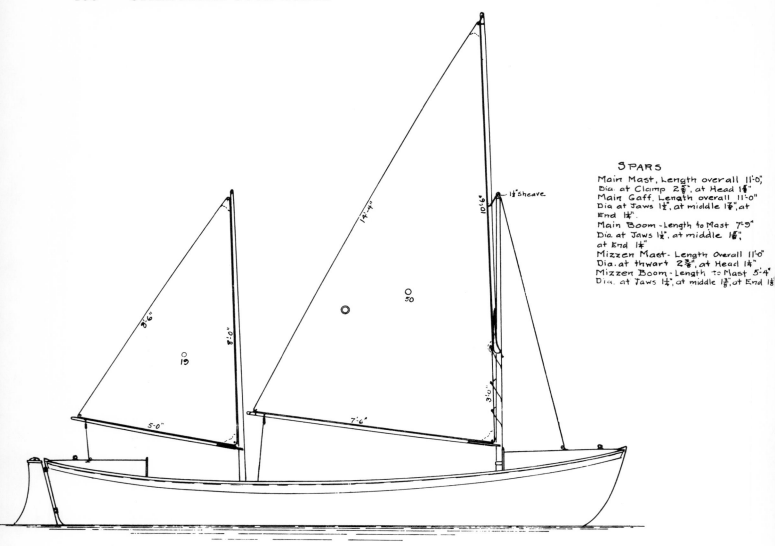

SPARS
Main Mast, Length overall 11'-0",
Dia. at Clamp 2⅞", at Head 1⅛"
Main Gaff, Length overall 11'-0"
Dia at Jaws 1¼", at middle 1⅞", at
End 1¼".
Main Boom - Length to Mast 7'-5"
Dia. at Jaws 1½", at middle 1⅞",
at End 1¼"
Mizzen Mast- Length Overall 11'-0"
Dia. at thwart 2⅜", at Head 1¼"
Mizzen Boom- Length to Mast 5'-4"
Dia. at Jaws 1¼", at middle 1⅜", at End 1⅛

The Carpenter *is an able little vessel, capable of much coastwise exploration under sail and oar.* (Sensible Cruising Designs *by L. Francis Herreshoff, International Marine Publishing Company*)

eye, it looked as if he was passing up a lot of perfectly good opportunities to get the boat out through the breakers, but this man had concentrated on this problem daily for many years. He exuded experience in what he was doing, and certainly his authority went unquestioned. At length, he found a smooth patch that satisfied him, gave the signal, and away they went in frantic haste. They made it, dry. You only have to think for a minute about the consequences of boat, gear, and men being flung back to the beach by the always surprisingly enormous power of even a small breaker to realize that the waiting and the concentrated study had been well worthwhile. The *Carpenter's* people, were they to use her in surf, would have to learn patience.

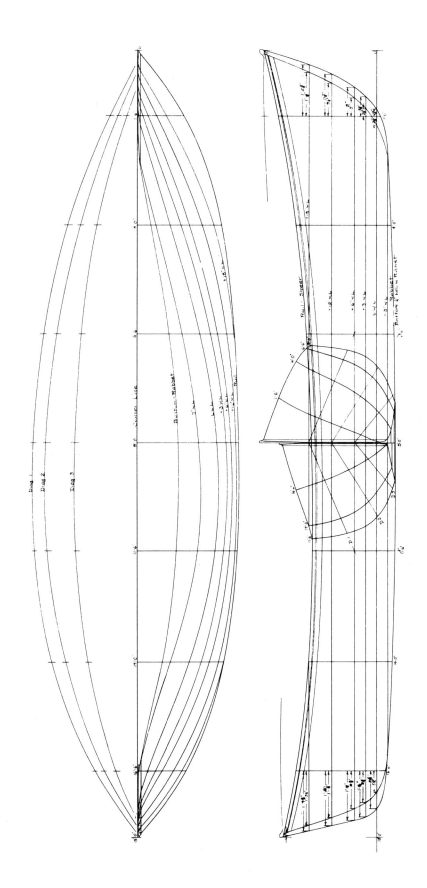

She is narrow and fine-lined and has a flat bottom for beaching. (Sensible Cruising Designs *by L. Francis Herreshoff, International Marine Publishing Company*)

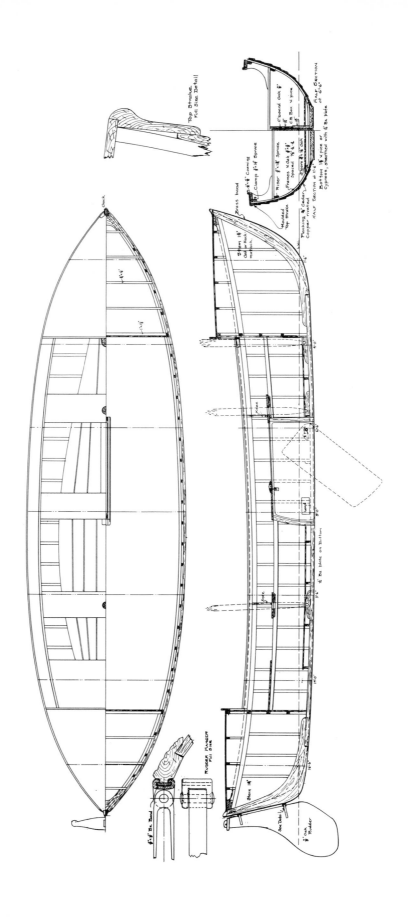

The Carpenter's scantlings are quite light. She has good-sized watertight compartments under her turtlebacks fore and aft. (Sensible Cruising Designs by L. Francis Herreshoff, International Marine Publishing Company)

The boat steers with lines to a rudder yoke. This would take some getting used to, but you'd have the advantage of being able to take the lines wherever you wanted to sit in the boat to steer. Running off in a gentle breeze, you could lollygag on the stern sheet using the turtle deck for a backrest, but on the wind in a hard breeze, you'd probably want to be up on the weather rail amidships.

The *Carpenter's* sails are small enough to be very easily handled. Her gunter mainsail has only 50 square feet, and the leg-o'-mutton mizzen has but 19 square feet. She has three mast positions (like a No Man's Land boat) so that you could sail her with either mainsail or mizzen alone with the mast of your choice stepped through the thwart at the forward end of the centerboard trunk. Her mainmast, mizzen mast, and main club are all 11-foot spars; they just fit inside the boat between the turtle deck bulkheads.

You'd want a topping lift on each of her booms.

You might also want a big gunter sloop rig for summer to give her more sail area for a light breeze or for showing off in harbor. I know I would.

Now with this fine pair of vessels, who wants to go up to Labrador?

20/ A Phil Rhodes Powerboat

> Length on deck: 45 feet
> Length on waterline: 42 feet
> Beam: 11 feet 3 inches
> Draft: 5 feet
> Sail area: 476 square feet
> Designer: Philip L. Rhodes

Sometimes it seems as if there are only two kinds of people in the world: those whose way of life, mode of dress and speech, and physical possessions — including boats — have to be those that somebody dreamt up no earlier than yesterday, and those who mistrust an idea, expression, or object that doesn't already have a history of at least a century. I suppose there really are some people who "combine the best of the new with the best of the old," as you so often hear, but most of us, I am afraid, are too prejudiced against either the new or the old to accomplish that feat.

Our prejudices show in so many little ways. Noting the rising cost of fuel, for instance, we use that phenomenon to condemn all high-speed, gas-guzzling planing powerboats and to strike a blow for the good old wholesome, slow, heavy-displacement powerboats that get there later but without having used very much of Earth's ancient, precious juice. Yet I don't know a single "modern" who has turned in his Boston Whaler for a Hampton boat. I think the price of fuel will have to double again and again before that happens, for prejudice runs deep. Imagine, if you can, the cataclysm that would

be required to convince the "traditionalist" to turn in his Hampton boat for a Boston Whaler!

Well, thank goodness for good old emotional, subjective, irrational prejudice! Were we all unemotional, objective, rational beings, I suppose we'd all analyze our way to the same few stereotypes of boats, one for each necessary activity on the water. Boring.

At any rate, if you were a traditionalist and had this heavy, 45-foot powerboat designed by Philip L. Rhodes a half century ago, you could claim to all your "modern" friends that you were right up to date with the "fuel crisis." She wouldn't be fast under power, but she'd be "economical" at 8 knots and her sails would save fuel on occasion.

The boat was designed as a sportfisherman and cruising boat to go offshore; she was designed for Luis Puig of Santiago, Cuba.

She is 45 feet long on deck, with a waterline length of 42 feet, a beam of only 11 feet 3 inches, and a draft of 5 feet. Her sail area is 476 square feet. She is powered with a 50-h.p. diesel.

The vessel has a handsome set of lines, in my opinion. I think Phil Rhodes drew the best

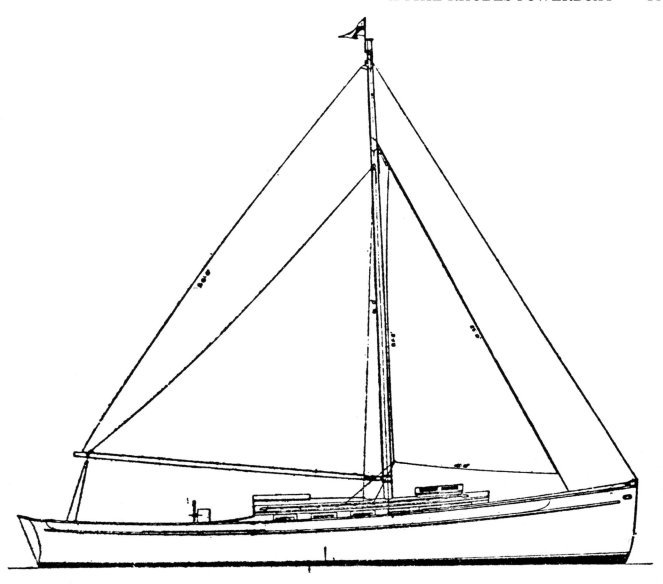

A handsome offshore cruiser and sportfisherman designed by Phil Rhodes. Look at that nice sheerline!
(The Rudder, *May 1929*)

sheerlines of any American designer to date, and I'd put him right up there with William Fife in the sheer department. Two big Rhodes motorsailers often lie at the Wayfarer Marine dock in Camden, and it is always a pleasure to look across the harbor at their lovely profiles. Phil Rhodes got his sheerlines down to the utter simplicity that is the essence of art.

And note how on this powerboat he enhanced the sheer in the stern by giving the transom just the right crown. That transom is nicely curved and not too bulky. She has a handsome stern.

Her forefoot is fairly deep, her entrance fine, and she has a bit of flare high on the bow. It's a shape that ought to cope well with a head sea.

Her midsection shows flare above the waterline, a hollow garboard, and a fairly deep keel; she shouldn't be a roller.

Her wheel and rudder are well protected by the skeg, and her rudder is big enough to turn her nicely at slow speed. All in all, she has the deep, heavy hull of the commercial boat, which would make her a mighty comfortable vessel.

Her rig and sails were designed for steadying and for trolling. And why wouldn't she sail reasonably well in a strong breeze? After all, she

*She's long and narrow, with the deep body of a
workboat. (The Rudder, May 1929)*

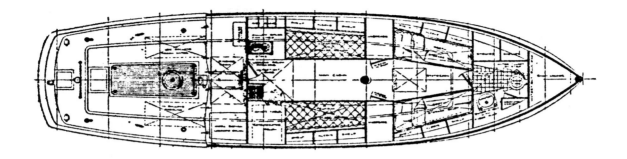

She's laid out for two people, but there is room for four. Her cockpit would be the envy of all. (The Rudder, May 1929)

has considerable lateral plane, a fine entry, and a good run.

The rig is simple and practical. A gaff sail would have made sense for its efficiency reaching, but the extra spar and halyard wouldn't be worth the gain. You'd want a couple of deep reefs in the mainsail for heavy weather and for setting a smaller steadying sail when heading up close to the wind. I'd have lazy jacks on the mainsail besides the topping lift shown.

At first you might think you ought to put a boom on the fore staysail, but then you realize you are going to be doing more running than tacking, so the loose-footed sail makes sense.

I'd have to add a bowsprit with a swordfishing pulpit to carry an anchor and to take the headstay moved out to set a big, high-cut jib.

I'd want to move the main sheet forward and put a cradle across the stern to take a nice rowing and sailing dinghy. A 10-foot boat would overhang each side of the transom by 10 inches. You'd use the boom for a derrick to hoist her in and out.

That long boom is partly to spread the generous mainsail and partly to spread a big awning for the tropics. Actually, a big piece of canvas over the boom would be just as useful in a cold, wet climate as it would be down near the equator. It ought to run almost the whole length of the boom, so it would protect the companionway as well as the big cockpit. You'd want to be

able to close it right down at the forward end to keep out the wind, or open it right up to let it in. You'd want to be able to tie the side flaps right down to the rail to protect the cockpit from wind and rain, or to batten them straight out from the boom to protect the cockpit from sun but let in a breeze. Such a piece of "sea cloth" would add greatly to the versatility of this boat's huge cockpit.

The steering pedestal up against the bridge deck at the forward end of the cockpit makes good sense. I'd also want a tiller aft as an emergency steering system and also to use when lazing along under sail with the engine shut down.

It would be a great temptation to give her a nice glass wheelhouse, but that would mean eliminating the bridge deck and losing headroom in the engine room in order to gain headroom in the wheelhouse without making it a skyscraper. The trade-off would depend on the intended use of the vessel and on the climate. For sportfishing in the tropics, the open cockpit makes good sense, of course, with the awning providing protection from the sun.

The engine under the bridge deck is accessible from on deck through a hatch and from below through a door from the galley.

She has six big rectangular ports on each side of her trunk cabin and a good-sized skylight in the top of the house above the forward stateroom, so she'd be quite light and airy below.

Even with her huge cockpit, she has enough room below for two people to live on board or for four people to cruise in her for lengthy periods. The location of the head away forward indicates she's laid out for two; for four, you'd want it back by the mast.

All in all, I think she'd make a wonderful exploration vessel. The combination of an able powerboat — able to "get there" in any reasonable weather at what seems to a sailor to be a very fast speed — and a good sailing and rowing dinghy on deck that can be readily launched would make it possible and most pleasant to get to know intimately a nice stretch of coast.

21/ The Herreshoff 15-Footer

Length on deck: 24 feet 6 inches
Length on waterline: 15 feet
Beam: 6 feet 9 inches
Draft: 2 feet 4 inches (board up)
Sail area: 330 square feet
Displacement: 2,800 pounds
Designer: Nathanael G.
   Herreshoff

One of the great things about growing up on the Pawcatuck River was that a half mile downstream lived Ed and Dave Cabot, father and son, just as crazy about boats as Pop and I were.

Ed had sailed and raced a lot on Buzzards Bay, mostly in the Herreshoff 15-footers. When his old boat, the *Ptiloris*, came on the market, he snapped her up, and then there was one of the early gaff-rigged Herreshoff 15s on a mooring right down the River at Avondale. We already knew the Marconi-rigged version, these being raced farther down at Watch Hill. Plenty of times, a Saturday afternoon sail in the yawl *Brownie* would include a leg over to see how my older cousin, Danny Larkin, was doing in the *Black Arrow*. Most of the time he'd be in the lead, running for home in Fishers Island Sound, spinnaker set perfectly to the sou'wester. Just knowing someone who raced a Watch Hill Herreshoff was heady stuff for a kid who still had to wear a life preserver to go out on the bowsprit.

Not long after the *Ptiloris* arrived in the River, Dave said his father allowed as how the two of us, then 14, could start sailing her. We were some excited.

I remember clearly the strong impressions the *Ptiloris* made on me both at the mooring and sailing the first time we took her out 35 years ago. We went on board and at first just sat in the cockpit, drinking her in. Her bow went out and up forever. It seemed to have unconquerable power and grace. What sea could worry us behind a bow like that? Underway, it was that quiet, smooth hiss of bubbles sweeping along the lee side that became indelible.

To me, the long, lean *Ptiloris* was like a cup defender. She had a huge, delicately proportioned rig with a great long boom overhanging her fine counter stern, low freeboard on the proportion of a much larger vessel, and a general feeling of steady speed.

Little wonder, for she had been designed by Nathanael G. Herreshoff. Her ancestors, a few generations back, were Herreshoff's experimental fin-keelers. She descended directly from a class of 15-foot-waterline racing sloops built with shoal hulls and conventional keels of moderate draft. These were the Newport 15s, of which eight were built.

Herreshoff Hull Number 503, the first of a 15-foot-waterline racing class for Buzzards Bay,

Nathanael Greene Herreshoff, from an oil painting. (The Boat-builders of Bristol *by Samuel Carter III*)

to be designated the E class at the Beverly Yacht Club and to become so popular that they were known simply as Herreshoff 15s, was built at the Herreshoff Manufacturing Company, Bristol, Rhode Island, in 1898. The contract price for the first boats in the class was $666.66. They were built from the same molds used for the Newport 15s but were given shoaler keels and sizable centerboards.

L. Francis Herreshoff estimated that over the years his father's company turned out about 150 Herreshoff 15s. On the company's list of the boats for which building contracts were written, I can count 71 E boats, but not all the relatively small craft built are on the list, so Mr. Herreshoff's estimate may well be right.

The 15s are 24 feet 6 inches long on deck, with a beam of 6 feet 9 inches and a draft, board up, of 2 feet 4 inches.

Captain Nat experimented with the draft on the 15s quite a bit and evidently settled on raising the lead ballast one inch to give a draft of 2 feet 3 inches. Forty-three of the 71 15s on the Company's list were built this way, including the *Ptiloris* and all of the Watch Hill Yacht Club 15s, which didn't come along until 1923. The *Toby,* Number 550, had her lead lowered 1½ inches, and 10 15s that followed her were built with their lead lowered five inches, bringing them to within an inch of the draft of the Newport 15s. The *Flicker,* Number 674, was built with a draft of 3 feet 4 inches, 6½ inches more than the Newport 15s. Like them, she had no centerboard.

Raymond Coleman, who still sails a Herreshoff 15 on Seneca Lake, New York, has made quite a study of the design. He says the displacement of the boats is 2,800 pounds. A Herreshoff Manufacturing Company catalog gives the weight of the lead outside ballast as 1,000 pounds.

Like most racing boats, the Herreshoff 15 gets her speed from very easy bow and buttock lines. Look at her long, flat run.

The boats differ a bit in shape. The high bow that so impressed me on the *Ptiloris* was notably absent on the Watch Hill boats — nor does it show up on Edson I. Schock's drawings of the *Fiddler,* the Herreshoff 15 preserved at the Mystic Seaport. I believe it was the older Herreshoff 15s that had the higher freeboard at the bow (we're talking about a difference of perhaps a couple of inches), and I don't think the later, gentler shape was an improvement.

As with all Herreshoff boats, the 15s have rather light scantlings. Frames are ¾ inch by ³⁄₁₆ inch, spaced with their centers 8 inches apart. Deck beams are ⅝ inch by 1¼ inches. Clamps are 1¼ inches square. Planking and deck are ⁹⁄₁₆-inch white cedar.

The boats were built with bulkheads sealing off big air tanks in the bow and stern for flotation. Each tank had a small deck plate, but most people cut holes in the bulkheads and installed

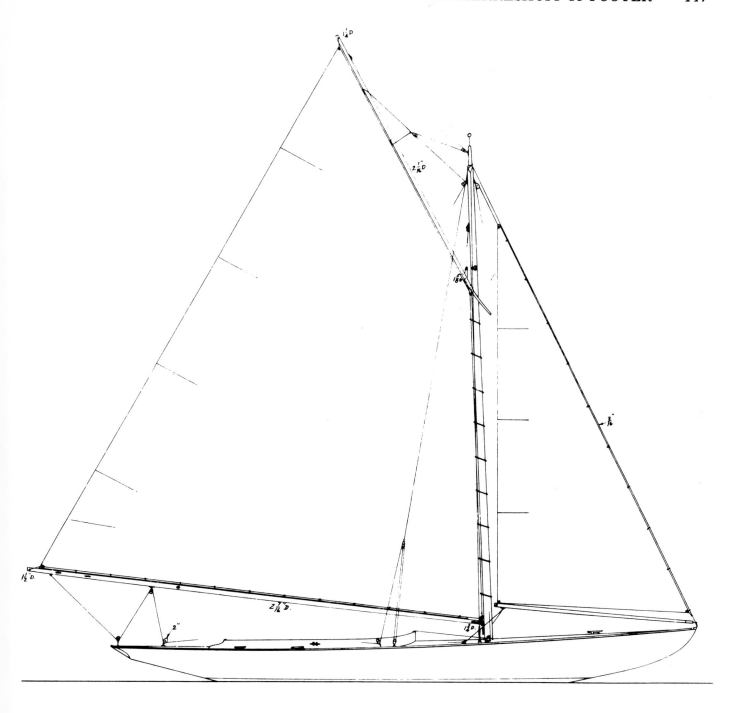

The Herreshoff 15 was designed in 1898 as a one-design racing class for Buzzards Bay. To a young sailor, she seemed like a cup defender. (Edson I. Schock, courtesy Mystic Seaport)

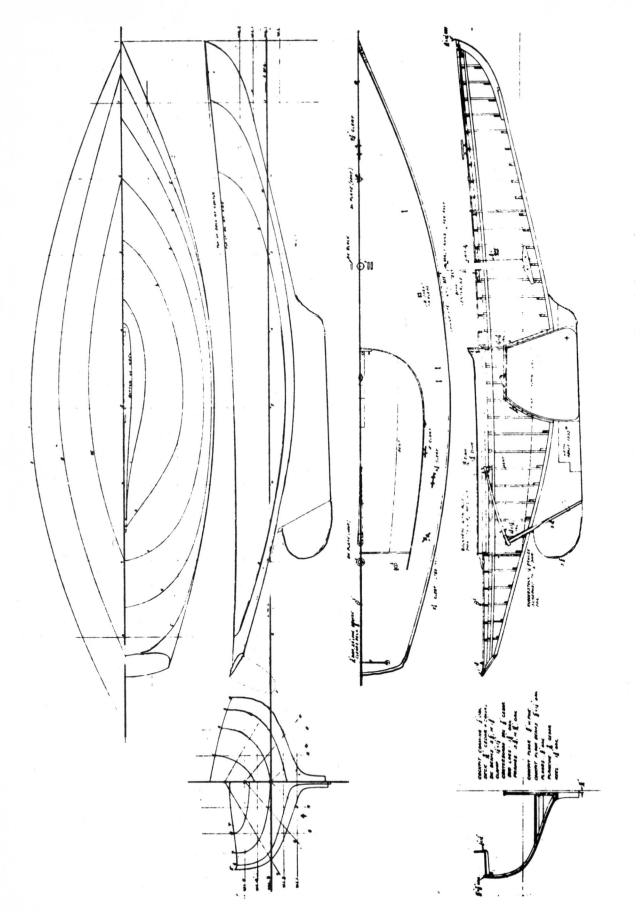

She is 24½ feet long on deck and quickly stretches out her 15-foot waterline when she heels over and gets going. (Edson I. Schock, courtesy Mystic Seaport)

more-or-less-watertight doors, so the tanks could be ventilated and even used for stowing gear if housekeeping outweighed safety.

Dave Cabot and I had a lot of fun in the *Ptiloris*. It wasn't long before we were cruising in her. We'd put a tarp over the boom and sleep on the cockpit floor. For comforts we had a mantle lantern, a portable radio, and a big picture of Jane Russell taped up across the frames in the crawl space up by the mast. We ate a lot of sardines. We had one of the early inflatable dinghies, which we deflated every day instead of dragging it from the stern.

The *Ptiloris'* shoal draft gave us courage to poke into harbors that our fathers' deeper cruising boats couldn't visit. For instance, one fine afternoon we worked her in through the obstructed entrance to Hay Harbor on the west end of Fishers Island and were rewarded with the adventure of The Night of the Swimming Girls (which, like Conan Doyle's tale of "The Giant Rat of Sumatra," shall remain untold).

Pop was a bit worried about our going off cruising in the *Ptiloris* and said we should not go outside Fishers Island Sound. We came back from Hay Harbor, however, by going outside Fishers Island. When we got back, Pop asked me if we had stayed in Fishers Island Sound. "Well," I replied, "we stayed on the Fishers Island Sound chart." Pop looked squally, and I felt small instead of big. My guilt vanished later when I learned that at that age he and a pal were supposed to be cruising on Quonochontaug Pond in a big St. Lawrence skiff, but when they got to the end of the Pond, they managed to drag her up over the beach, launched out through the surf into the ocean, and went merrily off to Point Judith to explore the ponds back of that rough, oceanic place.

At any rate, after a couple of summers of sailing the *Ptiloris* without drowning, Dave and I were allowed to go anywhere we pleased in her. We circumnavigated Shelter Island to the westward, and we went up into Narragansett Bay to the eastward.

On the latter trip, we were sailing easily into Potter's Cove on Prudence Island at the end of a long day's sail, when suddenly she refused to answer her helm. We trimmed sheets to get

where we wanted to anchor and, after furling up, donned flippers and face mask to see what was going on down there. A lot had happened. Most of the bronze drift pins holding the rudder to the stock had carried away, and the appendage was moving independently rather than merely carrying out the whims of somebody up in the cockpit holding the tiller.

The next day we beat down the bay to Newport, steering with the sails. With the main eased off a little, she would neither point nor foot at her best, but she was manageable. We spent that night in Brenton's Cove. Next morning we sailed her in to the dock at Williams and Manchester's yard in Newport, but they were too busy to haul us. We went across to Jamestown and tied up at the Round House Boat Yard, which hauled the boat, made and installed a new rudder, and put her back overboard in 24 hours. That gave us a night of camping at the yard, during which we were able to do a good deed. The lovely 60-foot Herreshoff powerboat *Thania* was tied up at the yard's dock and began pounding against it when a squall came up in the middle of the night. We helped her out with fenders until the yard folks came down and moved her around to the lee side.

With our new rudder we went out to Block Island, where we fell in with Pop and a couple of cronies in the *Brownie*. Next day we had a fine sail home across Block Island Sound just able to lay Watch Hill Point in a moderate westerly breeze. We started even with the *Brownie* (waterline length 23½ feet, one of Sam Crocker's best designs, shown in *Good Boats*) at Block Island and beat her by about a quarter of a mile at Watch Hill Point after 13½ miles of sailing full-and-by, rail down.

On that trip we sailed about 120 miles at an average-speed-made-good of just under four knots, including some drifting and a fair bit of beating.

Raymond Coleman says the rig of the Herreshoff 15 came in for a lot of experimentation also. The original sail area was 330 square feet, with 256 square feet in the mainsail and 74 in

The Fiddler *going out to race with an all-girl crew soon after the turn of the century. (Courtesy David Cheever)*

the jib. Bigger spreads of sail were tried, one rig including a bowsprit.

The *Ptiloris* had the 330-square-foot rig, or something close to it. That mainsail was a handsome sail, with its long boom, high-peaked gaff, and perfect, rather flat cut. The jib had a three-quarter-length club, which made it set very well indeed. You shifted the sheets when tacking; they belayed with a slippery hitch on horizontal oak pins on the after side of the forward end of the coaming. Her deep cockpit let you pull on her sheets, backstay tails, and halyards (which led aft) at a high enough level so that you could easily put some weight on them. With her big cockpit and her vast amount of deck space, she was a very easy boat to sail. Dave and I got so

we could put her through her paces quickly and easily. We sailed in her together enough so that each knew what to expect of the other. We shared steering and sail handling, thought alike about how she should be sailed, and so could maneuver her smartly while talking about something else.

Ed Cabot used to tell us stories about his racing days with his brother Nelson on Buzzards Bay. It always seems to blow harder there than almost anywhere else, and we came to understand that the Beverly Yacht Club sailors drove the Herreshoff 15s for fair. If the mast broke during a race, it was all in the day's work, we were told.

So we used to do a little sail-carrying our-

The race has started and the girls in the Fiddler *are third.*
It's one hand for the spinnaker and one hand for your skirt.
(Courtesy David Cheever)

selves when we were out in a breeze. We'd run with the spinnaker 'most any day and many a time would look back to see the stern wave bubbling merrily away, an inch or two above the top of the transom; and look up to see the forestay so slack it was starting to kink. Running like that, the helm would go all light and funny when she took off down a sea.

There are theories about how to trim the boat to take utmost advantage of such exciting conditions. Dave believed one of us should be riding the bow, legs dangling as the sea lifted under her and then stretched out straight ahead as she dipped her bow and tore down the face of the next one. He said having weight forward like that kept her going down the sea longer. Yet

Lloyd Bergeson, racing in his New York 30 (which is sort of a big, deep-keel version of this design), made us all huddle on the stern for the same reason. I like to stay sort of amidships.

Ed Cabot had an old spare mainsail for the *Ptiloris,* and Dave cut it into a big triangle for a balloon jib. Then we tried reaching along on a light day with two ballooners, the ex-mainsail set on the forestay, and the spinnaker set flying to the spinnaker pole lashed down as a huge bowsprit. That rig turned a few heads in Fishers Island Sound, I can tell you, as we whizzed through the ripples.

In a breeze, the Herreshoff 15 sails at a large angle of heel. Heeling way over doesn't seem to slow her down much, though. Her long, rather

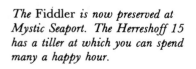

The Fiddler *is now preserved at Mystic Seaport. The Herreshoff 15 has a tiller at which you can spend many a happy hour.*

The Thistle, *a Watch Hill Herreshoff 15, beating out of Stonington harbor under reefed mainsail and small jib.* (Yachting, *May 1925)*

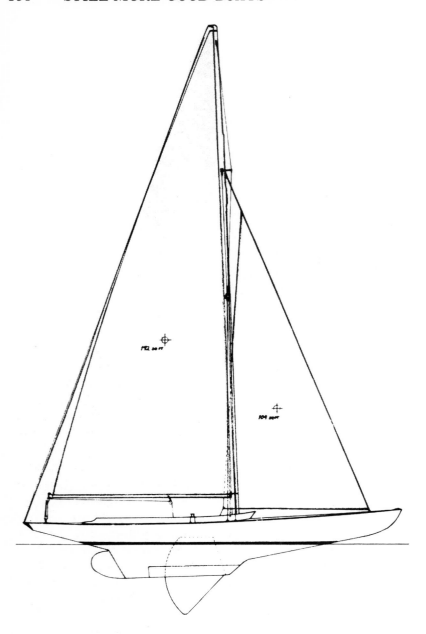

The sail plan of the new fiberglass Watch Hill Herreshoff 15. (Sailing)

flat bow can do some pounding going to windward in a steep chop. She can really punish herself a bit on occasion.

It's all right to lug sail off the wind, but all wrong to lug sail on the wind. Dave and I thought we had to be big sail carriers for quite a while. It took us a few years to learn that when thrashing to windward we wouldn't be flogged for tying in a reef or two to ease things up all around yet not slow her down.

We learned to grin and bear her considerable weather helm in a breeze on a broad reach.

We'd slack the main and trim in the jib all we could stand to (which wasn't very much, because we refused to do anything that would slow her down), held on to the tiller for dear life, and just watched that quarter wave hiss out astern. Maybe she would have gone faster with the jib trimmed flat and a little less weather helm, but we didn't think so at the time.

We used to keep asking the folks at the Watch Hill Yacht Club if we could race the old gaff-rigged *Ptiloris* against the Marconi-rigged Watch Hill Herreshoffs. The Powers That Be

One of the new Watch Hill Herreshoff 15s at rest and running with spinnaker. (Hubbard Phelps, courtesy Allan Vaitses)

said no, because the *Ptiloris* had too much sail. We persisted. Finally they gave in.

We got our chance, and we blew it. We made our big mistake out in Fishers Island Sound at the leeward mark, past which a healthy flood tide was flowing. The leaders rounded up on the wind to start the beat home and left the tide on their weather quarters. We, back in the middle of the fleet, tacked right after rounding to put the tide on the lee bow. We were allowed to go off like that all by ourselves with the tide setting us up to windward like anything and the tide knocking the other boats down to leeward like anything. We finished way ahead of the fleet and were never allowed to take that big gaff mainsail on a Watch Hill Yacht Club race course again.

When the Watch Hill Herreshoffs began to get a bit creaky, the Club set about replacing them with fiberglass replicas. A very nicely built class of new Herreshoff 15s was turned out in 1970. Allan Vaitses built the hulls at Mattapoisett, Massachusetts, and they were finished off by the Frank Hall Boat Yard at Avondale, right down the River. Sandy Van Zandt designed a tall Marconi rig for the boats. The sail area was reduced to 296 square feet.

When word about the new class got around I asked Emma Dean Larkin, Danny's sister, also a lifelong sailor of Watch Hill Herreshoff 15s, what she thought of the whole idea. She shook her head doubtfully and said, "It's sure going to be different not having that big mainsail to look up at." I'll say. In fact, I'd go all the way back to the gaff rig. If you want to go fast, spread a lot of sail.

A mere 15 years ago, I had another sail in the *Ptiloris*. John Hall, Frank's son, owned her by then and kindly lent her to me on a nice southwest day. My crew was our three young children. We beat down the River, close-reached across Little Narragansett Bay, beat around Stonington Point, and ran up into the harbor to anchor for lunch. The afternoon produced a single-reef breeze, and we let her go, full-and-by, out through Catumb Passage between Watch Hill Point and Fishers Island, stood offshore a couple of miles, then tacked and came rollicking back in on a great roller-coaster ride.

The *Ptiloris* is still on the River. I'd love to look up along that high bow again and let her play one more time her siren song of bubbles hissing down the lee side.

22/ The Dovekie

Length on deck: 21 feet 5 inches
Length on waterline: 19 feet
Beam: 6 feet 8 inches
Draft: 4 inches
Sail area: 143 square feet
Displacement: 600 pounds
Designer: Philip C. Bolger

When Phil Bolger's boat plans arrived at International Marine for his book *The Folding Schooner And Other Adventures in Boat Design,* eager hands opened the package and spread the contents on the office floor. We were expecting a fascinating fleet, and we weren't disappointed.

One of the most intriguing designs Phil sent us was that of the Dovekie, a 6.52-meter (for us old dogs, that translates to something like 21 feet 5 inches) sailing and rowing, engineless cruising boat. We studied the plans of this double-ended, leg-o'-mutton sharpie closely and tried to envision what it would be like to sail and row her. We read Phil's description of the boat closely.

He wrote that the boat had been built as an experiment by Edey and Duff, the people who make Stone Horse sloops and Doughdishes in Mattapoisett, Massachusetts. Phil's text said that no decision had been made whether or not to go into production. Then there was a footnote, we noted with some disappointment, that said: "After much discussion, it's been reluctantly concluded not to market her, or invest in production design or tooling."

But then, happily, that decision was reversed,

and Edey and Duff announced that you could buy Dovekies from them. I called up Peter Duff to admit that I was somewhat enamored of the boat, and he suggested I come and sail one. Then he went one better and said why didn't he and his wife, Maggie, bring a Dovekie to Maine? Before I could protest that that's a pretty long sail, Peter explained that the journey would be made at a steady 55 m.p.h.

Peter, Maggie, and the *Gray Dovekie* arrived on a Friday night. They slipped the boat into Rockport Harbor and spent the night quietly ensconced behind a ledge in a little pool that dries out at low tide, watching everybody else in Rockport pitch and roll to the usual surge that makes in from the Bay. By the time I got down there the next morning, they were tied up to a float at the new Marine Park. They said they had the morning to show me the boat; at midday a recent purchaser of a Dovekie would arrive with his new boat from Ipswich, Massachusetts, and they would go off cruising in company over around Vinalhaven.

I got out my index cards to make like a reporter. "How many of these things have you built and sold?"

Philip C. Bolger.

"Seventeen." (As of book-editing date, 20 more have been built.)

"What do they cost?"

"$4,870 for the boat ready to sail or row away, plus $885 if you want the special trailer for her." (Now $5,185 for the boat, same price for the trailer.)

No more notes; the rest of it I can look up or remember. She's 21 feet 5 inches long on deck, with a waterline length of 19 feet, a beam of 6 feet 8 inches, and a draft of all of 4 inches at her design displacement of all of 600 pounds. This is with gear on board, but no people, who would sink her an inch or two depending on the size of the crowd. Her sail area is 143 square feet.

She's a fiberglass boat, built of Airex foam sandwich construction. Her flat bottom, with ¾ inch of Airex between fiberglass skins, is perfectly stiff. The Airex in the boat gives her a lot of flotation. She is a boat that could capsize if mishandled or overwhelmed by wind and sea, but she would not sink.

She's all fiberglass; there is no relief of wood.

I went on board over the bow and made my way aft over her raised deck. Peter waited until I got back to the cockpit and then said gently that the whole idea of the two big hatches in the deck was to allow you to move from bow to stern without your feet leaving the bottom of the boat, yet have access to whatever you wanted to reach on deck. After a little more traveling around the

boat, I saw the wisdom and efficiency of this arrangement. It works beautifully.

The hatchways (the Old-Timer would call them standing rooms, and many a small workboat had them) have no hatch covers other than canvas ones. Hatch covers would only get in the way, and the canvas covers keep out all but the orneriest drops of driving spray.

The forward end of the cockpit is protected by a big dodger, and the after end can be covered by a tarpaulin, so that she may be entirely closed up.

In the middle of the cockpit is a high, tubular gallows frame. This is a great thing to hang onto or stand leaning against in the big cockpit of this boat. It also holds the mast and sprit in place in their lowered position, which is where they were when I came on board. The only time you have the mast up is when you're sailing. Rowing or at anchor or at 55 m.p.h., you strike the rig.

With the rig down, the forward ends of the mast and sprit lock into simple fittings on the foredeck. The gallows frame holds them up out of the way, one spar on each side of the boat. They lash in place on the gallows. As a matter of fact, far from being in the way, the spars make a nice cockpit railing and do provide a bit of relief of wood after all.

I had read Phil's description of how you put the rig up, and it sounded pretty complicated. Seeing spars, sail, shrouds, and Dacron forestay lying on deck confirmed my suspicion that sending it all aloft was going to be a tricky business. I won't list all the steps here, because that would only make you suspicious, too. Suffice it to say that the Dovekie's single shrouds snap-shackle to her chainplates, that her rope forestay leads aft to belay beside the midships hatch, which is where the mast-raiser operates, and that Peter had the rig up and secured pretty quickly. It's one of those things that takes a lot longer to tell about than to do.

The Dovekie's sprit rig is nice and simple; the sprit is up high where you don't have to worry about it hitting you on the head. The clew of the sail simply goes on a hook at the after end of the sprit and you take up on the snotter to stretch the sail aft where you want it. A lanyard on the

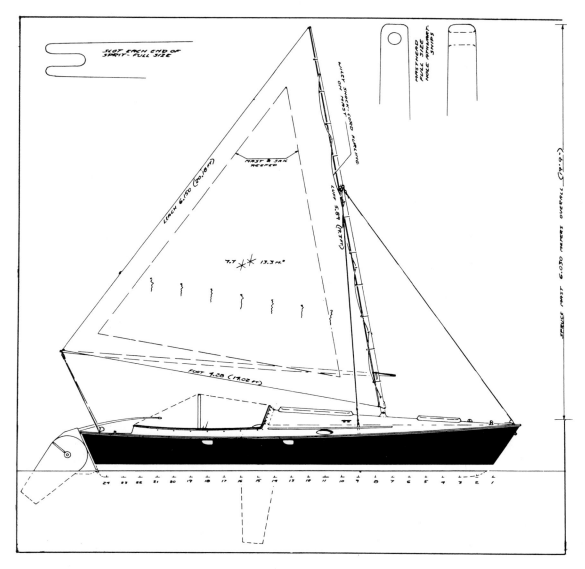

The Dovekie is a fascinating double-ended leeboard sharpie with a rakish leg-o'-mutton rig that lowers readily. (The Folding Schooner and Other Adventures in Boat Design *by Philip C. Bolger, International Marine Publishing Company)*

clew to pull out and make fast would probably be better for the singlehander, for the clew can come unhooked while you're setting up the forward end of the sprit if there's no one to hold the clew on its hook.

As shown in the sail plan, the sail has a fairly deep reef. When the sail is reefed, the mast is shifted from its normal step on deck down to a new step in the bottom of the boat. (The reefed position of the mast is shown in the construction profile drawing.)

We didn't reef the boat that morning, but Peter says it's a little bit of a chore. You furl the sail and take the mast down to reef her, and there is talk of having to hold her head to wind with an anchor to ease her motion while going

through the operation. Nothing difficult, but a bit tedious. You shift tack and clew and tie up the sail, but the whole thing is kind of in your lap. You let go the shrouds, which won't be used. You shift the mast to its new step (the mast now goes through the midships hatch), set up the mast, loose the reefed sail (its position and area are shown by dotted lines in the sail plan), get your anchor back on board from the forward cockpit, and then fill her away to see what she'll do.

We filled her away to a tiny little westerly breeze wafting down off the hills. The *Gray Dovekie's* battenless sail showed a fine shape. Like all Edey and Duff sails, it was made by Bill Harding of Marion, Massachusetts.

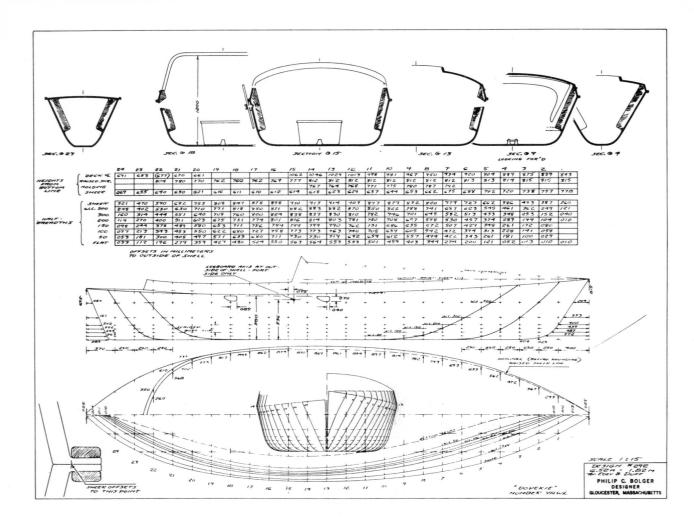

Her lines show a very shoal, light hull with a lot of room in it. (The Folding Schooner and Other Adventures in Boat Design by Philip C. Bolger, International Marine Publishing Company)

We sailed the boat that morning mostly reaching and with some beating and running in a land breeze with occasional fresh puffs.

The boat handled easily and surely, I thought, though I was hampered a bit by the main-sheet rig. It's just a single-part sheet leading through a turning block on the rudder head and in along the tiller where you take a couple of turns with it 'round a pin through the inboard end of the tiller. The boat steers steadily and with great sensitivity, and I'd want to get that sheet off the helm and make it a three-part tackle. At least that's my first reaction. Maybe I'd get used to the single-part sheet belaying on the tiller and like it, but I wished I could have gotten the feel of her helm unencumbered by the main sheet.

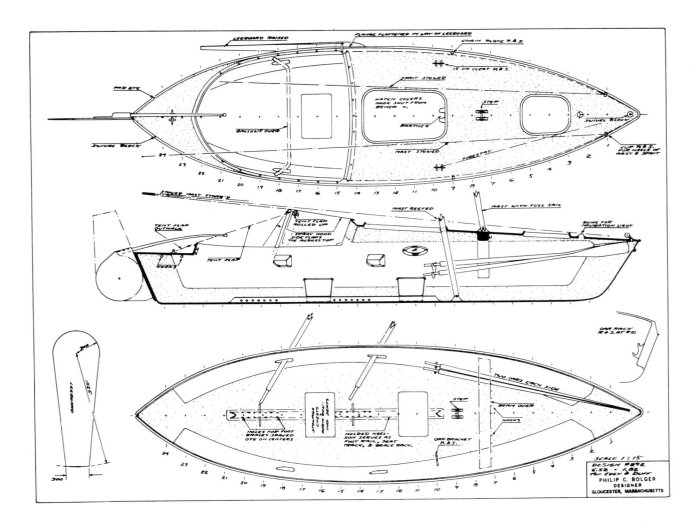

She is built of Airex foam-sandwich stuff. She has leeboards, a kick-up rudder, and rowing ports. (The Folding Schooner and Other Adventures in Boat Design by Philip C. Bolger, International Marine Publishing Company)

The *Gray Dovekie* was quite responsive and showed a good turn of speed. She does have a fairly quick motion, being a very light boat, and, of course, she can pound her flat bottom. Being a double-ender, she makes little fuss going through the water.

Her leeboards are heavily laminated of mahogany. They look plenty strong, which they should be. They operate nicely with ingenious cranks, the mechanical advantage coming from a fairly long crank arm rather than from any gearing. The cranks work the leeboards one-to-one. The crank handle folds out to unlock and turn the leeboard and then folds back against the side of the boat to lock the board in the desired position. The rudder pulls up and down

Above: *Peter Duff, the builder, enjoying a Dovekie. (Edey & Duff).* **Right:** *Her big midships hatch gives headroom and lets in plenty of light and air.*

She makes a great gunkholer. (Edey & Duff)

with a lanyard for shoal-water work and trailering.

As you sail the Dovekie and look around her, the sloping angle of her raised deck takes a bit of getting used to. To the uninitiated she looks as if she's going to try to dive under an approaching wave, but of course she does no such thing, and you begin to sense her lightness and buoyancy taking the apparent precariousness out of that downhill slope to the bow.

The boat's cockpit is very big and very deep. Its inhabitants could scarcely desire greater protection from the elements, especially with the dodger in place. The dodger does, however, restrict the view of the person steering. And if a non-steerer sits on the flat floor of the cockpit, he can't see ahead or to windward. It wasn't long before I started thinking about a jump seat on each side of the cockpit just abaft the leeboards, ones that would fold up against the side of the boat when not wanted.

You could have all kinds of furniture in this cockpit. There could be a chaise longue, or chairs and table, or perhaps a two-seater swing hung off the gallows. The *Gray Dovekie* may not have had any of these amenities, but she did have her sleeping mattresses, one on top of the other, stretching across the cockpit floor, giving the vessel an aura of Ancient Rome. As a matter of fact, I tried lying on this sumptuous couch, head propped on folded elbow, to look out the window of the oarport and watch the world go by. Not bad.

The boat's stern seat is very comfortable for the steering person, whether you elect to face forward or to leeward. I was told that under this seat is a Porta-Potti. Now that's about the last place in this boat that I would think of using a bucket, so I think I'd rather have the bucket, to use somewhere else.

In any event, you want a bucket and a big towel handy in this boat — as you do in any other small, open boat — because in a flat-bottomed boat, whatever water gets inside is right with you until you put it back where it belongs.

Below, forward, the Dovekie has topless bins for stowing gear. Peter Duff has quite properly resisted all suggestions to put covers on these bins. The covers would get in the way like anything, and there's nothing like simple access and seeing what you're reaching for.

The after ends of these bins form the support for a removable wooden seat in the middle of

Far from the madding crowd: a pair of Dovekies cruising in company. (Edey & Duff)

the big midships hatch. This is where you can sit to watch her go — or row to make her go. There's a curved seat in the forward hatch, which is another nice place to sit and watch her go, though unless there is a gang aft, your weight will put her a bit down by the head.

We got back to the float at noon, struck the rig, and tried out the *Gray Dovekie* under oars. Out came the transparent Lexan oarport covers, up folded the stainless steel "thole pins," and out went the 9½-foot Shaw and Tenney oars.

There was a light breeze up in Rockport Harbor, but she didn't feel it much with her rig down. She rowed as handily as a big heavy skiff, maneuvering well and carrying her way nicely. I can tell you that she rows quite a bit better than a 13-foot Boston Whaler; of course that admirable craft was not designed to be propelled by oars except in case of mechanical failure. I am told it's hard, because of steering difficulties, to row a Dovekie across a fresh breeze. It would be extremely difficult for me to row a

Dovekie across a fresh breeze even if she steered perfectly.

In Phil Bolger's description of the Dovekie, he reported that she had three failings: he said she sails around her anchor annoyingly; she is overpowered by a strong breeze if she has a light crew; and she makes a lot of noise slapping into a head sea. The middle one of these strikes me as being the most serious drawback, and I guess if I were going to go off cruising in this boat singlehanded, I'd pave her flat bottom with a few sandbags.

Peter Duff says a drawback to the boat when cruising is that you have no dinghy, so that to go ashore, you must tie her up at a dock or put her on the beach — where, if you leave her, you may have a security problem, since she is entirely open. There sure is a good market for that miracle boat, the easily inflatable, easily deflatable, handsome, nice rowing dinghy for small cruising boats.

I don't think the Dovekie is a pretty boat, but neither do I think she's ugly. She looks like what

A Dovekie ready to try a new cruising ground, perhaps a thousand miles from home. (Edey & Duff)

she is, a straightforward engineering-and-design solution to a problem: how to make a small cruising boat that will sail well and row reasonably well. Here is a boat with a purpose that could scarcely be more timely: cruising without an engine.

The keys to the success of this design, it seems to me, are the boat's extreme lightness, allowing her to move both under oars and a rig small enough to be set up and struck easily; and her flat bottom, which gives stiffness, maximum usable space, and extremely shallow draft. The Dovekie is big enough to handle some real sea and breeze, is easily the most spacious 21-footer I've ever been in, and gives you the ability to travel in very shoal water and to dry out upright, opening the way to a wonderful kind of peaceful cruising.

After rowing around a few of the boats in the harbor — I noticed that the *Gray Dovekie* under oars generated a few expressions of amused disbelief — we tied her up again and sat back to await the arrival of the other Dovekie and her

new owners. They soon came, towing the boat with a tiny car. The captain of this second Dovekie was a precise, careful sort of gentleman who knew what he wanted and how he wanted it. Though he allowed us all to help him launch his boat, rig her, and make her ready to get underway, I had the feeling that he could have done it more efficiently and quickly by himself. Even with us slowing him down, I don't think it was more than 20 minutes from the time he drove up in his car until the time he cast off from the float and followed the *Gray Dovekie* out of Rockport Harbor. And that included nearly five minutes of route planning over a chart. In addition, he took a moment to remark on the pleasure it had given him to tell his big-boat friends in Ipswich, "We're going cruising in Maine this weekend, but we'd love to cruise in company with you to Nantucket Wednesday."

Peter and Maggie Duff had the *Gray Dovekie* in Florida one spring. Now they are talking about a place called Thunder Bay that they tell me is part of Lake Superior.

23/ The Petrel

> Length on deck: 20 feet 9 inches
> Length on waterline: 16 feet
> Beam: 7 feet 1 inch
> Draft: 3 feet 1 inch
> Sail area: 265 square feet
> Displacement: 2,850 pounds
> Designer: Nathanael G.
>   Herreshoff

Years ago, cruising on the southern New England coast, we used to see a little green sloop sailing from harbor to harbor ably handled by what then looked to me like a quite elderly couple obviously enjoying the little boat hugely. She was only about 20 feet long but had a little cabin house with a square punt stowed upside down over it. She was gaff rigged and had a particularly handsome transom stern reminiscent of the type found on a Bahamian sloop.

Pop said she had been converted from a Herreshoff Fish class daysailer into the out-and-out cruiser we knew. She was close enough to the ideal pocket cruiser to set a young feller to thinking — and dreaming.

I never knew who her people were, but recently Dick Besse of Skaneateles, New York, wrote me that her skipper was Henry Lambert Knight of Vineyard Haven, "a great seaman with Cape Horn square-rigger experience." His boat was the *Pompano*. (Another green cruising Fish boat is kept at Marion, Massachusetts, by Dana Hayden. This confused me greatly, until Mr. Hayden kindly straightened me out.)

The *Pompano* always made the Herreshoff Fish class seem extra special to me. The folks at

Golden Era Boats in Noank, Connecticut, build a good replica of the Fish class called the Petrel, and they kindly asked me to come down and sail one of the boats. We were to sail the seventh Petrel built, the *Spring Tide*, owned by Dick Phillips and kept at Groton Long Point, Connecticut. We chose December 1 as a mutually convenient day for Dick, Justin Camarata (president of Golden Era), and me; then we assiduously ignored the dire predictions of the weather "forecasters."

Thanks to our combined efforts, the first day of December turned out to be a perfect sailing day — well, almost perfect. It was sunny and bright, temperature well above freezing, with a moderate westerly breeze. The only trouble was that the breeze thought it was a northwester and simply couldn't make up its mind what it wanted to do. Every other thing it would drop away to quite light. Nor could it come to a decision about its direction, swinging from southwest to north of west with no more warning than the ruffling of those tiny little ripples close aboard to windward. Since the "forecasters" said we were going to get a small blizzard the following day (another in a long string of

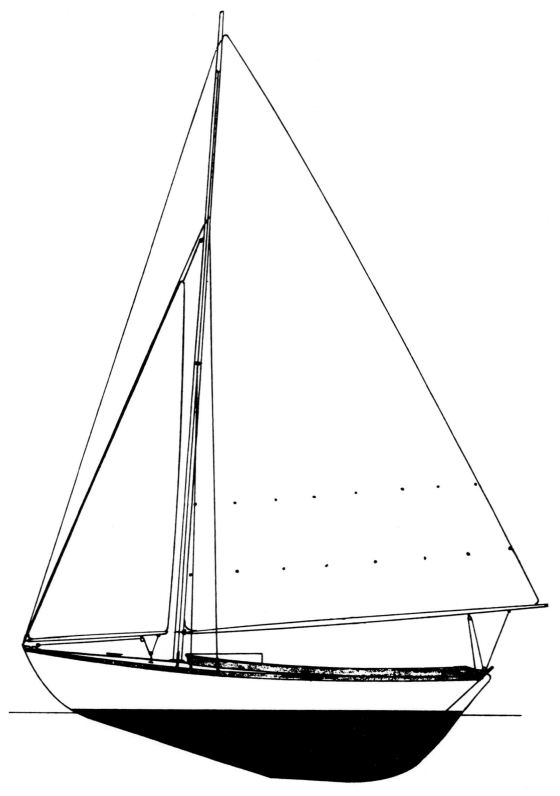

The Petrel's sail plan is the same as that used for the Marconi-rigged Fish class boats. (Golden Era Boats)

Justin Camarata's lines drawing of his replica of the Fish class. (Golden Era Boats)

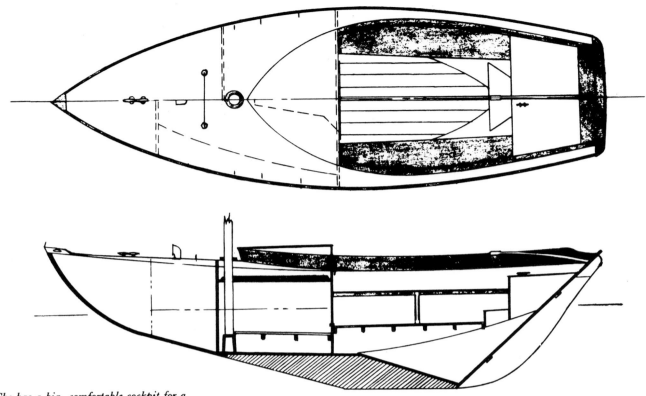

*She has a big, comfortable cockpit for a
21-footer. (Golden Era Boats)*

broken promises), we reveled in the sun and relative warmth allotted us and refused to complain about the wind's vagaries.

You have to look hard at the Fishers Island Sound chart to find the lagoon back of Groton Long Point. It's awfully skinny. Dave Cabot and I sailed the *Ptiloris* in there once and only managed to escape from the place after a quick succession of near collisions with moored boats, intermingled at random with near strandings on one or the other shore of the place.

That lagoon is where Dick Phillips moors the *Spring Tide,* and I was looking forward to seeing how he would get her out of the long, narrow slot. It was apparent from the wind direction that he couldn't quite fetch out the length of this slot and that, supposing he should manage to reach its far end, he would then be faced with going nearly dead to windward out of its bent mouth, into which a healthy little chop was rolling. Dick, who has been negotiating these horrors since the age of 12, remarked on the state of the tide — dead low.

We set mainsail and jib and Dick started her off on the long tack slanting diagonally across the lagoon. The long tack lasted quite a few seconds and was then followed by a short one across to the weather side of the place. And out we went, long-short, long-short, with Dick keeping the boat pointing way up, nearly into the eye of the wind, yet always maintaining at least good steerageway.

When we got to the lumpy corner where we had to go dead to windward, I really didn't see how he was going to make it. I would have been tempted to run back unscathed and say, "Well, how do you like her?" Neither helmsman nor boat faltered, however, and out she went, tacking bang-bang-bang. In the clear, we put her on a close reach, heading over toward the Dumplings and West Harbor on Fishers Island.

Nathanael G. Herreshoff designed and built the first of the Herreshoff Manufacturing Company's very popular 12½-foot-waterline sloops for children in 1914. Parents loved to sail them, too, but a father, going sailing after a day at the office, needed a place to hang up his business suit out of harm's way and change into sailing clothes. Such amenities were not provided in the 12½-footers, and so Captain Nat was asked to make a bigger version with the required "accommodations."

The great designer and builder responded in 1916 with the Fish class, blown up to 16 feet on the waterline. Twenty-three boats were built that year, the first ones for $875 each. Somebody must have figured something wrong, because buyers of the last of the 23 boats had to pay $925. (J.P. Morgan got in on the action at $875.) The lead boat in the class was the *Manatee,* Herreshoff hull Number 788. In 1917, three more Fish boats were built, still at the $925 contract price. One more was built in 1919; war-fueled inflation nearly doubled the price to $1,700. These boats, I believe, were all gaff rigged.

In 1925, six more Fish boats were built, these with Marconi rig, for $1,750. Then, that same year, seven additional Marconi-rigged boats were built at $1,900. These last were the Warwick Neck class.

The Herreshoff Fish class and the Petrel replica have a length on deck of 20 feet 9 inches, a waterline length of 16 feet, a beam of 7 feet 1 inch, and a draft of 3 feet 1 inch. The displacement is 2,850 pounds, with 1,400 pounds of lead outside ballast. The sail area of the Marconi rig (standard for the Petrel, with gaff rig optional) is 265 square feet.

The Fish boat and the Petrel are very lively sailers, like all Herreshoff boats, because of their high sail-area-to-displacement ratio and their ability to carry a big sail area due to a fairly high ballast-to-displacement ratio.

Justin Camarata has been careful to reproduce the same displacement, ballast, and rig so that the Petrel, judging by the *Spring Tide,* feels like a Herreshoff boat sailing.

Sailing the *Spring Tide* across Fishers Island Sound was just great. She put her rail down and just under at times in the puffs, which made her seem a trifle tender until we remembered that the air was a lot cooler and thus denser than in summer. When it's cold you have to shorten down more than when it's warm. We had full sail, and the puffs of dense breeze were maybe 15 knots.

A Petrel close-hauled in a light breeze.
(Golden Era Boats)

Dick Phillips sailing his Spring Tide. (Golden Era Boats)

Justin caught the sailing disease in a Herreshoff 12½-footer. He went to cruising with a growing family in the usual succession of bigger and bigger boats. Then, remembering the fun of the 12½-footer, he went back to a Fish boat. It was his appreciation for the sailing qualities, roominess, and beauty of the Fish boat that made him want to reproduce her.

For the lines of the Petrel, Justin took the lines off his own Fish boat. He feels that in the Petrel he didn't achieve quite as fine an entry as the Fish boat has. This is true, because his lines drawing shows a straight load waterline forward, whereas the Fish boat has a slightly hollow entrance. Also, the stem profile of the Petrel came out just a bit straighter than that of the Fish class. The stem profile in the Petrel's sail plan and arrangement profile look more like the Fish boat.

The stern of this boat is the handsomest flat-transomed stern I know of. It's very pleasing to look at from outside and in. Its broadness provides bearing as the boat heels, its rake gives lift in a following sea, and its general shape provides a great deal of room inside the boat.

The sections show lots of deadrise and lots of flare in the topsides, with an extremely easy turn of the bilge. She has moderately deep bow and buttock lines yet a remarkably long, straight run for such a short, fairly full boat.

Justin increased the chord of the rudder by 1½ inches to make her a bit surer to turn (at the expense of a slightly increased heeling moment when applying weather helm to the heeled hull). This is probably an improvement; I have experienced being unable to head off in a 12½-footer, when pressed, without easing the main sheet — not a bad feature for a children's boat but perhaps a rather rigorous quality for general sailing.

The Petrel is built with a fiberglass hull and deck. The hull consists of ⅜ inch of Airex sandwiched between two layers of fiberglass. The fiberglass is laid up more heavily than is required for normal strength in order to bring the displacement of the hull up to that of the original Fish boat. The deck construction is a lighter version of that of the hull; the fine fiberglass cloth on top has a surface approximating that of heavy canvas.

The Petrel has positive buoyancy when full of water. She gets her flotation from the Airex in her hull, an air tank in each end of the boat, and additional flotation under the cockpit seats and under bunks in the cuddy when the latter are fitted.

This flotation is obviously a valuable feature in a heavily ballasted open boat. To me the most important advantage of the Petrel's flotation is not that she will stay afloat if completely

The Shark, *one of the early Fish boats, hard at it.* (The Rudder, *September 1919*)

The Sea Robin *on a fast reach.* (The Rudder, *September 1919*)

The original sail plan of the Fish class. (The Rudder, *February 1916)*

filled, but that she will float high enough when half filled to give her crew a good chance of wielding the two big buckets she ought to carry to get rid of the water before she does fill completely.

The Petrel's sheer strake, coaming, seats, cockpit and cuddy soles and cuddy doors are all teak. The sheer strake doesn't have the handsome and unique Herreshoff molded shape to it, but Golden Era may offer that as an (expensive) extra in future boats. The Petrel's spars are very well made of Sitka spruce. The *Spring Tide* impressed me as being nicely built.

A standard Petrel costs $15,200 today. The price would vary somewhat, depending on the kind of arrangements you want in the cockpit and in the cuddy. Fourteen Petrels have been turned out to date.

After reaching across the Sound, we worked up toward the entrance to West Harbor, tacked, and stood back toward Groton Long Point, passing to weather of the Flat Hummock and to leeward of the Dumplings. We reached fast through the edge of a tide rip in which she was docile as a lamb. We were just far enough off the wind so that neither Dick nor Justin was too worried about my getting him wet, even though I had sinned in that regard (though not greatly) on at least two inattentive occasions coming across the Sound.

Off Groton Long Point we converged with a very-modern-looking sloop beating to windward under a tall, skinny mainsail and big genoa jib. Nearly covered with people and circled by two doting power launches, she seemed to be somebody's new creation out on trials. The jib was so glossy it fairly glistened in the bright sun. It looked like the sailcloth had been covered with a layer of celluloid.

We tacked under the stern of this machine and put the *Spring Tide* up on the wind to see how fast the thing would pull away from us. Instead, we sailed through her lee, because the celluloid jib split from luff to leech.

The big mainsail on the Petrel is a great joy, just driving her constantly with no fuss or bother. She has a permanent backstay rigged each side of the mast pulling against the forestay, a very sensible arrangement, I

thought. These stays are far enough forward not to interfere with the boom when running. The mainsail does bear on them when well off the wind, of course, and it would probably make sense to build Petrel mainsails with long, narrow reinforcing strips on each side of the sail where they touch the backstays. Sort of like putting elbow patches on a new wool sweater.

Her little jib helps a whole lot for its area; it helps the mainsail. The masthead stay carries no sail (unless somebody wants to fool with a big ballooner) but keeps the masthead from bending aft and generally steadies things aloft in a head sea.

The Petrel has bronze hardware closely resembling that to be found on a Fish boat. She is an extremely handy boat for singlehanding, since there is nothing to touch when tacking but the tiller. Dick Phillips has installed a nice little tiller comb for self-steering and to hold the helm over a bit when jibing singlehanded. It folds down out of the way when you're not using it.

After witnessing the trials (and tribulations) of the celluloid-jibbed boat, we fell in with a Luders 16 that had sailed out of West Harbor. We trailed her on a close reach for a ways and couldn't tell whether or not we were gaining. We certainly didn't think we were falling back any. Then she tacked and came back, and we tacked too as she drew abeam to weather. She was being sailed singlehanded. The two boats converged, both reaching along fast, and we exchanged compliments. It was fun to watch her long, sleek hull sliding easily through the waves.

It was quite a stroke of luck to fall in with another boat of the same waterline length but quite a different hull form. The Luders 16 is longer on deck than the Petrel, narrower, deeper, and has less sail area. On that point of sailing and in that breeze, the two boats sailed dead even. Later, as we approached Fishers Island again, and both ran off farther in a lighter breeze under the shore, our big mainsail began to do its work and we gradually pulled away.

The *Spring Tide's* auxiliary propulsion consists of a pair of 8½-foot oars that stow nicely in the cockpit back of the seats out under the deck. There are oarlock sockets on the coaming and the boat can be rowed with two oars or one (in the latter case, that tiller comb comes in mighty handy). I'd want a third oarlock socket on the quarter for sculling.

She has a bilge pump mounted permanently under the cockpit sole, a sensible arrangement. There are lockers under the cockpit seats.

The cuddy arrangement on the Petrel is the same as that on the Fish boat. It looks good and works well. The *Spring Tide* has stowage arrangements in the cuddy well thought out by Dick Phillips for an icebox, a tool kit, life jackets, and so forth. She also has a head in the cuddy. Oh yes, and there is an outboard motor in there for some strange reason.

The standard position of the Petrel's forward watertight bulkhead is (as shown in the arrangement profile) just forward of the mast. But if you want to use the boat as a short-range cruiser, she can be built with this bulkhead moved farther forward to allow room for a bunk on each side of the cuddy. That's what I'd do.

We went over to West Harbor and back twice and then ran her off for the Mystic River. It sure was great to be out sailing around in a good boat in Fishers Island Sound. It's always fun to return to once-familiar waters. Names and vistas that you haven't thought of for a long time come flooding back effortlessly, and it seems as if you must have been sailing there just last week.

Fishers Island Sound is an ideal sailing ground for a boat like the Petrel. It has just the right combination of openness and protection, and there are plenty of coves to explore and points to round. Mother, in her "old age," used to cruise these waters in a Fish boat that was owned and skippered by one of her many lady cousins. As they voyaged from harbor to harbor (not very long distances are involved), the cousin's husband, worried for their safety, would follow in his car from point to point. This amused Mother greatly, but I'm not sure how the cousin felt about it.

Why is it so many people come to an able, roomy daysailer with minimal cruising accommodations when they get older? I like to think it is because they also get wiser.

That's the kind of boat Nathanael Greene Herreshoff himself sailed in his later life. As a matter of fact, his very last boat was the *Water Lily*, a slightly enlarged centerboard version of the Fish boat.

We ran the *Spring Tide* quietly up the Mystic River, landed at the Mystic Shipyard where she was to spend the winter, and tied her off in a slip. There were still a handful of boats afloat at the yard. Looking at them and at the *Spring Tide*, it was easy to see that in that fair sampling of boats, the Petrel was the most distinguished vessel. It's good to have boats available again built to such an outstanding design.

24/ The *Sabot*

> **Length on deck: 19 feet 6 inches**
> **Length on waterline: 16 feet**
> **Beam: 6 feet 4 inches**
> **Draft: 3 feet**
> **Sail area: 189 square feet**
> **Displacement: 3,450 pounds**
> **Designer: William W. Atkin**

One of the most generous souls I know on the face of the earth is John Atkin. John is — as I suppose 'most every sailor of small boats is aware — a designer of good cruising boats with an ability probably to be blamed, at least in part, on his father, William Atkin, who designed in his lifetime score upon score of fine vessels, boats and craft.

A few years back, when I visited John's utterly fascinating designing room in southern Connecticut, he pressed into my hands a small pamphlet entitled "Small Yachts and Boats," edited by his brother, Bill W. Atkin, and published a good many years ago by an organization known as Silvermine Associates of Norwalk, Connecticut.

It is from this little booklet that I quote the next two paragraphs:

"I share Bill Atkin's [Bill, the father] fondness for very small cruisers. At bottom it is not a matter of reason. I like them, and that's that. But they do have some real advantages. They can be gotten under way easily and quickly and put to bed at the day's end in a few minutes. Their ground tackle is light. Their sails are small and easily handled. They can go into little places. They are inexpensive to build. They can be kept up with a minimum of labor. And last of all, if they are *good boats* [emphasis added] they are flexible and responsive and great fun to sail.

"On the other hand, all very little cruisers have faults. Some of these are inherent and cannot be cured. For instance, their maximum speed is limited by their waterline length. The best of them have great difficulty in beating against strong head winds or heavy seas. And they can't carry sail as a large boat would. I think the design of this little boat goes as far as it can in getting speed, stability and weatherly qualities out of a tiny craft."

The writer was Elihu Root, Jr., an experienced sailor and owner of a number of successful small cruising boats, and "this little boat" is a 19-foot cruising sloop designed by William Atkin in 1934. The two men must have collaborated on the basic idea, for on the little sloop's plans, Atkin printed: "Designed from data compiled by Mr. Elihu Root, Jr."

Her name is the *Sabot*, which is what a Frenchman calls a wooden shoe.

Now, it is true that this little craft does have a long turtleback, sufficient in itself to bring her

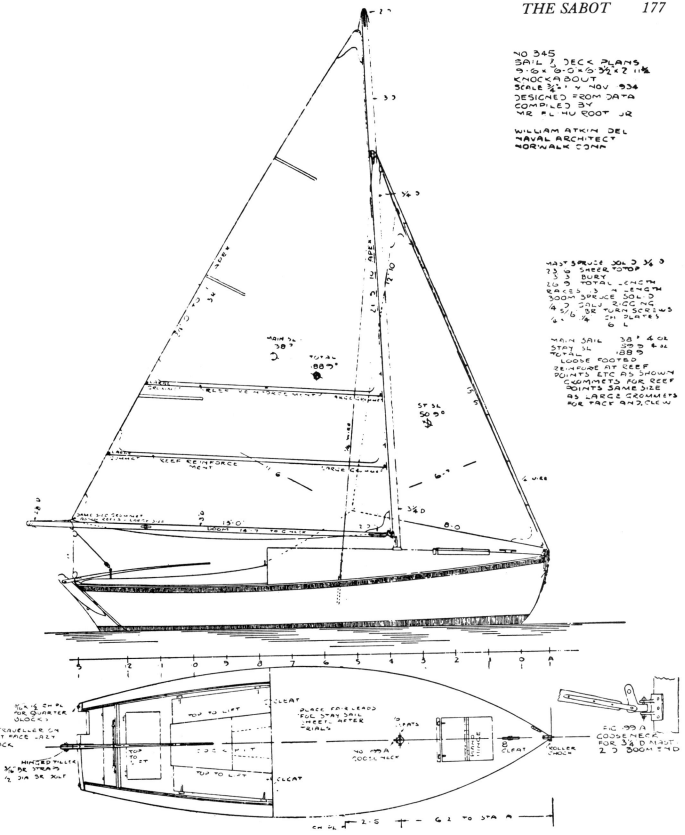

The Sabot *is a 19-foot cruising sloop that Billy Atkin designed "from data compiled by Elihu Root, Jr."* (Small Yachts and Boats *edited by William Atkin)*

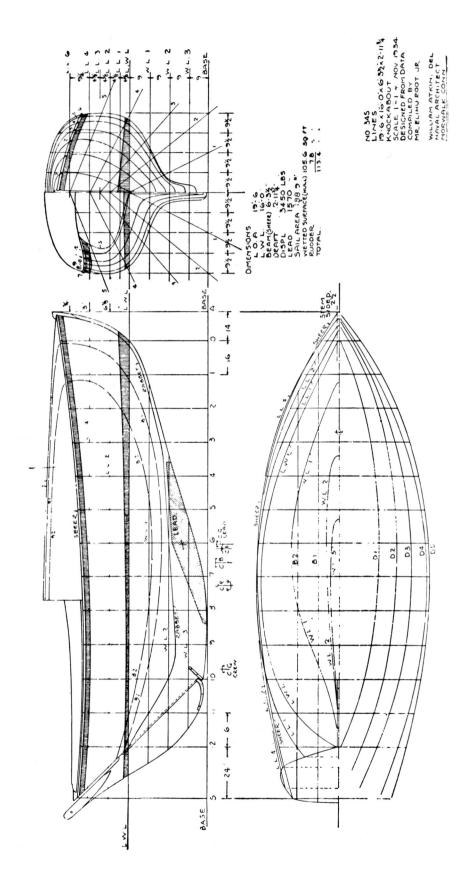

DIMENSIONS
L.O.A.   19'·6
L.W.L.   16'·0
BEAM (SHEER) 6·3½
DRAFT   2·11¼
DISPL   3,450 LBS
LEAD   1,570
SAIL AREA 198·7
WETTED SURFACE (HULL) 105.6 SQ FT
RUDDER   7·8
TOTAL   113·4

NO 345
LINES
19·6 × 16·0 × 6·3½ × 2·11¼
KNOCKABOUT
SCALE 1½" = 1' NOV 1934
DESIGNED FROM DATA
COMPILED BY
MR. ELIHU ROOT JR.

WILLIAM ATKIN, DEL
NAVAL ARCHITECT
NORWALK, CONN

Her turtleback gives her a roomy enough hull so that she can be fine-lined and fast for a tabloid cruiser. (Small Yachts and Boats edited by William Atkin)

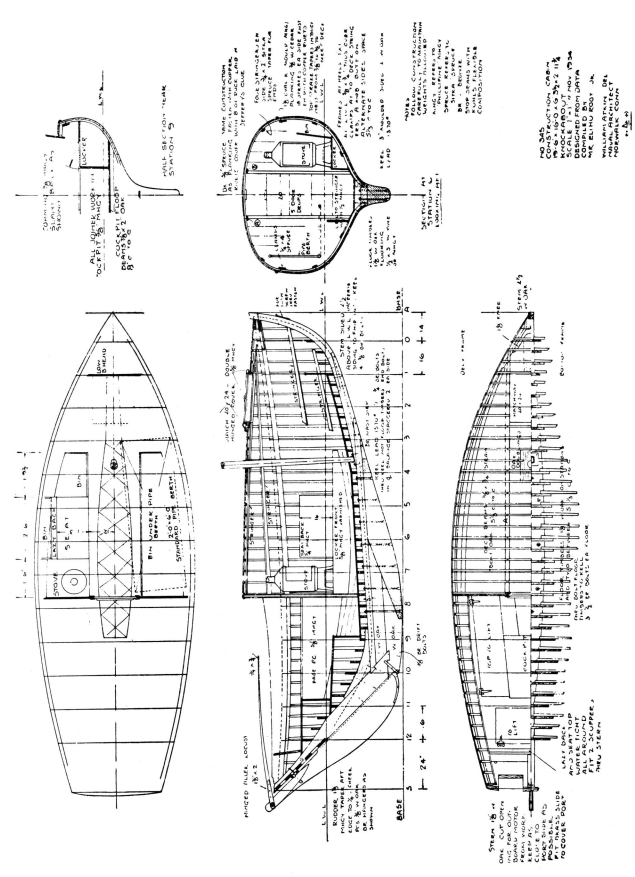

Inside her strong, oval-shaped hull, she can be laid out for one or two people. (Small Yachts and Boats edited by William Atkin)

looks of scorn and expressions of derision from many a sailor.

We boys certainly had no kind words for a 35-footer that we used to see cruising occasionally that was one big white turtleback from bow to stern. We never knew whether to laugh or cry when we saw her coming. She was, of course, named the *Moby Dick,* and her tender, always chasing along after her on a towline, was naturally named the *Captain Ahab.*

What does the turtleback do for this little wooden shoe? Well, a number of things, but basically it gives her the space below so that she can be a practical little cruising boat with a set of quite fine lines showing a hull that will really sail, instead of a tubby wallower of a hull.

You say you don't like the looks of a turtleback? Well, I'll admit that it takes a bit of getting used to, but it does give her a sort of seagoing look a bit reminiscent of a lifeboat, doesn't it? And, yes, by all means, when you paint her up, do emphasize that nice sheer strake!

The *Sabot* is 19 feet 6 inches long on deck, with a waterline length of 16 feet, a beam of 6 feet 4 inches, and a draft of 3 feet. She displaces 3,450 pounds, of which 1,570 pounds are in her lead keel. Her sail area is 189 square feet. The *Sabot* is quite fine below the waterline; she has a remarkably long, flat run for such a little boat.

She'd be quite stiff, small as she is, because of her considerable outside ballast and her flare just above the waterline all the way 'round her, especially at the stern.

Her transom is big and has every potential for ugliness, but Mr. Atkin gave it so much shape and rake that it turns out to be one of her handsomest features.

The boat is strongly built; her frames are one inch square at their heels and taper to ⅝ inch by ¾ inch. She has four stringers on each side, one in the bilge, one just above the waterline, and two in the turtleback. Her planking is ⅝-inch white cedar. The turtleback is built just the same as the hull.

Her mast is 27 feet long and has a diameter of 3¼ inches at the gooseneck. The mainsail has 138 square feet and the jib, 51.

There's a single shroud led well aft to eliminate the need for backstays. With a fore-

and-aft sail, we think we're squaring the boom well off when running, but with the *Sabot's* boom just clear of that aft-leading shroud, the sail would be far enough out so that its head would be square to the mast. We don't let the boom out as far as we think we do.

The mainsail is loose-footed. Mr. Atkin's notes on the sail plan specify that the reefing grommets shall be the same size as the clew and tack grommets. This is only common sense, but how often do you see it? Even back in the "good old days," the great designer had to spell it out.

I'd want the feet of the sails a bit higher for visibility to leeward. Six inches would make all the difference.

You'd want a good, flat trysail and storm jib on a boat like this for those times you're out when you shouldn't be. And for those times that you dream of during the winter — chasing away before a gentle breeze with the sun on your back — you'd want a nice big ballooner and a pole for it.

She has a removable section in the port side of her transom so that an outboard motor could be mounted thereon fairly close to the water. If you must have one of these contraptions — working cat's paws and oars will give you more satisfaction every time — then I would recommend mounting the thing on the side of the boat. The *Arete,* described in the first chapter, has a very satisfactory rig consisting of a heavy bronze track bolted onto the planking amidships, one on each side. A bracket slides down into this, a long hook going to a heavy screw eye giving additional support to take the thrust of the motor. There is little to go wrong; the rig is strong and simple. And the permanently installed tracks are quite unobtrusive, particularly if painted the color of the topsides.

And don't forget that a dinghy with an outboard can make a fine tow boat, pushing, pulling, or lashed alongside. A dinghy under oars can also tow this boat right along. It's that declaration of independence from fallible machinery and a limited fuel supply that makes the oar so appealing to me. Part of the fun of a boat this size is to fool around with oars, dinghies, yulohs, or what-have-you to learn the easiest way to move her.

The *Sabot* has a very deep, snug cockpit that lets you sit or stand well down inside the boat. Yes, if she ships a sea you have to bring both buckets into play ferociously, you'll be plenty scared, and she'll be quite a mess for a while. You could even lose her with threat to life. You have to make up your mind you're not going to ship a big sea, which means being plenty conservative about weather and open water. She's not a boat in which to go "offshore"; she's a "puddle jumper." Watch your chance, then jump the next puddle. You don't have time to wait for the weather? You what?

But 'vast heaving! This is supposed to be comment about a good boat, not a seamanship sermon. We're still all free to learn to go on the water after our own fashion. Now let's just settle down in the *Sabot's* big cockpit and look around us to see why we're so comfortable. First of all, we notice that the coaming is high enough to lean back against and that it slants outboard like the back of a comfortable chair. At the after end of the cockpit there is an additional backrest, and it's made watertight so that any slop over the transom will drain back overboard instead of wetting the cockpit seats.

Actually this cockpit is a three-level affair. There is the level of the seats, one on each side and the broad one in the stern. Then there is the cockpit floor extending well forward from the stern seat and all the way to the bulkhead in front of the side seats. The third level is a narrow footwell that is a small extension of the cabin sole out into the cockpit. This would be a

great place to stand down out of the wind and steer with that long locust tiller, beating up into the harbor on a late fall afternoon. Of course you'd have to learn just where that well is so you wouldn't always be falling down it.

This footwell also allows you to duck below (literally) without a need for a companionway hatch. And, as a matter of fact, the idea is that when you sail up to your mooring singlehanded, you confound your friends, who expect you to scramble awkwardly up over the turtleback, by slipping below and re-emerging almost instantly halfway out of the forward hatch, from which secure position you pluck your buoy from the sea.

The *Sabot's* arrangement plan shows her laid out for a singlehander with a pipe berth over the transom to starboard and a seat, bin, and stove to port. She could also, of course, have a pipe berth on each side. And pipe berths make good sense when otherwise bunks would have to double as seats. The good old pipe berth folds back during the day, keeping bedding secure and forming a backrest to the now-exposed transom seat.

Yes, she is fine-lined below the waterline and that's what makes her so much fun to sail; turtleback and all, her headroom is 4 feet 4 inches.

I've waxed a bit philosophical here and there about this little vessel, because I find her intriguing and well worth considerable study. Maybe now the best way to conclude is simply by saying that if this wooden shoe fits . . . .

25/ The *Trilby*
And Other Friendship Sloops

> **Trilby**
> **Length on deck: 28 feet 6 inches**
> **Length on waterline: 23 feet**
> **10 inches**
> **Beam: 9 feet 5 inches**
> **Draft: 5 feet 4 inches**
> **Sail area: 634 square feet**

One of my favorite growing-up books was Howard I. Chapelle's *American Sailing Craft.* My older brother had gotten a copy for Christmas not long after it was published in 1936, so the book was around the house.

My favorite vessels in there were the Nova Scotia tern schooners and the Boston pilot schooners, but there were plenty of good small boats, too, and I used to keep returning to Mr. Chapelle's example of a Friendship sloop of 1900 to study her handsome lines and sail plan.

A couple of years ago, I found another Friendship sloop I liked just about as much as the Chapelle example. The plans for this boat were printed in a 1907 issue of *The Yachting and Boating Monthly.* This British magazine had picked them up from a then-recent issue of the American magazine *Boating,* in which William Lambert Barnard had used them to illustrate an article on what he called "the Maine sloop" in a series called "The Working Boats of New England." Mr. Barnard identified the boat as the *Hattie* or *Little Hattie* and said that she had originally been named the *Trilby.* She was a creation of Wilbur Morse, Barnard wrote.

Soon after I had "finished" the "research"

for this chapter, Jon Wilson of *WoodenBoat* and I were talking things over on the telephone and somehow we got onto Friendship sloops. I mentioned that my favorite one was Howard Chapelle's example of the type for 1900. Jon said he liked that boat too, and he never could understand why Mr. Chapelle hadn't identified her as William Lambert Barnard's *Trilby.* Jon reminded me that he had reprinted the whole Barnard business on the Maine sloop in his second issue, way back in 1974.

Since I believe very little of what I hear about boats, particularly on the telephone, I had to go back and compare the plans of the *Trilby* (and her given dimensions) against those of Mr. Chapelle's example for 1900.

Great jumping sheerlines, but Jon is right again! The *Trilby* must be where Howard Chapelle got his example. My excuse for not noticing this before is that the *Trilby's* plans were printed big in both *The Yachting and Boating Monthly* and *WoodenBoat,* whereas Mr. Chapelle's redrawn plans of the handsome little vessel were printed quite small in *American Sailing Craft.* I feel lucky (and indebted to Jon) to be able to offer this excuse before publication (as it

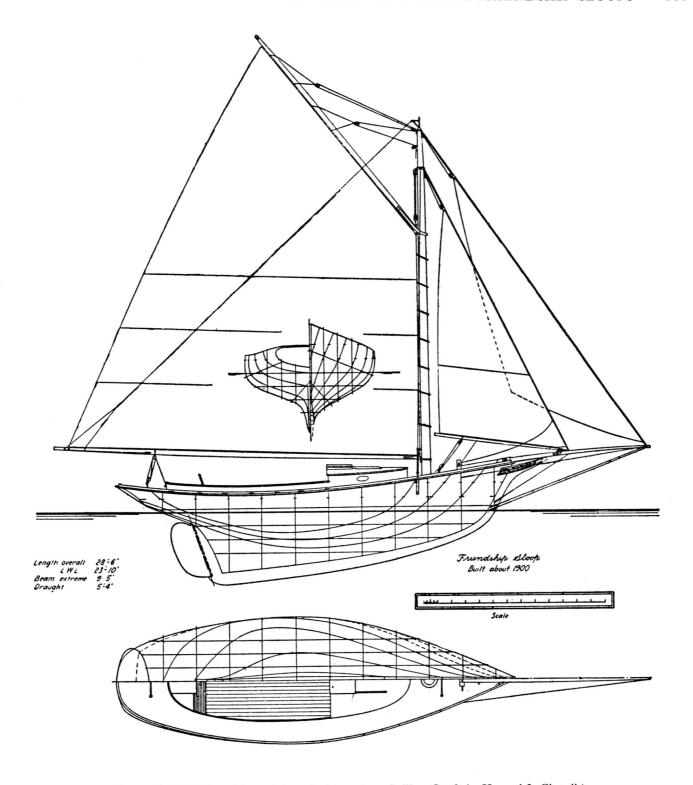

Length overall   28'6"
LWL   23'10"
Beam extreme   9'5"
Draught   5'4"

Friendship Sloop
Built about 1900

Scale

The wonderful Trilby, *fairest of them all.* (American Sailing Craft *by Howard I. Chapelle*)

were), rather than in embarrassment afterward. And when Jon reprinted the *Trilby's* plans, he reproduced the information (unlike *The Yachting and Boating Monthly*) that they had been drawn by Martin Coryell Erismann from data taken by Mr. Erismann and Mr. Barnard.

Now with the pedigree of my favorite Friendship sloop well established, I can sit back and enjoy her more than ever. She is 28 feet 6 inches long on deck, with a waterline length of 23 feet 10 inches, a beam of 9 feet 5 inches, and a draft of 5 feet 4 inches. Her sail area is 634 square feet.

Part of this boat's charm for me is her low freeboard. Least freeboard is 1 foot 4½ inches, for the *Trilby* does sit deep in the water. She is ballasted with 1½ tons of iron and 2 tons of stone, all inside.

The *Trilby* has oak frames 1½ inches by 2¼ inches, spaced 9 inches apart center to center. Her planking is of 1-inch stuff, the top three strakes being of oak and the rest of white pine. Her deck is 2-inch-wide strips of white pine. She cost between $700 and $800.

I suppose it is rather obvious to say that most of the sloop's sail area is in her mainsail. It has an area of 484 square feet, while her jumbo has but 74 square feet and her jib but 65.

She has a huge open cockpit 12 feet long and a small cuddy boasting headroom of 4 feet 8 inches.

Let's see where these Maine sloops, or Friendship sloops, came from. You can get an idea of it, even today, if you try to travel along the Maine coast by land. You spend all your time going up and down long peninsulas to get where you want to go. Someone traveling to the same places by boat can go in relatively straight lines. If you keep this geographical fact in mind while considering how tedious was land travel 100 years ago, you can see how useful it would have been to have a boat like the *Trilby* if you lived on the Maine coast. And if most or part of your income came from fishing, there was just nothing to beat a boat like this. The *Trilby* and her sisters and her cousins and her aunts spent plenty of time taking their people lobster fishing and handlining.

The fishermen had to compete for a market, so speed was a requirement in their boats. They fished winter and summer, so their boats had to have enough sail for light airs and be weatherly enough to get them home against a freezing northwest gale.

Mr. Chapelle wrote that these sloops demonstrate the "practical use of power to carry sail in heavy weather in order to obtain weatherliness in hard conditions." He also wrote: "The low sails, the great beam, the weight of ballast, and the deep draft, part of which was the flat-sided false keel, made these boats very weatherly, and they could beat off a lee shore when a less stiff and powerful boat would be knocked down and driven to leeward. This was their great quality — they would bring you home as well as they took you out."

Mr. Barnard wrote that these "Maine sloops" were built all along the Maine coast. Mr. Chapelle and most later historians call them Friendship sloops and point out that the part of the Maine coast where the boats were most popular was the Muscongus Bay area and that one of the biggest building centers was the town of Friendship. In his *Mystic Seaport Museum Watercraft*, Maynard Bray wrote: "Friendship sloops are what these boats are called now, but to the Maine fishermen who used them they were known simply as 'sloop boats.'" That's a sensible statement. (I'll bet Eric called his Viking longship something that would translate simply as "the vessel," as in, for example, "C'mon, boys, let's take the vessel to sea.")

Malcolm Barter has estimated that in 1880 there were something like a thousand fishermen living on or near the shores of Muscongus Bay, the main centers of population being the villages of Friendship, Bremen, and Bristol. It is the history and use of the boats built and sailed by these men that we shall now consider briefly. We are only able to do this because of the research and recording by Howard I. Chapelle in his books *American Sailing Craft* and *American Small Sailing Craft*.

The fishermen of the Muscongus Bay area began building fishing sloops that could be termed a distinctive type of the locality about 1850. Some fishermen favored rather deep-draft keel sloops, while others built shoaler-draft keel-and-centerboarders. The choice probably depended on whether a man thought he could make more money fishing offshore or mostly inshore. At any rate, the two types seemed to develop together until the late 1880s, when the centerboarders died out rapidly and everybody seemed to want the deep-keel boats. It was the latter that became known as the Friendship sloops, while the former were called Muscongus Bay sloops. (The Muscongus Bay sloop was described in *More Good Boats*.)

The Muscongus Bay fishermen of a hundred years ago weren't as isolated as you might think. When things were slow in Maine, particularly in the winter, they made many a trip to the Grand Banks in the fo'c's'les of Gloucester schooners and Gloucester sloop boats. These Gloucester craft were thought to be the finest fishing vessels around, so a Muscongus Bay fisherman, building his next boat, was influenced by what he had seen up to the westward.

What he saw in Gloucester in the 1880s was sloop-rigged fishing boats similar in hull form to the schooners but scaled down to 50 or 60 feet long, these smaller vessels being spawned by economic depression. At the same time, the Gloucester schooners themselves were changing. Too many shoal, centerboard schooners were foundering, and the Gloucester fishermen were moving to narrower, deeper vessels with greater ultimate stability. The great trend-setter in this regard was evidently a schooner designed by the yacht designer Edward Burgess that came out in 1889 — the *Fredonia*.

These important changes in Gloucester were reflected in Muscongus Bay. The centerboard Muscongus Bay sloops fell out of favor and deep-keel Friendship sloops became popular. And the deep-keel Friendship sloops were built finer and longer-ended, like the *Fredonia*. This new *Fredonia* type of Friendship sloop, introduced in the 1890s, brought the type to its full development. Some were built up to a length of 40 feet.

The heyday of all these well-developed sailing fishing vessels was short. Sailing fishing craft began to have internal combustion engines soon after the turn of the century, and by World War I the development of sailing fishing vessels had stopped. It will probably never start again, although fishing vessels with both engines and

sails are being developed now and obviously will be in the future. (I wonder how fishing boats propelled by sail only would be designed today if practical engines hadn't yet been made.)

But let's turn back now to how the Friendship sloops were built. They were built with a weather eye on the dollar, the construction being unfancy to the point of corner-cutting. Yet the boats were strong and lasted well, primarily because of their heavy scantlings.

Keels were particularly substantial. And on a 30-footer, the bent oak frames would be, say, 1½ inches by 2¾ inches with centers 10 inches apart. The lower ends of the frames were nailed into the keel. There were no floor timbers, and few knees were worked into the construction.

Planking was of oak, yellow pine, white pine, or cedar, depending upon availability. Plank as thick as 2½ inches has been reported. And the boats were ceiled throughout, often with stuff up to an inch thick, which certainly added to their strength if not their ventilation. Decks were laid with pine as much as two inches square. The boats were fastened with galvanized nails.

One interesting construction detail of the Friendship sloops was the use of a "lock plank" of 2-inch-thick oak used as a sheer timber in place of a shelf or clamp. The lock plank was laid horizontally up under the deck at the sheer. The heads of the frames were nailed to the outside of the lock plank and the deck beams were notched into its inboard edge so that they were flush on top. The decking laid over the lock plank was nailed into it as well as into the beams.

Some of the sloops were built as smacks with wet wells installed just abaft the cuddy bulkhead.

The cockpits were always big and open, and cuddies always small and somewhat cramped.

Boatbuilding in the Muscongus Bay area often ran in families. The best-known family building Friendship sloops was undoubtedly the Morses. Wilbur Morse didn't fool around. His very definition of a Friendship sloop was: "A sloop built in Friendship by Wilbur Morse." Wilbur built his first sloop in 1874 at the age of 21. Eventually he had quite a gang of builders working for him, and they sometimes turned out as many as eight boats a year. By the time he got through building boats in 1915, Wilbur had built something like 400 sloops plus dozens of other craft.

Wilbur built plenty of great Friendship sloops besides the *Trilby*. One of the best is the *Sazerac*, a 33-footer he turned out in 1913, and, happily, she is still going strong. I think she's about the handsomest Friendship still sailing.

Wilbur Morse built boats first in Bremen and later in Friendship. His brother Charles built plenty of sloops over in Thomaston, and his brother Albion built plenty more over in Cushing. Jonah, another brother, was Wilbur's foreman for years. (Wilbur's father's name was also Jonah.) Then there was Warren Morse, who built boats on Morse's Island. He was a distant cousin to all these Morse brothers.

Robert McLain built sloops on Bremen Long Island, as did his sons Robert E., Eugene, Armand, and Alexander. Robert McLain married Wilbur Morse's sister.

Robert E. McLain built the *Estella A.*, a 34-foot sloop, at Bremen in 1904. She was nicely restored at the yard of Newbert and Wallace in Thomaston from 1970 to 1972 and is now preserved in good condition at the Mystic Seaport.

George Washington Carter and his sons George, Abden, and Norris built a good many sloops on Bremen Long Island. Charles Carter was another builder.

It was Abden Carter who built a nice little 25-footer in 1914 called the *Florida*. She later became the *Pemaquid*, was used as a yacht, had her lines taken off by the Boston naval architect Charles G. MacGregor, and eventually inspired quite a few replicas.

Winfield Carter built a big 38-footer at Friendship in 1937. She is the *Tannis II* and is one of the bigger Friendship sloops still sailing.

Vincent Collamore and William and George Prior built sloops on Bremen Long Island. Clifford Winchenbach built sloops at West Waldoboro.

It became a custom to give the Friendship sloops carved trailboards and for the builder to carve his name into the board. The stuff of an historian's dreams.

These trailboards adorned bows given a graceful clipper shape by nicely curved stemheads. The Friendship sloop's nice bow was balanced by her beautiful elliptical transom, probably imported from Gloucester.

A distinction of these boats is the extreme tumblehome in the quarters, a pretty shape (I just love it) and one that has the practical value of streamlining so the main sheet won't catch.

Down near the waterline the quarters are wide and flat, producing stability as she heels. Of course these boats have considerable initial stability due to their fairly generous beam. The garboards are quite deep and wide to provide a good place for the big load of inside ballast.

The Friendship sloops had to have a big sail area to drive their heavy hulls. The basic rule of thumb for the rig was that the length of the boom should equal the length of the boat on deck. All other dimensions of the rig were proportioned around the boom: for example, the mast stood above the deck to a height about equal to the boom length. The mast was typically set back from the stem about one-fifth of the waterline length. The boats had long bowsprits producing, with the boom overhang, a large rig with a relatively low center of effort. Mr. Barnard wrote that the boom was kept nearly parallel to the water so that it wouldn't swing much when she rolled.

The Friendship sloops generally carried three or four men in the crew if they were going well off into the Gulf of Maine to Three-Dory Ridge, say, or maybe all the way out to Cashes. For inshore work, two men were enough.

If a sloop had a topmast, it would be left ashore in winter. Nor would the jib usually be set when fishing. The jib was used for light weather or to get back and forth to the grounds. When fishing, the sloops were handy under mainsail and jumbo. There were generally three deep reefs in the mainsail and two in the jumbo. In a real breeze, the sloops were worked under close-reefed mainsail alone. A trysail was sometimes used as a riding sail.

Being handsome and able boats, Friendship sloops have found considerable favor with a certain breed of yachtsman. (The kind who have both romance and practicality in their genes.)

(Continued on page 196)

The Sazerac *full-and-by. She was built in 1913. (William Thon)*

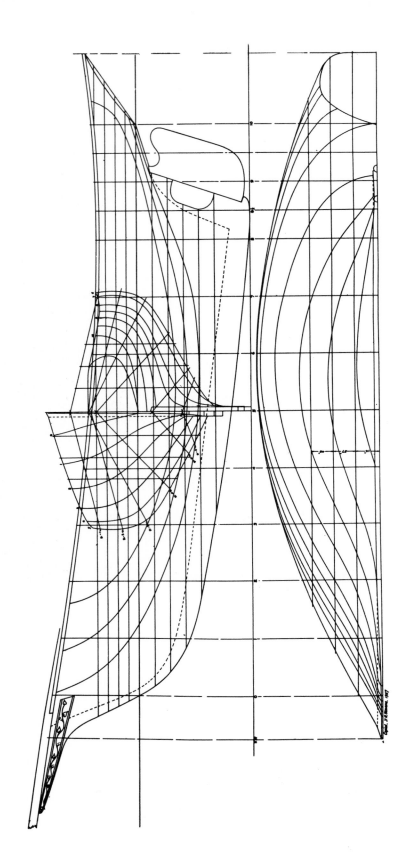

The lines of the Estella A., *which is now at the Mystic Seaport. (Mystic Seaport Museum)*

The Estella A. *reaching down Fishers Island Sound. (Mystic Seaport Museum)*

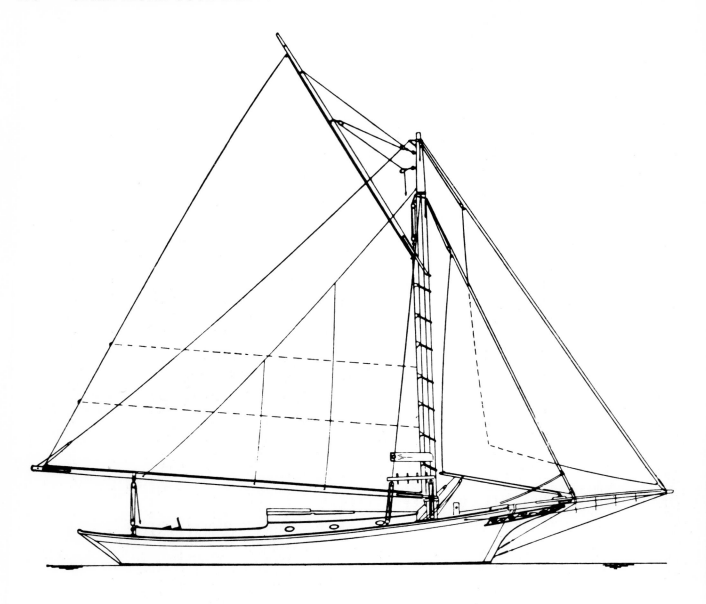

Geerd Hendel's sail plan of the Old Baldy, *a replica of the* Pemaquid *except for the lengthened cabin house.* (Yachting, *July 1966)*

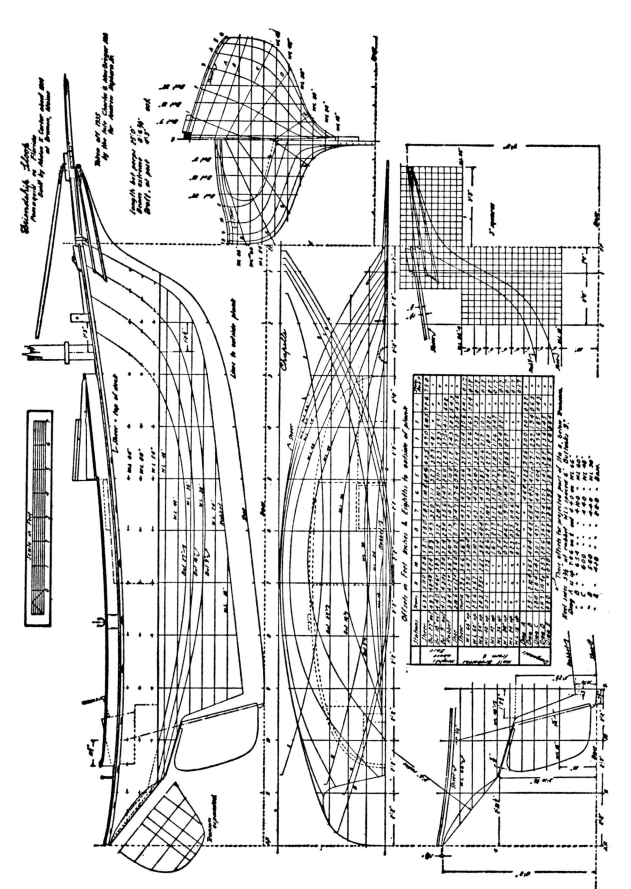

The lines of the Pemaquid. (American Small Sailing Craft by Howard I. Chapelle, W. W. Norton & Co.)

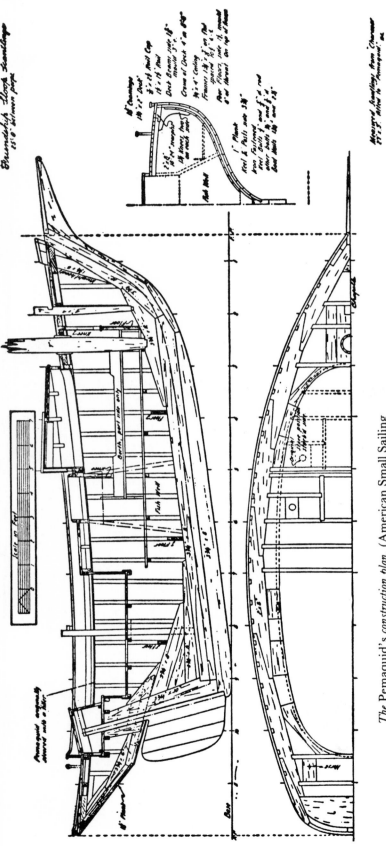

The Pemaquid's construction plan. (American Small Sailing Craft by Howard I. Chapelle, W. W. Norton & Co.)

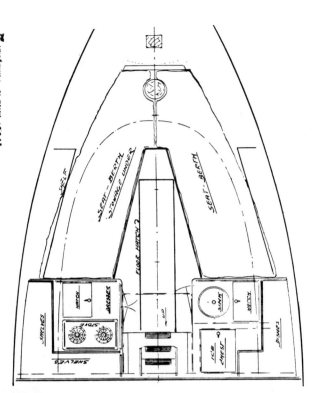

The Old Baldy's cabin arrangement. (Yachting, July 1966)

The Old Baldy *spreads her wings.*
(James S. Rockefeller, Jr.)

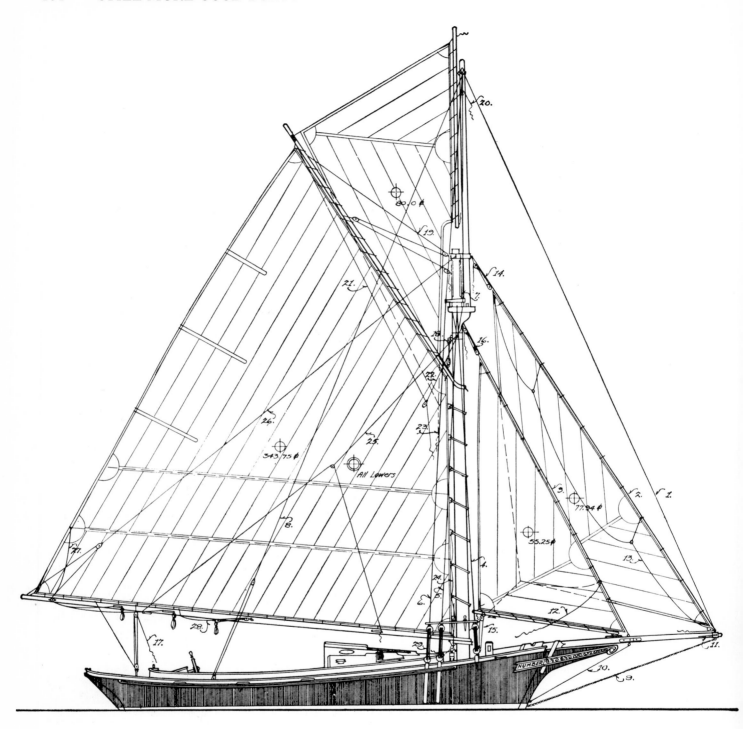

The Maggie, *designed by Walter J. Skinner. Her sail area is 556 square feet.* (The Rudder)

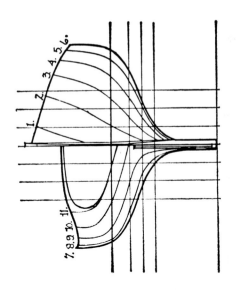

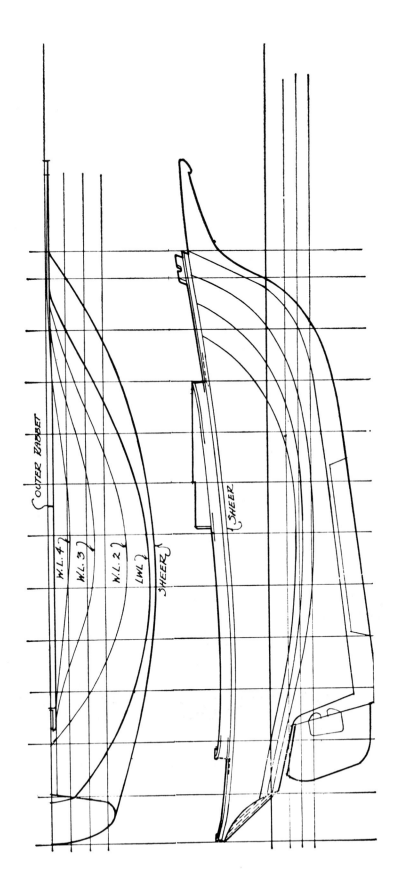

The Maggie's lines. She is 24 feet 10 inches long on deck, with a waterline length of 21 feet 11 inches, a beam of 8 feet 8 inches, and a draft of 4 feet 3 inches. (The Rudder)

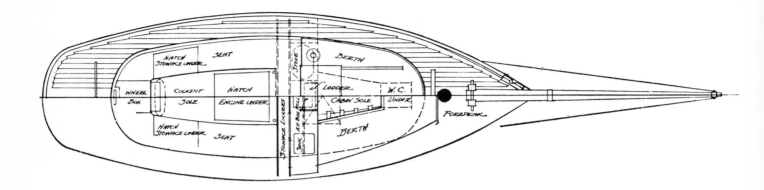

The arrangement plan of the Maggie. *(The Rudder)*

(Continued from page 186)

An amazing number of the old Friendship sloops have been restored for use as yachts; replicas of Friendship sloops have been built as yachts; and a number of cruising boats have been built along the general lines of Friendship sloops.

Of course you know what has happened to the cost of these boats. In 1900, a 25-foot Friendship sloop cost, say, $675. It took until the early 1930s for this cost to double. By the time things settled down after the Great Depression, that same boat would have cost you something like $2,000. And today I suppose she'd be 10 times that.

One basic change almost always made to a Friendship sloop when she retires from fishing to a life of leisure is that she is given a watertight cockpit. The same feature is built into yacht replicas and near replicas. Putting in such a barrier to the sea makes sense. Fishermen were willing to use their excellent judgment and take their chances, for they couldn't imagine working every day from up on top of a little boat as opposed to working from down inside her. I'll bet if a yachtsman took his Friendship sloop fishing, his back would tell him after three days that he had better either chop away the cockpit floor or forget about the whole business.

Perhaps the most popular Friendship sloop replica is that of the *Pemaquid*. She is a good choice, for she has an excellent sailing model. She has a flatter run than many Friendship sloops. She ought to be quite handy and fast.

Jim Rockefeller built a *Pemaquid* in 1965.

Geerd Hendel did some design work on her, giving her outside lead ballast and a somewhat bigger cabin. Jim built her at his place on Bald Mountain and named her the *Old Baldy*. He hauled her to the sea (or rather eased her down to the sea) in the old manner with oxen. Jarvis Newman has built a number of *Pemaquid* replicas using fiberglass. Carl Chase is finishing off one of these now for his cousin George, and George and I threaten to rendezvous in the Barred Islands next summer with his *Pemaquid* and my Tancook whaler of the same length to see what's what. (You probably won't be spared the details.)

Philip J. Nichols of Round Pond built four fine-looking Friendship sloops for his own use. In 1932, he launched the *Result;* 10 years later he built the *Pressure;* in 1965, he finished the *Surprise,* so naming her because he didn't think he ever would get her done; and a few years later, he finished the *Secret.* When John Chandler asked Mr. Nichols why he was still building Friendship sloops in his seventies, Mr. Nichols said, "I guess I just can't quit."

Murray Peterson, the great designer of coasting-schooner-like yachts, designed a fine 32-foot Friendship sloop in 1956 for Roger Duncan. This is the *Eastward*, built at Pemaquid Beach by James Chadwick and used ever since by Roger and Mary Duncan to cruise with and without paying guests and with and without doing research for *The Cruising Guide to the New England Coast.* Mr. Duncan even wrote a book about her, also called *Eastward.*

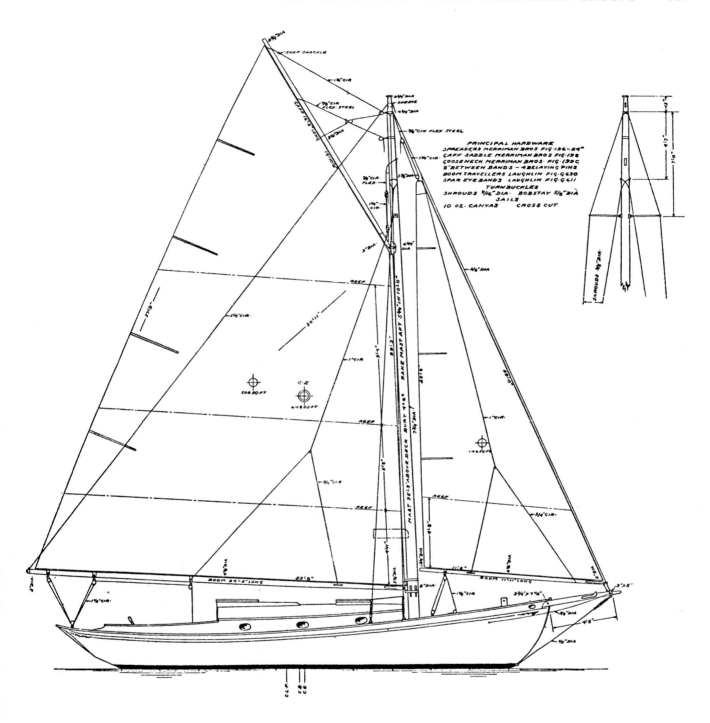

A modified Friendship with a spoon bow designed by Ralph E. Winslow. (The Rudder, *March 1931*)

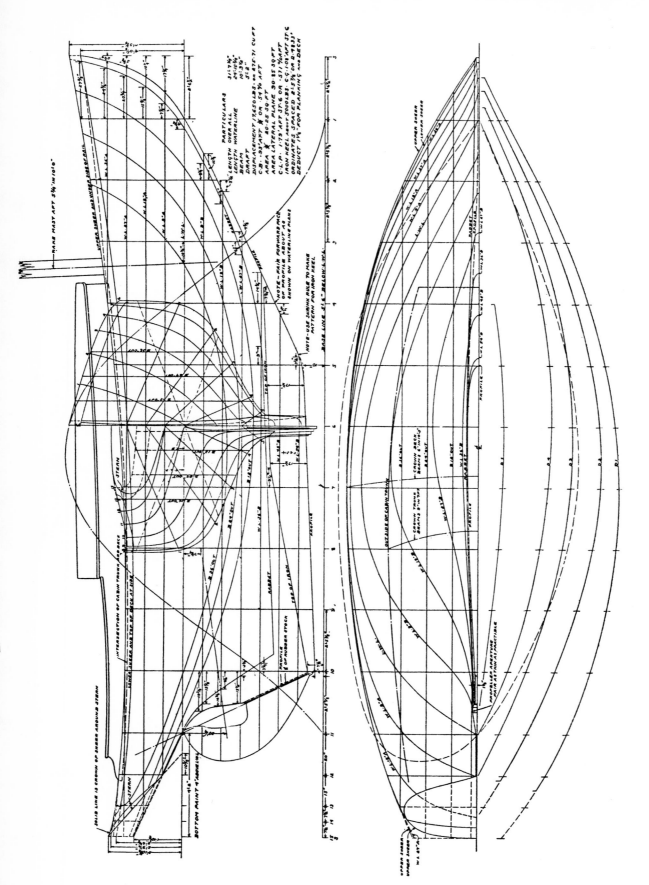

The lines of the Winslow Friendship. (The Rudder, *March 1931*)

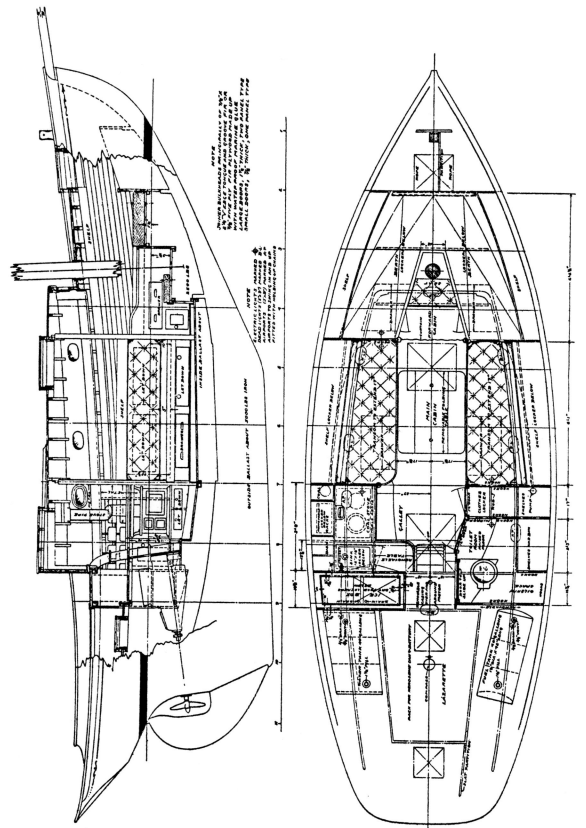

The arrangement plan of the Winslow sloop. (The Rudder, *March 1931*)

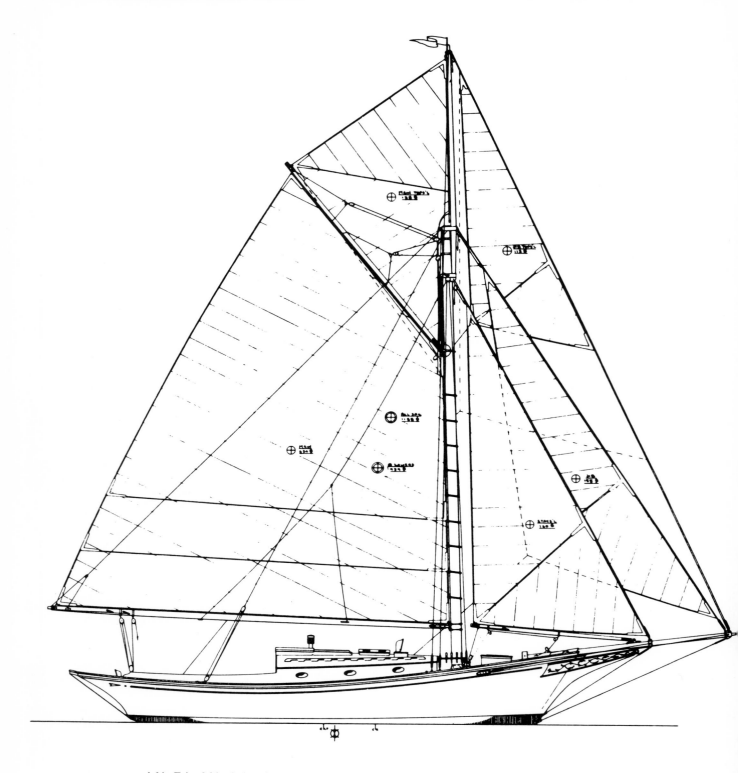

A big Friendship designed by Edward S. Brewer. Her sail area is 1,188 square feet. (Understanding Boat Design *by Edward S. Brewer and Jim Betts, International Marine Publishing Company)*

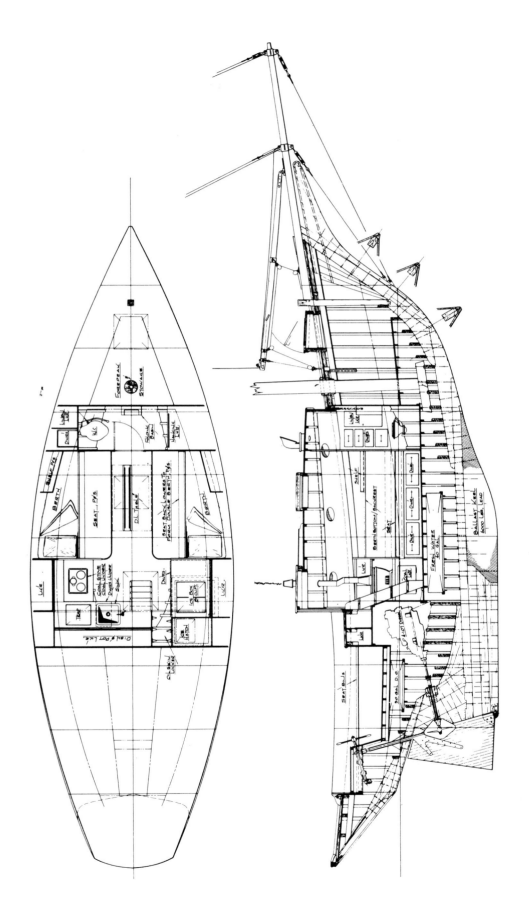

The Brewer Friendship is 38 feet 9 inches long on deck, with a waterline length of 29 feet 6 inches, a beam of 11 feet 10 inches, and a draft of 5 feet 9 inches. She displaces 10 tons. (Understanding Boat Design by Edward S. Brewer and Jim Betts, International Marine Publishing Company)

Bill Thon, the artist and master of the Friendship sloop Echo *at Port Clyde, Maine, has transferred to paper some of the thousands of the little vessels sailing through his mind, like this one. (Bill Thon)*

Walter J. Skinner, of Bridgeport, Connecticut, designed a very nice 25-foot Friendship sloop called the *Maggie.* She's quite similar to the *Pemaquid* but has a fair bit more sail.

Newbert and Wallace built some very fine wooden Friendship sloop replicas in the 30-foot range in the 1960s. I was lucky enough to sail several times in one of these boats, the *Sarah Mead.*

Bruno and Stillman of Newington, New Hampshire, built several 30-footers also. These are fiberglass boats and are rigged with topmasts.

Some of the last Friendship sloops were built with spoon bows instead of clipper bows, and often when yacht designers drew the plans for cruising boats reminiscent of Friendship sloops, they used the spoon bow. Ralph Winslow did

that when he designed a 32-foot cruising sloop somewhat along Friendship sloop lines in 1930 for *The Rudder* magazine. John G. Hanna, who was then writing a sort of ombudsman column in *The Rudder,* immediately jumped on the design as pure Winslow and wanted to know what a Friendship sloop had to do with it. He also said she was a good boat. I agree with Hanna on both counts.

The Winslow sloop is a big, rugged affair. She is 31 feet 7 inches long on deck, with a waterline length of 24 feet 11 inches, a beam of 10 feet 4 inches, and a draft of 5 feet 2 inches. Her sail area is 648 square feet. She displaces 17,650 pounds, with 7,500 pounds of iron ballast, 5,000 pounds outside and 2,500 pounds inside.

Phil Bolger has designed a couple of most interesting little Friendship sloop types, the 18-foot Monhegan and the 22½-foot Master Hand. These boats have more drag to the keel and wider transoms than the original type. Their plans may be studied in Phil's book *Small Boats.*

Joe Richards, the artist and writer, has done a fair bit to popularize the Friendship sloop with his two books about his beloved *Princess.* (I hope you don't mind getting your bibliography in text form.)

Friendship sloops, being able little vessels, have naturally made some notable voyages.

There is a possibly true story about one being stolen in 1931 at Quincy, Massachusetts, and next being sighted wrecked on a beach in Holland. She was apparently sailed there by a singlehanded thief. (That's someone who sails the boat he stole by himself, not a one-armed bandit.)

A better documented voyage is that of the *Ochito,* a 36-foot, spoon-bowed Friendship that sailed in the same year as that in which the above pilferage was alleged to have occurred from Gloucester to Bermuda and then, the next year, from Bermuda to the Azores and on to Lagos, Portugal.

There is a persistent rumor about one of Wilbur Morse's sloops being wrecked on an island off the boot of Italy.

And Jim Rockefeller sailed out to Tahiti in his ketch-rigged Friendship sloop type, the *Mandalay.*

After all this, you won't be surprised to learn (as if you didn't already know) that in 1961 there was formed the Friendship Sloop Society. The Society has run Friendship Sloop regattas every summer since then at Friendship. One of the many good things about those races is that they use distance handicapping, in which the bigger, faster sloops have to sail farther than the smaller, slower ones. If everyone sailed the perfect race, all the sloops would start together and finish together. Of course it doesn't work out quite that way, but it makes for exciting racing compared to wondering if you really beat that guy who is well astern at the finish.

The Friendship Sloop Society has published an interesting program each year and has also produced three books: *Ships That Came Home,* 1962; *It's a Friendship,* 1965; and *Enduring Friendships,* 1970. They started a museum for the town and the sloops named after it in 1964.

So what is a Friendship sloop? Roger Duncan said it best: "A Friendship sloop is a gaff-rigged sloop with a fisherman look about her. A Friendship sloop is a beautiful fusion of form and function. A Friendship sloop is a state of mind composed of independence, tradition, resourcefulness, and a most fortuitous combination of geography and language in the name Friendship."

26/ The Alerion Class Sloop

> **Length on deck: 26 feet**
> **Length on waterline: 21 feet**
> **9 inches**
> **Beam: 7 feet 7 inches**
> **Draft: 2 feet 5 inches**
> **Sail area: 364 square feet**
> **Displacement: 6,000 pounds**
> **Designer: Nathanael G.**
> **Herreshoff**

Sixty-seven years ago, the world's greatest yacht designer, Nathanael G. Herreshoff, designed himself a 26-foot daysailing sloop and had her built at his plant, the Herreshoff Manufacturing Company of Bristol, Rhode Island. He named her the *Alerion* (his third boat of that name) and sailed her for 17 years — often singlehanded — in Narragansett Bay, Rhode Island; Biscayne Bay, Florida; and Bermuda. He only sold her when he became too old to sail her by himself.

The *Alerion* is a lovely boat and was appreciated by a series of owners, the last of whom, Ike Merriman, donated her to the Mystic Seaport, where she is preserved in impeccable condition.

The *Alerion* is 26 feet long on deck, with a waterline length of 21 feet 9 inches, a beam of 7 feet 7 inches, and a draft of 2 feet 5 inches with her centerboard up. She displaces just over 6,000 pounds and has a sail area of 364 square feet.

Like many another successful Herreshoff boat, she spawned a number of closely related designs. In 1914, when the *Alerion* was only two years old, along came a near-sister ship, the *Sadie* (now preserved at the Chesapeake Bay

Maritime Museum at St. Michaels, Maryland); a class of four one-design racing boats for Buzzards Bay stretched out to a waterline length of 25 feet; three identical racing-cruisers (the concept is hardly new), the Newport 29s, further stretched out to that waterline length.

I was lucky enough to have one of the Buzzards Bay 25-footers, the *Aria*, described in *More Good Boats*.

Every time I go to the Mystic Seaport, I make the pilgrimage to the shed where the *Alerion* lies in state, painted just as Captain Nat had her, with his own white bottom paint and his own special light green topsides, the two colors separated by a nicely contrasting thin boottop of dark blue. All this is set off by a beautifully molded sheer strake of varnished mahogany. She is a lovely piece of sculpture.

I have never had to wait in line to see the *Alerion*, but plenty of people must make this same pilgrimage. Two who did were Alfred and Ed Sanford. They appreciated the boat, and, like many others, thought that, in a way, it was too bad the wonderful boat was in a museum so that she'd no longer be sailed. They decided to try to rectify the situation.

They formed the Sanford Boat Company on

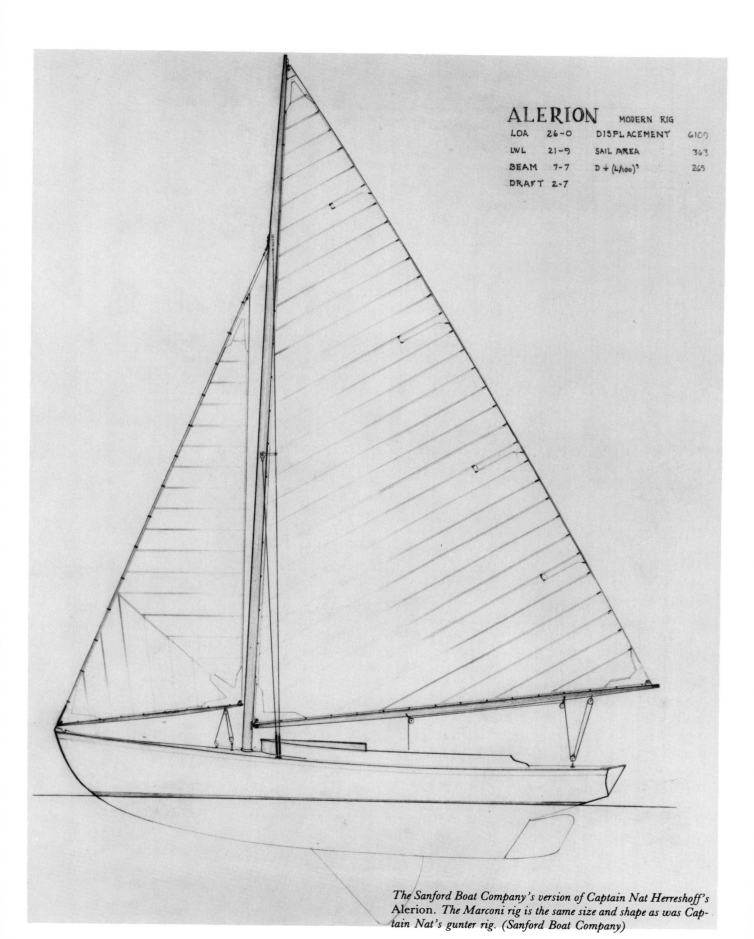

ALERION   MODERN RIG

LOA   26-0   DISPLACEMENT   6100
LWL   21-9   SAIL AREA   363
BEAM   7-7   D ÷ (L/100)³   265
DRAFT   2-7

The Sanford Boat Company's version of Captain Nat Herreshoff's
Alerion. The Marconi rig is the same size and shape as was Cap-
tain Nat's gunter rig. (Sanford Boat Company)

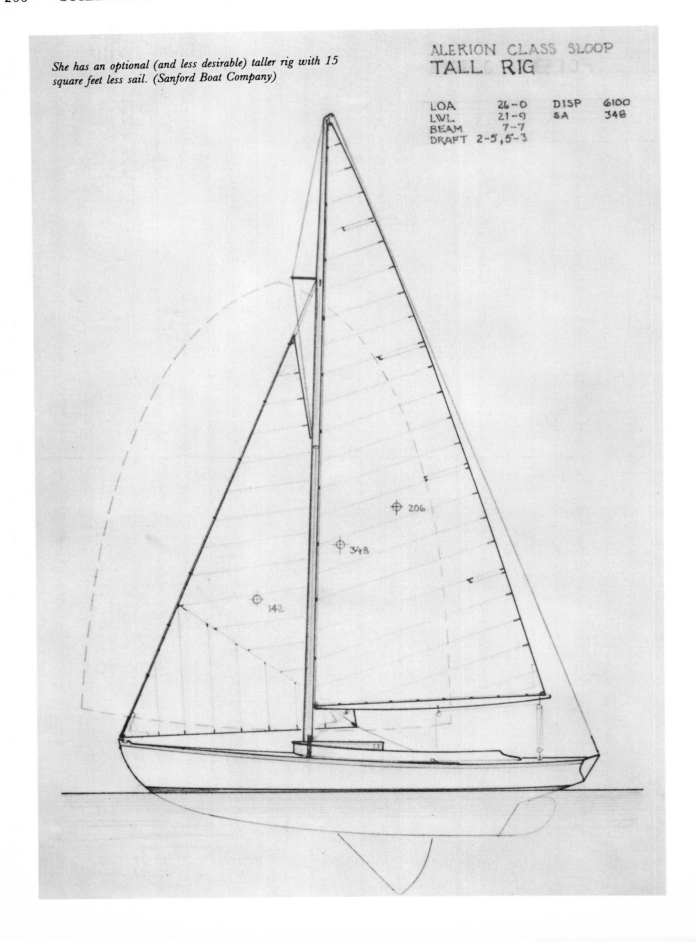

She has an optional (and less desirable) taller rig with 15 square feet less sail. (Sanford Boat Company)

ALERION CLASS SLOOP
TALL RIG

LOA	26-0	DISP	6100
LWL	21-9	SA	348
BEAM	7-7		
DRAFT	2-5,5-3		

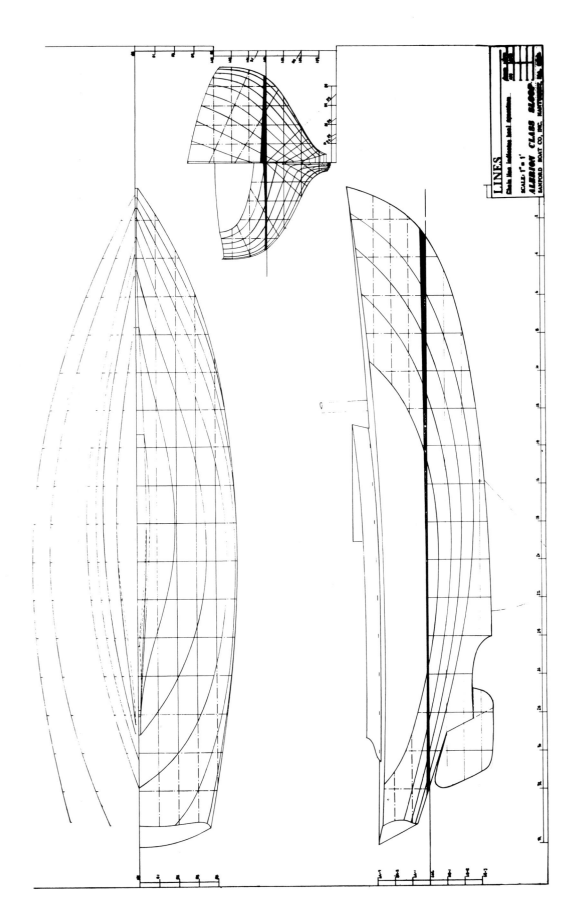

The Alerion Class Sloop has almost as sweet a set of lines as does her larger sister, the Buzzards Bay 25-footer, and that's mighty sweet. (Sanford Boat Company)

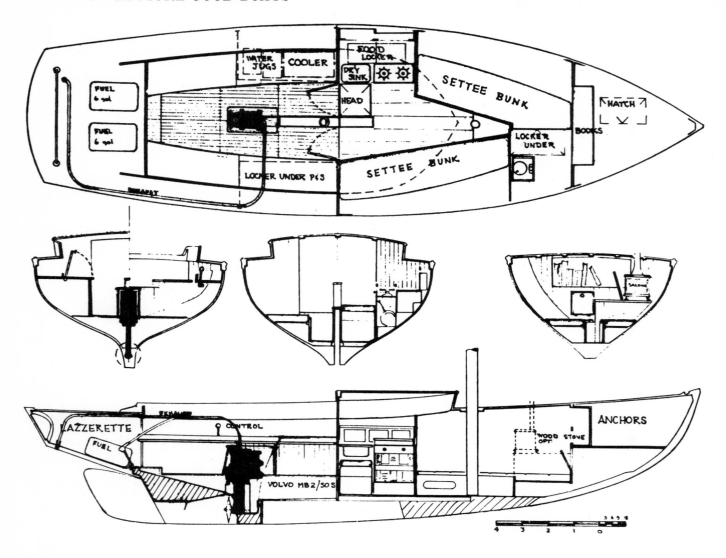

She can be all rigged out for cruising for two. That black thing in the middle of the cockpit is a little Volvo engine. (Sanford Boat Company)

Nantucket Island for the purpose of building production replicas of the *Alerion*. They call the boat the Alerion Class Sloop. They have built 11 of them.

The Sanfords kindly invited me to go to Nantucket to sail Alerion Class Sloop Number 3. Nantucket is a beautiful place to sail, and the late summer day I arrived was perfect, with a light southerly breeze in the morning and a moderate sou'wester in the afternoon.

Alfie Sanford took me straight from the airport to the boat, we made sail and reached out of the basin between two long docks where she was tied up. Right away, she felt like a Herre-

shoff, going faster than she had any right to. We crossed the harbor and ran out the channel between the jetties against the tide. Then we beat back in with it, making long tacks with the flood and short ones lee-bowing across it.

Of course I couldn't help constantly comparing her mentally with the *Aria*. The *Alerion* has a bit more freeboard, less overhang, and is a tiny bit narrower and somewhat shoaler in proportion to the *Aria*.

As I looked along the deck, something seemed peculiar. The bow didn't seem to have the rise it ought to have. The stern certainly did, maybe a bit more than I expected. Aha! I

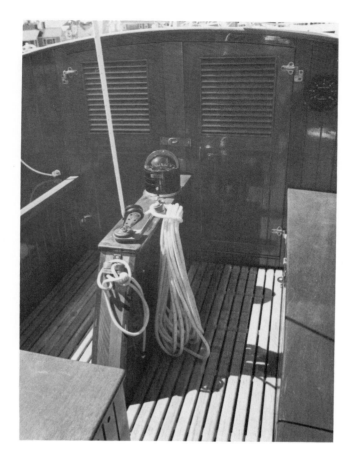

Some of the boats are fitted with the latest gimmicks and some with real bronze hardware. (Sanford Boat Company)

opined to Alfie that she might be a bit down by the head. He agreed she probably was, with only two of us in the cockpit. (This was confirmed later when we got off the boat and looked closely at how she lay on her waterline, carefully painted to a horizontal checked by transit.)

All of which makes me wonder what's happened to the old-fashioned concept of trimming ballast in a boat. I remember having miscellaneous hunks of lead years ago, but you don't see such things very much in small boats today. Two or three hundred pounds of extra weight tucked into the stern of Alerion Class Sloop Number 3 that day would have done wonders.

One change Alfie Sanford made on Hull Number 3 was to cut away the deadwood a bit aft and give her a balanced rudder with the part of the rudder forward of the rudderpost projecting partway into the area cut out of the deadwood. Hull Number 3 had suffered a minor accident to her balanced rudder the day before.

She'd sailed over a mooring pendant and it caught between the top of the balanced part of the rudder and the deadwood. Clearing it required enough force to spring open the lower gudgeon. It still held the lower pintle, and the rudder worked all right, but with enough friction to spoil the feel of her helm.

After our morning sail, Alfie had her lifted out of the water, tapped the bronze gudgeon back to very near its original shape, thus removing the cause of the binding, and then had her put back overboard again. We took another sail in the afternoon, now with more breeze, reaching up the length of the harbor a ways. Now, the helm did feel light and airy compared with the *Aria's.*

Another underwater change Alfie made to the *Alerion* is in the shape of the centerboard. Instead of just a straight, planked board, he has built a thicker board with an airfoil section. Whatever its shape, the board soon performed for us that admirable function of such a device, the automatic proclamation of a gentle warning that, yes, the reason the sandy bottom looks closer is because it is closer. We took the hint, found a deeper hole ahead, tacked, and stood back close-hauled.

She roared up the harbor and went through the anchored fleet so fast I hardly had time to look the boats over. There was what to me was certainly a unique skipjack, emigrated north from the Chesapeake Bay, with not only a patent stern, but also a round stern under it. I think her name might have been the *Sallie Bramble,* but she went by in a bit of a blur. I vaguely remember a bright red six-meter, a number of small catboats, and a green yawl with a canoe stern. It occurred to me that this last vessel might have been designed by Albert Strange, but there was no time to ask.

We did tack beside another *Alerion,* a smaller and considerably modified type designed and built for Ike Merriman (after he gave the original boat to Mystic) by Halsey Herreshoff, Captain Nat's grandson. This boat had a somewhat longer bow, more like that of the Buzzards Bay 25-footers, and had a much longer, narrower counter stern, by comparison with the original *Alerion.*

A more fundamental change the Sanfords

A pair of Alerion Class Sloops having a brush. (Sanford Boat Company)

have made to the *Alerion's* design is the increasing of her ballast, since her hull construction is lighter. The original *Alerion* had about 3,100 pounds of lead in her keel; the production boat has about 3,800 pounds. Displacement is just over 6,000 pounds. The Sanfords build their keel by making a fiberglass shell and filling it with lead ingots (the word seems more appropriate than "pigs" in view of the current price of the stuff) embedded in plastic gunk to form a solid mass. This keel is bigger than that of the original boat and thus comes up into the boat more, giving her an extremely shallow bilge under the cabin floor. This is not really a problem, because the boat doesn't leak.

She doesn't leak because her hull is made of four layers of laminated wood planking. The fiberglass keel shell is attached by lowering it

down inside the hull through the opening between the "garboards," to which its wide flange is both glued and fastened. The boat's hull planking is ¾ inch thick, made up of an outer fore-and-aft run of planking of ¼-inch mahogany, an inner fore-and-aft run of planking of ¼-inch mahogany or fir, and, sandwiched in between these runs, two opposing diagonal runs of ⅛-inch planking. This planking is all sealed and bonded with epoxy.

The planking is temporarily held in place with staples, and these are removed after the epoxy sets up. Then the staple holes are filled with epoxy. Alfie Sanford said it was too bad but you could see some of the tiny imperfections in the planking caused by these filled staple holes. Hull Number 3 is finished bright, and while she was out of the water, he pointed out

Here she comes . . .
(Sanford Boat Company)

. . . and there she goes.
(Sanford Boat Company)

some of these imperfections to me as we stood with our noses all but pressed against her side. I'm still not sure I saw what he was talking about.

The sloop's deck is made of ½-inch plywood laid on quite a few longitudinals and not very many beams. The plywood is sealed with epoxy and is then covered with canvas, which is painted.

The deck beam construction is interesting. Each beam is a truss, with the plywood deck itself forming the top part of the truss and a very light beam forming the bottom part of the truss. The two parts are held apart with rectangular wood separators spaced along the tops of the beams. The resulting structure has a bit of an Eiffel Tower look to it; just for appearance' sake, I think I'd fill in the whole space between the longitudinals with the separators so the structure would look solid instead of lattice-like.

The centerboard trunk bolts to the keel structure and can be removed for cleaning and painting. Now there's progress!

Of course all these newfangled construction ideas raise the question: Will the boats last? The *Aria* is still going strong at age 65. Yes, she undoubtedly leaks a bit when sailed hard; at least she did when I had her when she was only 45. I guess Father Time can answer the question, "Will the Alerion Class Sloop Hull Number 3 be around in 2044, and if so, how much water will she make driving into a head sea?"

In the middle part of the day, we went through the Sanford Boat Company itself. Everything is new — the neat, well-designed building nestling into the Nantucket landscape, the array of power tools, and the office equipment. It's a nice facility.

Of course it's hard to tell on a short visit, but my guess is that the handful of young men building Alerion Class Sloops for the Sanford brothers are a happy gang; a couple of them were still talking pleasantly to the bosses after some hours of assembling Keel Number 5 by bedding down chunks of lead in yellow goo.

The Sanfords themselves are sailors of some experience recently come to boatbuilding. Yes, a veteran boatbuilder could say they are wet behind the ears. A cynic could say they are like

kids with new toys. I say they are building a good boat to one of the very best designs ever created.

These boats are not cheap. The current price is $35,000 if you want the cuddy all fitted out for cruising. But if the Alerion Class Sloop is expensive on a dollar-per-foot basis, I suspect she is relatively inexpensive if her price is computed on the basis of dollars-per-average-lifetime-speed-under-sail.

The original *Alerion* had a gaff rig with a big, high-peaked mainsail. In 1924, Captain Nat gave her a gunter mainsail, with a tall yard extending the luff of the sail nearly vertically. Alfred Sanford gave the Alerion Class Sloop a Marconi rig based almost exactly on Captain Nat's gunter rig by simply combining Captain Nat's mast and yard into a single mast to support Captain Nat's gunter mainsail. The result is a relatively low-aspect-ratio mainsail with plenty of area.

It's interesting that two of the boats have been ordered with Captain Nat's gunter rig. Either way, it's a wonderful sail. You can really feel that big mainsail driving her.

The Alerion Class Sloop has no running backstays, and Alfie and I discussed the pros and cons of these devices in the ivory tower of Nantucket harbor. I'm conservative enough to want something to be able to set up on the weather quarter to hold things together when she is plunging and thrashing on a really rough day. Leave them made up to the shrouds the rest of the time, where, to be sure, they'll lollygag around, chafing and getting in the way to some extent.

Hull Number 3 was rigged up with some fancy new hardware. I went to ease the main sheet a mite in a fresh puff. Took it out of the cam cleat and away the whole thing smoked through more frictionless black plastic blocks than I could count. People ordering Alerion Class Sloops can specify old-fashioned friction-prone bronze blocks and those funny old cleats with horns on them where you have to wrap the rope back and forth around them. I know I would.

There is an anchor locker up in the bow. You put a lightweight, streamlined anchor in there and shut a flush hatch down over it (if the locker should fill with water, it can drain out through a pipe going through the hull), and you'd never know you had an anchor up there at all. Of course if your beard is white, you can relive your youth by tying down on the bow one of those big, heavy symbols of hope with its strangely crossed projections sticking out all over the place and then I suppose you could seal up the locker so it couldn't flood at all. Then you'd have to look at the anchor all the time. I think those funny old anchors are quite nice to look at.

Hull Number 3 is all fitted out for cruising. Her cabin seemed like the lap of luxury compared with what the *Aria* had. There are two real bunks that double as seats, a real galley, and a good-sized flat forward to starboard. The plan shows a little coal stove on this flat, but it turns out there is really not quite enough room for it up there. The forward end of the centerboard trunk is made into a fine seat for the cook.

Although the *Alerion* is smaller than the *Aria,* she has that same wonderful feeling of space, with her huge cockpit and her nice cuddy. There is plenty of room for two people for cruising, and you can take as many as six out for a day sail.

Dare we speculate on what Captain Nat himself would think of the Alerion Class Sloop? I think he'd be delighted that a couple of young men are building boats to the design after all these years. And I think he'd approve of their trying laminated, glued construction with a keel assembly that spreads out the stress in keeping with that hull construction. He might or might not agree with Alfie Sanford's modification of his deadwood and rudder, but my hunch is that even if he thought, as I do, that that is probably a mistake, he would be sympathetic with the Sanfords' attempt to improve the design. After all, that's how Mr. Herreshoff spent his life, and that's why he was responsible for more innovations in yacht construction and design than have been thought up by anyone before or after him.

27/ A Sloop by George Stadel

> **Length on deck: 26 feet**
> **Length on waterline: 22 feet**
>   **2 inches**
> **Beam: 8 feet**
> **Draft: 4 feet**
> **Sail area: 376 square feet**
> **Designer: George H. Stadel, Jr.**

I get completely carried away by the whole business of pilots and pilot boats.

The idea of a seaman so skillful he can board 'most any kind of vessel, take over from her master, bring her into a congested port, and tie her up without hitting anything — well, that's really something. And the boats pilots have used for their own goings and comings, particularly in the days of sail, have been among the handsomest, ablest, and fastest of all.

Howard I. Chapelle recorded his research on the history and development of American pilot schooners in his *American Sailing Craft.* (His last book, *The American Fishing Schooners,* was to have been followed by one titled, *The American Pilot Schooners.*) In the chapter on the Boston pilot boats, he mentions one of their top designers, Dennison J. Lawlor. He lists a half-dozen Lawlor pilot schooners ending with, "and the great *Hesper,* built in 1884." Then he gives you Figure 71, the lines of the *Hesper,* and the caption, "*Hesper* was deeper and narrower than Lawlor's other schooners. Her speed and weatherliness were phenomenal." The great *Hesper. There* is a vessel to conjure with. Just imagine her plumb bow knifing through the seas. As I say, I get all carried away with this stuff.

Chap's first words on pilot boats in *American Sailing Craft* were, "Taking all types of commercial schooners into consideration, the pilot boat most closely approaches the yacht and her requirements, since she carries no cargo and has to be fast and seaworthy." One who read that statement and believed it was George H. Stadel, Jr., of Stamford, Connecticut. Pilot boats influenced a number of his yacht designs. Forty years ago, for instance, he designed a fine little 26-foot sloop with strong pilot boat resemblances. He wrote that he tried to make her "as near to these old [pilot] boats as a small boat can be and still be any good."

The published pilot boat lines that look closest to Mr. Stadel's sloop (that I can find) are those of the *George Steers,* a New York pilot schooner named after her designer and modeled in about 1852. That would be not long after he designed the yacht *America,* on whose model Mr. Chapelle said the *Steers* was an improvement. The *Steers,* thought of as a small pilot schooner, was 71 feet long on the waterline.

Mr. Stadel says he was inspired by the pilot schooners *Phantom* and *Pet.* When he scaled the type down for a small cruising boat, he naturally had to change such proportions as beam-to-

George H. Stadel, Jr.

The Stadel sloop was inspired by such vessels as the pilot schooner George Steers (named for her designer), whose lines are shown here, and more specifically by the pilot schooners Phantom and Pet. (American Sailing Craft by Howard I. Chapelle)

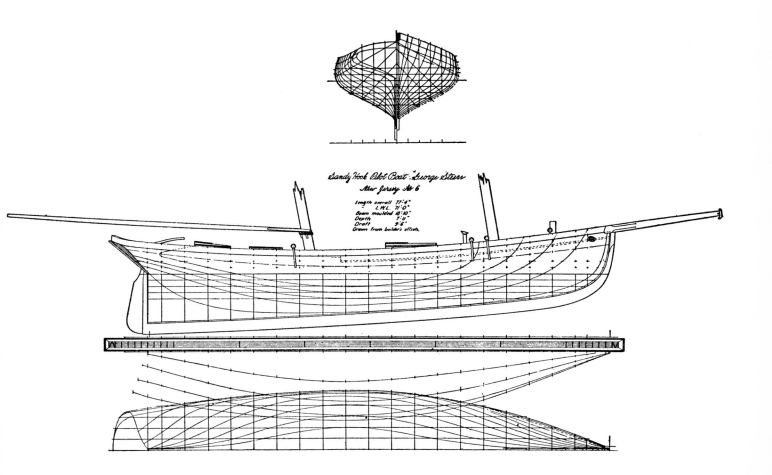

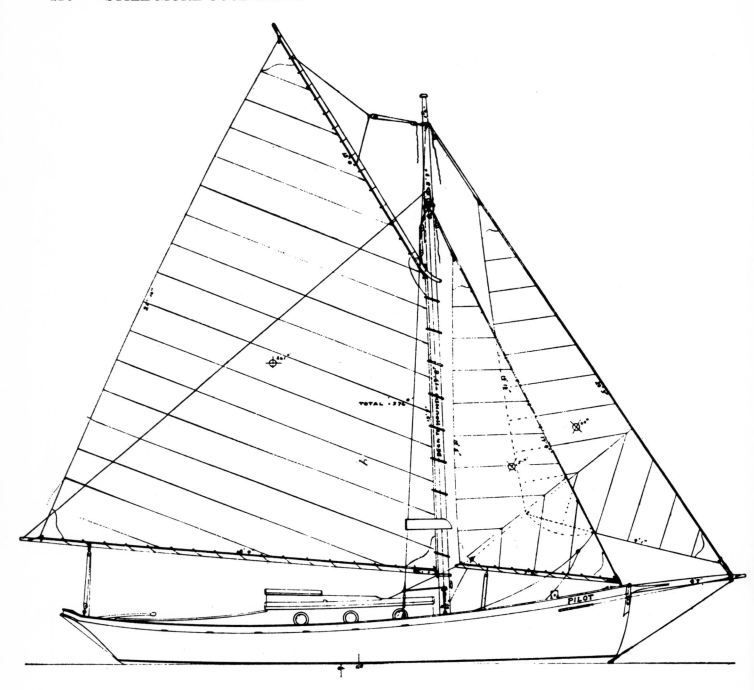

Everything about her looks just right. (Yachting, *December 1939*)

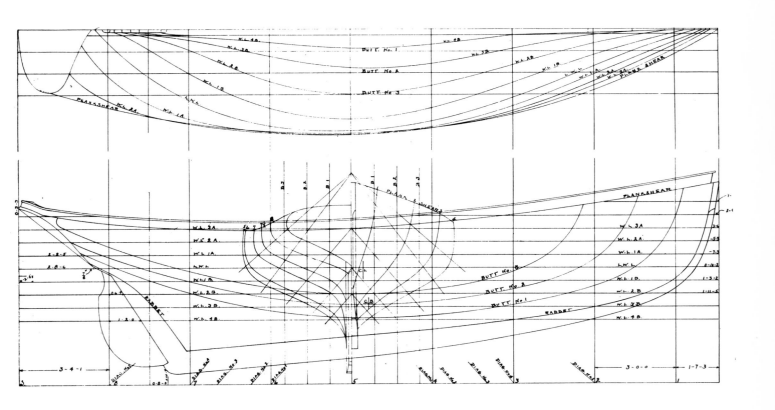

Above: *She has the beauty and ability of her ancestors.* (Yachting, *December 1939*). **Below:** *She has room for four people on a short cruise, or two on a long one.* (Yachting, *December 1939*)

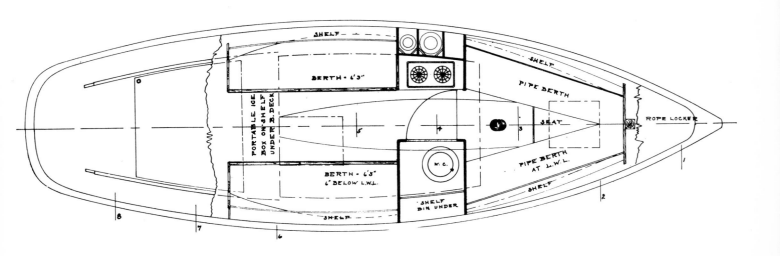

Bill Letts' West Indian, *shown in Florida in 1949, was the first boat built to the design. She was launched at Provincetown, Massachusetts, in 1939, by Blaney and Foster. (George H. Stadel, Jr.)*

length and freeboard-to-length, but he didn't change the basic shape of the hull much. He cut her away a bit at the forefoot, gave her a little more drag to the keel, and gave her a raking sternpost instead of a vertical one. He gave her a little more deadrise and hollowed the garboards a bit more.

George Stadel made his sloop 26 feet long on deck, with a waterline length of 22 feet 2 inches, a beam of 8 feet, and a draft of 4 feet. The rig he drew spread 376 square feet of sail. She has outside ballast of 1,400 pounds of iron, and, sensibly, has some lead inside trimming ballast.

The boat was built by Joel Johnson at Fairfield, Connecticut.

I think she has a very handsome set of lines. I love her fine, hollow entry, and she has as handsome a counter stern as there is. To say nothing of a very pretty, springy sheerline.

Mr. Stadel's pilot boat offspring has the good characteristics of her forebears, for she would be able and would have a good turn of speed. I can't quite bring myself to say she would be fast, at least in gentle weather, for she barely escapes the stinging epithet, "Not enough sail." She does escape it, however, and you could always carry on board a balloon staysail, main topsail, and overlapping jib.

Her rig looks good. The gaff is nearly parallel to the headstay, the bowsprit is steeved up nicely, and the angles of her main boom and staysail club are just right.

The sloop has a big mainsail and small headsails, like a Friendship sloop. You'd shorten down by reefing the mainsail, everything being rove off so there'd be no temptation to put off the tiny task. A gallows frame, nicely curved to complement that handsome stern, would help. (I have an artist friend who staunchly resists such a notion, saying that the structure interferes with vistas from the cockpit. My practical arguments readily cave in before such wisdom.)

The engine specified for this boat is a Universal Bluejacket Twin. It's supposed to develop 10 h.p. at 2,000 r.p.m. The thing is tucked away beneath her self-bailing cockpit.

The sloop's arrangement plan is simple. The transoms are cleverly placed to use space under the bridge deck as quarterberths but still be far enough out into the saloon to double as seats with the bedding stowed aft. A portable icebox goes on a shelf under the bridge deck.

She'd be a bit cramped with four people on board for a long cruise. Better to go two at a time, use the fo'c's'le for stowage, and have elbow room and peace and quiet.

Whatever the number of companions, I'd love to get carried away in this little pilot boat.

28/ The *Boadicea*

> **Length on deck: 30 feet**
> **Length on waterline: 24 feet**
> **Beam: 10 feet 3 inches**
> **Draft: 4 feet 6 inches**
> **Displacement: 11 tons**

The *Boadicea*, an "unobtrusive" — her owner's word — little gaff-rigger lying moored off in Bussand Creek at West Mersea, was pointed out to me by Maurice Griffiths, the cruising boat designer and editor from 1927 to 1967 of *Yachting Monthly*, the leading English cruising magazine. I had taken time out during a business trip to England to go pay my respects to Maurice at his lovely waterfront home on Mersea Island, a ways north of the Thames Estuary. He was kindly driving me 'round and didn't want me to miss the little green fishing smack.

I was excited to see her, having remembered reading about her rebuilding in an English book we had published in the United States, *Restoring Vintage Boats* by John Lewis. "She's the oldest one we have, you know," said Maurice. "Built in 1808." I had forgotten she was quite that old and made some appropriate exclamation. Yet the fact of her age didn't really sink in at the time. Mr. Griffiths might as well have told me that a light year is 5,865,696,000,000 miles.

When was 1808, anyway? Well, on this side of the Atlantic, Thomas Jefferson was the president of our country, in his second term. (In his first term, he made the Louisiana Purchase, extending the western boundary all the way to the Rockies.) In England, from whom we had declared independence more than 30 years earlier, George III was still king. (Not until 1811 would he be declared insane and be replaced by a regent.)

The year before 1808, the *Clermont* had made her famous run from New York to Albany. The three-masted schooner had recently been "invented," but Chebacco boats had not yet developed into pinkies, and such new, specialized types as the Cape Cod catboat and the Friendship sloop were still decades in the future. That's when 1808 was.

I spent the next couple of days not far from the *Boadicea's* mooring with my friend John Leather, the marine surveyor, writer, sailor, and designer. About the first thing John told me after I arrived at his Ballast Quay Farm was, "Michael Frost is going to take us out for a day's trawling in the *Boadicea* tomorrow." Now I really was excited. Trawling under sail in a 170-year-old smack! Talk about your lessons in maritime history!

John filled me in a bit on Mike Frost and his

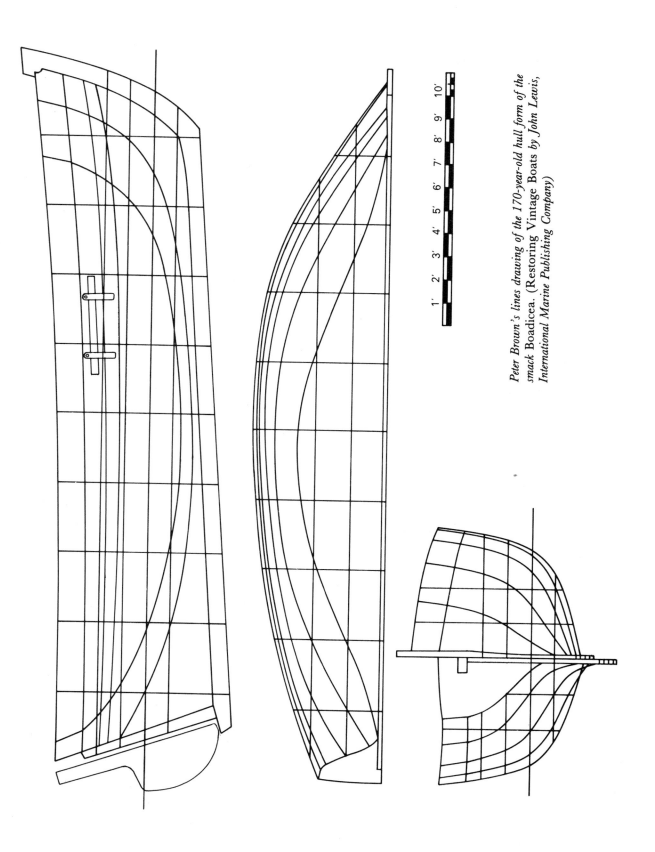

Peter Brown's lines drawing of the 170-year-old hull form of the smack Boadicea. (Restoring Vintage Boats by John Lewis, International Marine Publishing Company)

1' 2' 3' 4' 5' 6' 7' 8' 9' 10'

Boadicea. "You know," he said, "he's had her more than 40 years."

Michael Frost bought the *Boadicea* in 1938. Except for World War II and a major rebuilding, he's been sailing her year-round since 1938. Another mind-boggler.

When was 1938? FDR was in his second term, and King George VI had Neville Chamberlain as his Prime Minister.

The *Boadicea* was built by James Williamson at Maldon, a few miles up the Blackwater River from her present mooring. She worked out of Maldon, dredging oysters, and was owned by Bradwell and Burnham until 1825. From that year until 1871 she was owned and fished by John Pewter out of nearby Tollesbury. From 1871 until 1917 she was owned and fished by a man named Binks and then by his son, Isaiah Binks. The elder Mr. Binks rebuilt the boat extensively in 1890. From 1917 until 1938 she was owned and fished by E.W. French of West Mersea. Michael Frost gave the *Boadicea* a complete rebuild, which took from 1963 until 1972. The *Boadicea's* five owners each had her an average of about 34½ years.

One thing about a wooden boat: she *can* be rebuilt as necessary to withstand the ravages of time. The *Boadicea* now has just one bit of wood in her deadwood that is perhaps original. So, is she still the *Boadicea?* I won't attempt to argue "the *Constellation* question" here, but my simple answer to it is a resounding and unequivocal "*Yes!*" (My reasoning doesn't depend on that possibly original chunk of deadwood.)

The *Boadicea* is named for the East Anglian queen who fought a losing battle against Roman occupiers of Britain in 61 A.D. Scholars say her name should be spelled Boudiccea. Anyway, *Boadicea* has a soft *C* and the accent is on the next-to-last of her five syllables. Those who know her well get away with calling her the "Bodasher," or, more affectionately, the "Bodie."

She's a normal English fishing smack (in England the word "smack" indicates neither a carry-boat nor a boat with a wet well, as it does in America) of her time, but, as I have emphasized, that time was long ago. She has an old form of hull.

The lines drawing reproduced from *Restoring Vintage Boats* by the kind permission of John Lewis was drawn by Peter Brown in 1974. The drawing doesn't show great detail but certainly gives a general idea of the hull shape. My impression is that the boat presently sits deeper in the water than this drawing shows, the actual load waterline being perhaps halfway between the one shown and the next waterline above.

There is great balance in this set of lines. The bow is short and curved and the flat transom and sternpost are moderately raked. She is at least as fine aft as she is forward. She has generous beam amidships.

Her sections are gentle with an easy turn to the bilge. She has a long run and a long, straight keel.

The *Boadicea* is 30 feet long on deck, with a waterline length of 24 feet, a beam of 10 feet 3 inches, and a draft of 4 feet 6 inches. Her displacement is about 11 tons, and she now has about 4 tons of inside lead ballast.

The day we were to go trawling with Michael Frost in the *Boadicea* was warm and sunny, particularly warm for October. I always think of English sailing weather as being abominable, but this sailing day was absolutely lovely.

When you go sailing on the east coast of England, the first thing you contend with and the last thing you contend with are the same: mud. Lifelong East Anglian sailors, like Maurice Griffiths, can write eloquently about the beauties of the stuff, but they are usually referring to watching from the cockpit at sunset, as the tide creeps back in over it. As we made our way toward "the Hard" (that's a gravelly place along the shore where you don't sink in above your ankles), John Leather warned that there might be slippery patches here and there. In his three-sizes-too-big boots, I approached the foreshore as if I were crossing Niagara Falls on a tightrope. Speechless with concentration, I didn't dare nod acknowledgment of his message for fear of losing my balance. We made it to the water's edge without mishap.

Mike Frost had seen us coming and, with his little daughter and the ship's dog, had tumbled into his dinghy and sculled along so that he arrived at the Hard just as we did. We boarded the tiny craft, Mike pushed her off with his oar, and he quietly sculled us out to the *Boadicea*. The dinghy was burdensome, heavily built, nicely balanced fore and aft, beamy amidships, and rather low all along the gunwale. Mike admitted having designed and built her himself and, looking down at her shape as he sculled her along, shook his head and said, "I am afraid that unwittingly I just made her a small *Boadicea*."

Mike's wife, who had been keeping ship while the rest of the *Boadicea's* company had gone to fetch us off, greeted us as we came over the rail. Then she went forward and was ready to cast off the mooring by the time Mike had the Sabb 2-cylinder diesel turning over. Mike said he regretted running the engine, but otherwise we'd have a long, slow beat in a head tide. No doubt of that, for the wind was light, she wouldn't quite lay out the creek, and the flood was running hard. The *Boadicea* has a solid, off-center wheel. Driven smoothly by the Sabb, it shoved us out over the flood.

As soon as we were underway, we started making sail to help her along. It was immediately apparent that the Frosts had worked out just the nicest ways to handle the *Boadicea's* traditional cutter rig. John and I pitched in to help, and the Frosts explained the ship's ways to keep us from doing things out of order, or according to — in my case — some strange foreign custom. Soon we had the mainsail and staysail up and sheeted flat to draw a bit, and then we bent on and set a tiny spitfire jib. All these sails are very heavy canvas, tanned and thoroughly waterproofed.

The tack of the loose-footed mainsail is left free rather than being bowsed down. Mike said he only lashes down the tack when he is double reefed and it is blowing really hard or when he has the third reef tied in. The sail is heavy enough so that the luff stands well without being stretched taut.

There is no parrel line on the boom jaws, but evidently she's never jumped her boom off the mast. I suppose after 170 years you can trust it.

The bitter ends of all the halyards are made fast, not only so they can't get aloft by accident, but also to keep the rope from unlaying.

The sheet of the loose-footed staysail makes fast back on itself and works on a horse running across the deck. To flatten the sail, there is a bowline on each forward shroud to go right 'round the sheet and bowse it aft and outboard.

The spitfire sets flying on a ring 'round the bowsprit, held forward by an outhaul, and a two-part halyard. The sheet trims in through a hole in the bulwarks and belays right forward. There's no inhaul on the ring, a pull on the sheet being sufficient to bring the whole sail inboard with the outhaul let go. The little sail sets well back from the bowsprit end.

Like many traditional boats, the old English smacks are rigged according to a series of rules of thumb. Mike explained that the *Boadicea's* boom length was determined by the formula: two-thirds of the length of the smack (two-thirds of 30 equals 20) plus 4 feet for overhang (20 plus 4 equals 24). Then her 24-foot boom determined all the other dimensions of her rig according to set proportions.

Once clear of the creek, we laid her off a little to a close reach heading out along the edge of Mersea Flats, already well covered by the flood. We were to trawl in company with another smack in sight to seaward of us. She turned out to be a pretty, young thing. She wasn't even 100 years old yet, and her relatively recent design, by comparison with that of the "Bodie," had been influenced by turn-of-the-century racing yachts.

We got the trawl ready to go overboard. The net was maybe 15 feet across its mouth and twice that from head to cod end. We hoisted it aloft on a single-part whip just to be sure it was clear and then faked it down on the quarter. The buoy on its rope was made fast to the cod end and the cod end was tied shut with a fancy knot that wove back and forth in such a way that its bulk plugged the cod end, yet it could be released completely with one pull when the time came. A pair of otter boards, maybe 2 feet by 1 foot and quite heavy, were rigged to the sides of the trawl. Then the warp was taken down from its place hanging in the shrouds and was faked down to run clear. It was led from the stern through a single block on a fairly long bridle leading to the otter boards, then forward outside everything to the big, heavy wooden windlass

On a nice reach with the little spitfire holding her head off. (Michael Frost)

around which turns were taken and the warp then belayed. In the bitter end of the warp back aft, a stopper knot was tied so that if that end of the warp should somehow be lost overboard, it couldn't run out through the block on the bridle and so lose the net.

Not long after the trawl was ready to go overboard, we had gained enough offing and were ready to let her go back in toward Mersea Island towing her gear with the tide. Our companion smack had done this; we went out a ways beyond him, shut down the engine, and were ready to follow suit.

The operation of shooting the net has been well described by Michael Frost in his book, *Boadicea: CK 213,* published in England by Angus & Robertson in 1974. He wrote:

> A sailing trawler works with the tide and only exceptionally does she tow her gear behind her. Almost always she works broadside on to the wind and tide and is usually more or less hove-to while working. I say more or less because there are any number of variant combinations of sail areas which can be employed

and altered at will to adjust the amount of pull the vessel is exerting.

> When the vessel is in this broadside-on working attitude she is referred to as being 'put-to,' and the term goes back beyond memory. It is an apt term and means simply that she has been put to work.

> A distinction should be drawn between the act of putting-to and the steady state of being put-to which results. The one is a complex evolution, while the other is a state of moving equilibrium relatively easy to maintain.

> The evolution took us years to learn and, even when learned, practice allows it to be polished until it becomes one of the most graceful manoeuvres in the whole of seamanship. In contrast the steady state can be maintained by simple rule of thumb.

> It would be out of place to describe the act of putting-to in detail when talking about our trawling of that first winter, but in broad outline, the trawl is made ready in the lee scuppers. At the time of putting-to the vessel is wended [tacked] to come round hove-to on the other tack and while she does so the net is cleared over the side. After she is round the vessel will be making more leeway than for-

On the wind with a big working jib. (Michael Frost)

She has the feeling of a vessel much bigger than 30 feet long.
(Photo by John Lewis, courtesy Michael Frost)

ward way, so the net streams clear on the weather quarter. When it has streamed to its full length it opens out rather like a parachute and at that moment the beam [in our case that day, otter doors] is pushed over the side and the warp is lowered away until the trawl reaches the bottom.

We put-to in the *Boadicea* and as Mike checked away the bridle to the otter doors, one part in each hand, he looked like a sorcerer imploring spirits of the deep to open his trawl doors.

Once the warp was slacked away and belayed, we began to experience ''the steady state of being put-to,'' myself for the first time. I enjoyed it hugely.

Being put-to is, if anything, more peaceful than being hove-to. Wind and sea are abaft the beam, rather than on the bow, so that the vessel gives more readily to the seas. The trawl tethers her enough so that she moves very slowly through the water. Being off the wind, she pitches but little. She is even quieter than when hove-to. And, as you sit along the weather rail, the wind is at your back. Who wouldn't sell his farm and go to sea?

Maybe putting-to should be studied as a heavy-weather tactic. In a discussion of this sort of thing with Melbourne Smith some years ago, I remember him opining that perhaps a good way to take care of a vessel in a heavy breaking sea would be to run off with wind and sea on the quarter, and slow her down, control her heading, and even give her a bit of a lee by towing one or more heavy warps made fast on the weather side, one end forward and the other aft to form a big bight up to windward of the vessel. Such a maneuver would approximate being put-to.

As Mike wrote in his book, it was very easy to keep the *Boadicea* put-to nicely. We controlled her heading by shifting the lead of either the forward or after part of the warp, leading them 'round thole pins stuck in a number of holes along the rail. Speed through the water was controlled with the staysail, letting it draw for maximum power, hauling it aback for medium power, or dropping it for low power.

Once she was put-to, Mike took the tiller out, since the rudder wouldn't be used. With his vessel happily put-to, Michael Frost really relaxed. So did we all, lounging around on deck in the sun watching the little vessel do her work and drinking Mrs. Frost's good coffee.

While the tide carried us back toward Mersea Island, Mike told us about a few of his experiences with the *Boadicea*. It seemed that on occasion he had done a bit of what he called "playing about" with the little vessel. He told about being out in a gale one time when he and his crew got to talking about whether or not she could be driven under. Mike didn't think she could be, and, to prove his point, instead of luffing in a heavy gust, he pulled the helm up to drive her off. He managed to drive her bow under, and she went right over, mast in the

water. He thought she was gone, but up she came slowly to right herself. Once she had pitched off her deck the water trapped by her bulwarks, she popped up like a cork. Mike said he doesn't play about with her as much as he used to.

Mike was quick to point out that he still has much to learn about handling the *Boadicea,* things he said any smacksman used to know. You can take Michael Frost at his word on this, rather than putting such a statement down to undue modesty, because you can sense from sailing with him and from reading his book how deeply involved he is with the minute details of handling his vessel under all conditions. He was talking here about fine points, let me assure you, though his argument was that they weren't so much fine points to the fishermen as practical necessities of everyday life.

As we talked, the breeze increased to moderate. It was fun to watch the little "Bodie" going quietly about her trawling untended except for some occasional attention to the staysail or the moving of one or the other parts of the warp forward or aft one hole 'round a different thole pin. How many and many a time must she have been put-to just this way to let the tide drag her trawl over this same bottom! Had her log been kept every day, it might now run to 32,000 pages!

We made an hour's tow and hauled back — all too easily. These waters are overfished. We pulled the trawl on board over the weather rail, and it was a "water haul." There were a half-dozen plaice too small to keep, lots of little crabs, a bit of seaweed, surprisingly little sand, mud, or stones, one good-sized starfish, and some tiny shrimp. The haul was barren of edible fish, but of course no haul is barren of the excitement of dumping it out on deck and sorting through it to see what was on the bottom.

Mike had been experimenting recently with the otter trawl. He normally uses a beam trawl, which is what the smack accompanying us had over. She got one big plaice and a stone crab big enough to keep.

A couple of us now went below into the cabin. The smack has no cabin house, just a slightly raised hatch in the deck. So all the time you are on deck there is no evidence that the boat has a

Dried out on the hard. (Michael Frost)

cabin; and once you have dropped below, you are absolutely removed from the deck and there is no suggestion that the boat is anything but cabin. On the *Boadicea,* deck and cabin are two totally separate worlds. You can pass easily from one world to the other through the hatch, but as you enter one world you leave the other completely behind.

That's a nice feeling that I had never experienced so completely before in any boat. The arrangement enables you to have the best of both worlds, actually. You have your choice of remembering or forgetting the world you are not in, depending on circumstances. If it's rough and cold and you've just come below, you can forget all about the world of the deck. If it's rough and cold, and you've just come on deck, you can remember and look forward to re-entering that other warm, dry, quiet world that you know must still exist below.

The *Boadicea* is arranged very simply below deck. Forward, there are two wide, comfortable transoms for sleeping or sitting on, leaning back against the curve of the frames. At the after end of the cabin are lockers and stoves. A gimbaled Primus enabled Mrs. Frost to produce hot coffee and tea all day long. The cabin was warm and cozy. Aft under the rest of the deck is a steerage where lives the engine and where there is lots of stowage for all sorts of odds and ends of ship's gear.

We beat up into the River Blackwater a ways, and I thoroughly enjoyed sailing the *Boadicea.* She has no cockpit; her tiller is relatively short and stout. Because of the smack's heavy displacement and the extremely hefty appearance of her tiller, I expected she would be something of a brute to steer. When Mike turned her over to me, I sprawled on deck to weather of the great helm, grasped it firmly with both hands, and gritted my teeth a bit, determined not to let her luff too much. Ten seconds later I relaxed and grinned all over inside. There was simply nothing to pull against; she had no will of her own except to forge steadily ahead, responding quickly to the slightest whim mentioned to her rudder by her tree trunk of a tiller. She's some actress! She has the soul of a lively dinghy and has been masquerading about the seas all these years hiding it behind her heavy timbers and planks.

Mike said diplomatically, ''I think she'll go a little higher.'' Indeed she would. She was just the nicest kind of a boat to sail, somehow at once very serene and very lively.

Mike Frost has written that the fishermen steered standing to leeward of the tiller, hands on knees, nudging the tiller a bit as necessary with the inboard leg. In such a position they were certainly more ready for action than I was, spread out on deck, and they certainly would have kept warmer in cold weather, but that day

I would not willingly have given over the subtle feel of the *Boadicea's* tiller to a mere knee.

For a while, we were able to keep our younger cousin smack tucked away astern and to leeward, but then I began reaching off a tiny bit, assuming it was Mike's intention to head back for his mooring in Bussand Creek, whereas both smacks were to continue beating up into the River Blackwater. By the time I came to, the new smack had worked up well to weather of us.

But Mike seemed pleased that we had held him for awhile. He said the *Boadicea* always sails at her best when there is no regatta on. He suspects it may be because on regatta days he finds it necessary to replace his beloved little spitfire with a much bigger headsail that gives her a bit of lee helm and kills her responsiveness.

A funny thing happened while I was sailing the *Boadicea.* I began to like the angle of her bowsprit! It's parallel to the water, thus spoiling her gentle sheerline, which it fails to carry out, and looking generally droopy when you look at her side view at rest. But there was something very purposeful about that long, straight spar pointing right level at the horizon instead of at some point above it. I am not converted, mind you, but for the first time I saw the possibilities of the level English bowsprit.

Later, we ran off back down toward Mersea Island, jibed, and headed up the creek for the mooring. By now the tide was ebbing strongly. We took in the jib and eased up over the tide. Fifty yards from the mooring, Mike signaled to drop the peak. Then, when he was sure he had way enough to come up to the mooring and carry it up against the tide a bit before she lost way over the ground, we dropped the staysail and mainsail. Mike had a kedge anchor all ready to let go forward in case he had found his mooring buoy towed under by the tide.

We folded the mainsail down atop the boom, tied its stops 'round the gaff only, and then hoisted the throat up out of the way. Mike bowsed the bobstay up under the bowsprit so it would clear the mooring pendant.

While we were forward after straightening her up, Mike explained how a skipper, mate, and boy would position themselves to handle the smack. The skipper would be aft steering and handling the main sheet. The mate was at the mast to starboard. Here he could reach all the important running rigging: the peak halyard, main topping lift, jib halyard, staysail bowline, and, a step or two forward, the jib sheet. The boy would be at the mast to port with the throat halyard and staysail halyard — far less used and less critical when used than the mate's lines — and the staysail bowline and jib sheet on that side. Little needed to be said among these three to carry out the most precise maneuvers.

We now settled down on the bow, got out our sandwiches, and enjoyed a four o'clock lunch in the last of the glorious sun. It had been a good day with good people, Mike enjoying the day's sail, their precocious daughter wheedling very poor jokes indeed out of "the American one," and John Leather increasing his already great familiarity with the "Bodie." The ship's dog seemed to have been on board forever. I was just trying to drink in as much as possible of the whole new experience and was enjoying every minute of it.

At length, as it got cool, we went below to that other world and leaned back at ease. It took a while to absorb the massiveness of the smack's construction and the massiveness of Michael Frost's task and accomplishment in renewing it all.

The *Boadicea* was originally clinker-built, but when she was rebuilt in 1890, her planking was changed to carvel. Old Isaiah Binks had told Mike Frost that he "thought that the change had not improved the hull. The water did not flow as smoothly past the new skin as it had done with the old one and, although the change had made the vessel stronger, it had also made her pitch more in a seaway, so that she became heavier and rather wetter. She had never been quite as fast with the new skin."

This business keeps coming up. How many times have you read that such and such a type of indigenous boat originally had overlapping planks but gradually evolved into a smooth-skinned craft? And that the change was no improvement? Will the America's Cup eventually be lifted by a clinker-built racer? Maybe we'd best feed in one lapstrake defender each time, just to be safe. You see what imaginings can take place in a cabin like the *Boadicea's?*

Michael Frost's herculean rebuilding of the *Boadicea* involved a greenheart keel, frames of English oak, bottom planking of greenheart, 1½-inch larch for topside planking, a teak transom, and many a pound of Monel nails. John Lewis gives a very complete description of the rebuilding in *Restoring Vintage Boats*.

Michael Frost's perseverance, skill, and workmanship appear to assure that the *Boadicea's* long life will continue far into the future. How could her owners in future centuries fail to respond to the way he has cared for his vessel with their own care? Could it be that this little smack is just getting started?

29/ The *Binker*

Length on deck: 39 feet 10 inches
Length on waterline: 30 feet
Beam: 10 feet
Draft: 6 feet 2 inches
Sail area: 901 square feet
Displacement: 11 tons
Designer: W. Starling Burgess

One of the drawbacks to living way up the Pawcatuck River was that the four miles of rather tortuous channel from Stonington Point to our home mooring — coupled with the fact that there was scarcely room to turn around once you got up there — discouraged all but the gunkholiest cruising boats from using the place as a port of call. The only cruising vessels we got to see were the handful that, like ourselves, had permanent moorings in the River.

So it was always a great treat to include a run up into Stonington Harbor on a sail so that we could see the many good boats moored there, together with, we hoped, some interesting visitors.

One of the Stonington regulars that we always hoped to see was the 35-foot cutter *Little Dipper* designed by W. Starling Burgess. She was a very handsome and weatherly looking boat, with, for some years, her topsides finished bright. She had a really pretty, delicate, fine counter.

It wasn't too often, though, that we found her on her home mooring, for her owner, Richard Baum, cruised in her from Nova Scotia to the Caribbean (as described in his book, *By the Wind*, published in 1962 by D. Van Nostrand). It was always a pleasant surprise to find her back where we could admire her.

I wrote to Mr. Baum some years ago asking if he had any plans of the *Little Dipper*, and unfortunately he didn't. He sings her praises in his book and wrote me, "She is an unusual little ship and marvelously well behaved in heavy weather."

It's funny how it sometimes takes so long to pull things together. Only recently did I realize that a design I have long admired, the *Binker*, a 40-foot Starling Burgess cutter, is to my liking because she shares a lot of the characteristics of the *Little Dipper*. I believe Starling Burgess designed the *Binker* shortly after he drew the plans for the *Little Dipper*. This was in the early Thirties, and Mr. Burgess designed the *Binker* for Boyd Donaldson, his business partner at the time.

Mr. Donaldson wanted a boat in which he and his 15-year-old son could cruise comfortably, his chief specification being that the boat should perform well going to windward. I suspect Mr. Donaldson got what he wanted — a fine, weatherly cruising boat.

The *Binker* has been owned since 1966 by

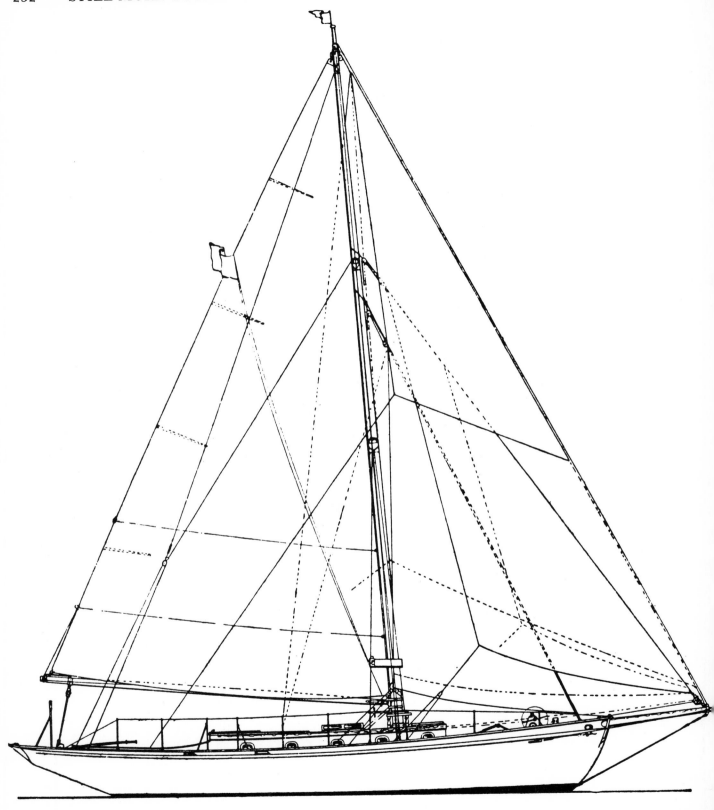

Starling Burgess gave the Binker *the cutter's traditional three-headsail rig. (Uffa Fox's Second Book by Uffa Fox, International Marine Publishing Company)*

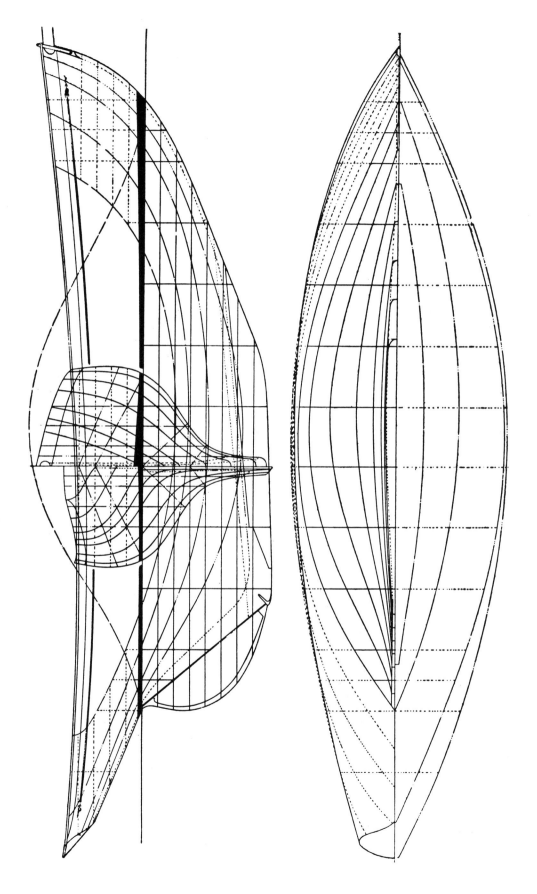

Her lines show a powerful, well-proportioned hull well able to carry out her owner's desire for a comfortable cruiser that will sail well to windward. (Uffa Fox's Second Book by Uffa Fox, International Marine Publishing Company)

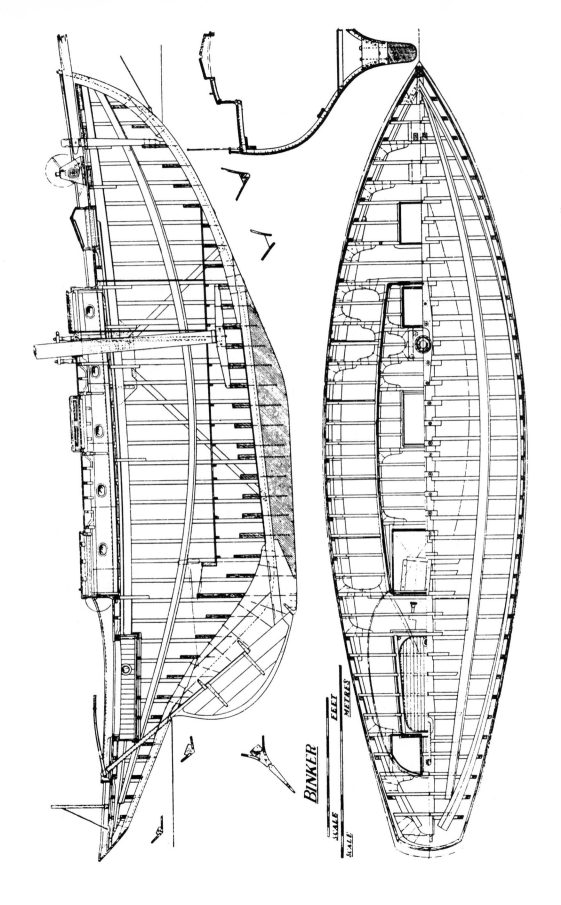

BINKER

SCALE

FEET

SCALE

METRES

She was well and truly built by Julius Peterson. Note her bilge stringers, bronze strapping, and all those knees. (Uffa Fox's Second Book by Uffa Fox, International Marine Publishing Company)

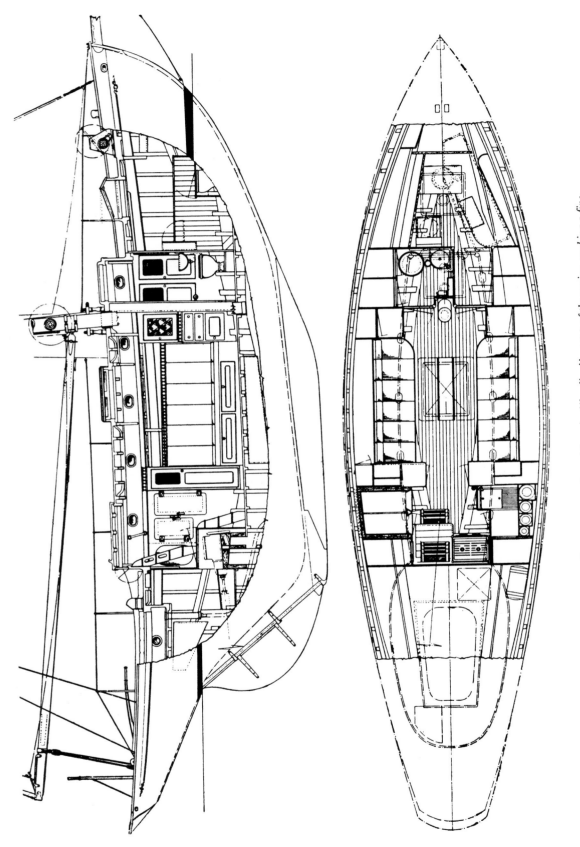

She has a "standard" arrangement plan with a nice "landing" on top of the engine, making a fine place to stand and see what's going on. (Uffa Fox's Second Book by Uffa Fox, International Marine Publishing Company)

Melvin and Anne Marie Seddon, who sail her out of Manhasset Bay, New York. They obviously love their vessel, and they take very good care of her.

She is 39 feet 10 inches long on deck, with a waterline length of 30 feet, a beam of 10 feet, and a draft of 6 feet 2 inches. She displaces 22,000 pounds, of which 8,250 pounds is outside ballast in a lead keel. Her sail area is 901 square feet.

I think this boat has very nice basic proportions of length, beam, draft, displacement, and sail area. Her hull looks powerful and able, with considerable ballast on a fairly deep keel and big shoulders in her topsides.

She has fine waterlines, deep bow and buttock lines, and curvy wineglass sections. I particularly like the curve and tumblehome of her topsides.

The *Binker* has a fairly short bow and a longish, fine counter (the *Little Dipper* has proportionally an even shorter bow and longer counter) somewhat reminiscent of British cutters, from which breed she may have received some rather distant inspiration.

The *Binker* was carefully and soundly built by Julius Peterson. Her 1⅛-inch planking was fastened to 2½-inch by 2⅛-inch frames on 12-inch centers. She was given substantial bilge stringers 1½ inches thick by 6⅛ inches wide amidships, tapering to 4½ inches wide at the ends. She has diagonal bronze strapping of 3½-inch by 3/32-inch stock let into the planking in way of the mast. As may be seen in her construction drawing, she has no fewer than 42 knees in the deck and house.

"I am the deck-caulker in the family," Mrs. Seddon wrote me, "and have recaulked the entire boat 1½ times. This is a very frustrating and time-consuming job requiring much patience and fortitude. The satisfaction comes in having a dry bunk to sleep in!"

I think the *Binker* sail plan shows a handsome profile, with her bowsprit to balance her long counter and her mast nicely raked.

The sail area of her mainsail was originally 486 square feet. It's a little less now, for her boom has been chopped off just enough to give her a permanent backstay. "With such a big mainsail, *Binker* is rather tender and so we reef

often. Eighteen knots of wind require that we take one reef, and then she sails beautifully . . . . Another recent improvement to the boat was the addition of 'lazy jacks' for the main. Dropping the main in heavy wind and sea is no longer a problem. They also make reefing while underway so much easier and safer."

The cutter's sail plan shows a nice array of headsails. Besides the three working headsails, there is a small jib, an overlapping fore staysail (hurray!), a big Yankee jib topsail, a jib filling the whole of the fore triangle, and a huge overlapping ballooner. I'd add a tiny storm fore staysail, as well as a main trysail.

Her jib is shown set flying on a roller. This makes good sense, for a jib stay isn't really needed and with the jib taken down there will be plenty of room for tacking with the big, overlapping jib topsails.

Maybe this is as good a place as any to digress a minute on this business of roller-furling jibs. I get a fair bit of correspondence on the subject, all the way from people who chastise me for tolerating them on a boat at all to those who upbraid me for not realizing that the modern ones are absolutely foolproof. I am afraid I am right in the middle on this one. I think roller jibs are fine on certain boats and with certain rigs (including this one on the *Binker*) as long as you are cruising alongshore, where a lot of maneuvering and fairly rapid sail changing makes the handiness of the roll-up sail valuable, but I'd never take one offshore, where sail changing should be a bit more deliberate and where the main thing you are after is extreme simplicity, reliability, and repairability. I love to make a big jib disappear just before entering a harbor, but offshore, give me no gimmicks. The Seddons cruise coastwise in the *Binker*. "All of our headsails are now roller-furled with the exception of the drifter."

The *Binker's* engine is a 4-cylinder Gray 112 turning a 16-inch wheel. As you can see, the power plant is off-center to port but is canted so its thrust won't turn the boat to starboard. Of course there is some loss of direct forward thrust with this arrangement. "When the bottom is clean, *Binker* will move along at 8 knots wide open. We cruise at 6½ to 7 knots comfortably."

With her considerable depth of hull, the cut-

The Binker *knocking off the miles with the help of a big, quadrilateral jib.* (Yachting, *July 1937)*

ter's house can be low and narrow, leaving much deck space and not detracting from her good looks. There is room for a 9-foot dinghy on top of the house. Her oval cockpit is a handsome feature. There's a bilge pump in the cockpit floor.

I'd prefer a wheel to steer with in this boat (*Little Dipper* has a wheel), for she would pull a bit at times, and the wheel takes up less room than the tiller.

"You might be interested to know that *Binker's* tiller was replaced by a wheel soon after she was originally commissioned."

The *Binker* has what I call a standard arrangement, simply because it seems to be the most common one used in a boat of 35 to 40 feet: galley aft and saloon amidships separated from a forward sleeping cabin by a head and lockers. In the *Binker,* the forward sleeping cabin wasn't to be used much, so it got squeezed down to a fo'c's'le with a single pipe berth.

"A couple of years ago I started to refinish the varnish below and really have been pleased with the results so far; butternut is a beautiful wood! I still have plenty more to do and plan to tackle it by sections, so that it won't overwhelm me."

The "landing" halfway down the companionway would make a fine place to stand in the hatchway to watch her go. And she is worth watching: "We were tickled this summer when a flashy new one-tonner tried to overtake us in a 10-knot breeze and could not stay as high as we could. He finally came alongside and asked if we were motorsailing, because he could not believe we could sail so close to the wind in our 'old' boat!

"She is a joy to sail, and a beauty to behold. I can't recall a day's sail when we haven't been photographed and/or admired by other yachtsmen," wrote Mrs. Seddon. Little wonder in such a good boat, write I.

30/ The *Heart's Desire*

Length on deck: 52 feet
Length on waterline: 36 feet
Beam: 11 feet 6 inches
Draft: 7 feet
Sail area: 1,000 square feet
Displacement: 14 tons
Designer: Uffa Fox

Uffa Fox, the great English sailor and yacht designer, drew the plans in 1934 of what he then conceived to be his ultimate cruising vessel. He wanted a boat in which he and his wife could cruise or in which he could sail alone, a boat that would be so able she would seldom be weatherbound, a boat that would be fast enough so that he could enter her in races with a straight face.

Uffa named the design the *Heart's Desire,* for as a boy he had sung in the choir, "Oh rest in the Lord, wait patiently for him and he shall give thee thy heart's desire." I don't know whether or not Uffa was too impatient, but he never did get this particular heart's desire, and she has remained a dream ship.

Uffa Fox wrote, "It is a remarkable fact that all things naturally developed without rule or restriction for passage through air and water in this world are pointed at the stern, for example birds, fishes, tadpoles, the Indian canoe, Viking ships, whaleboats, lifeboats (of all nations), racing eights and funneys (single sculls).

"And so as rating rules which govern length and those which govern cost have produced the square-sterned boat and not the laws of nature,

and as the laws of nature will endure to the end, it is far better to design to these than to artificial conditions."

At any rate, Uffa gave his *Heart's Desire* a pointed stern.

The year after Uffa designed the *Heart's Desire,* he was commissioned to produce the design of a large cruising yacht, and he gave the great 83-foot *Wishbone* a very similar hull form to that of the *Heart's Desire.*

The *Heart's Desire* is 52 feet long on deck, with a waterline length of 36 feet, a beam of 11 feet 6 inches, and a draft of 7 feet. She displaces 14 tons and spreads an even 1,000 square feet of sail. Uffa felt that 1,000 square feet of sail, with no sail bigger than 500 square feet, was the most sail that should be set on a boat that was to be sailed singlehanded at times.

It would be hard to put the *Heart's Desire's* rail under, what with her considerable turn of bilge above the waterline and her tumblehome. She has quite deep bow lines and a rather long, straight run. By contrast, her waterlines forward are fine, and those aft are a bit full.

Mr. Fox believed that well-designed overhangs help a boat in a seaway. He felt the canoe

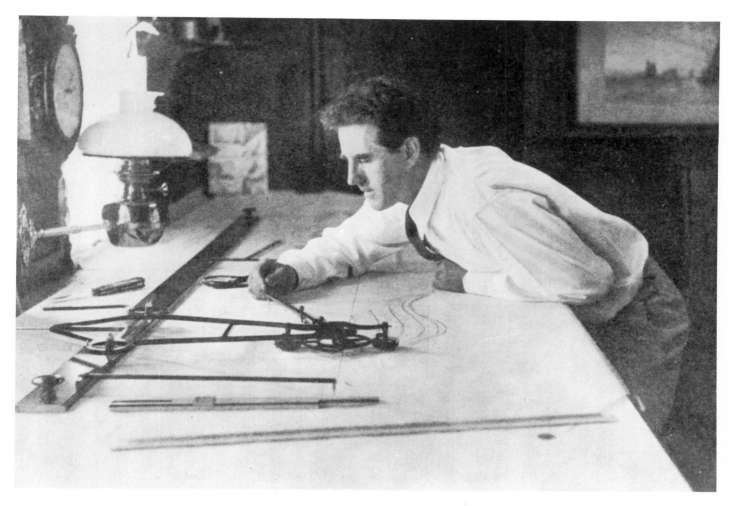

Uffa Fox at his drawing board. (Uffa Fox's Second Book *by Uffa Fox, International Marine Publishing Company*)

stern of the *Heart's Desire* was Vee'd enough so it wouldn't pound if the boat were becalmed in a leftover sea. You don't often think of the stern pounding, yet it can happen. The water presents a lot of different shapes, and I guess at some angle of heel any boat can probably pound at either end.

With her restricted sail area for singlehanded sailing, the *Heart's Desire* looks a bit underrigged, but she's easily driven and has big, overlapping headsails for reaching in light weather.

Her mast is well aft to keep her mainsail down to 500 square feet. The lower mast stands only 35 feet above the deck. Her 21-foot topmast is hollow and is designed to be struck.

The cutter's sails were to be made of tan flax to retain the original strength of the material and yet be soft to handle. The cloths of the mainsail were to run parallel to the leech for maximum strength and so the reefpoints could be positioned at the seams. The sail was to have no battens. It has three deep reefs and a diagonal balance reef for keeping the boom up out of the water when running in a seaway. She has a main trysail of 150 square feet following the exact shape of the forward part of the mainsail. She has quite an array of headsails, only two of which would be set at once. The fore staysail can be reefed, there is a modest working jib, small and big jib topsails, a big balloon fore staysail, and a huge balloon jib. There are running backstays on both the lower mast and the topmast.

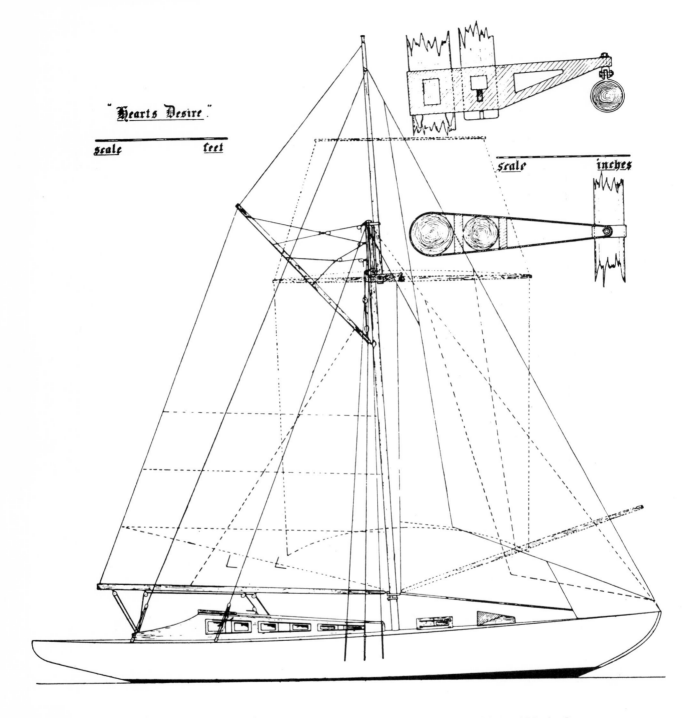

Uffa Fox's idea of his own ultimate cruiser as of 1934. (Sailing, Seamanship and Yacht Construction by Uffa Fox)

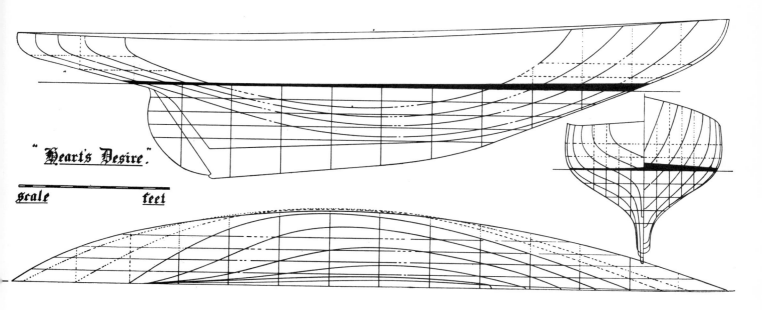

"Heart's Desire."

scale _____ feet

Above: *Uffa Fox believed that, like so many things designed according to the laws of nature to travel through air or water, cruising boats should have pointed sterns. (Sailing, Seamanship and Yacht Construction by Uffa Fox).* **Below:** *Her deck layout is ingenious, with its streamlined deckhouse with bunk and chart table, its protected steering well, and its neat stowage for an 8-foot dinghy. (Sailing, Seamanship and Yacht Construction by Uffa Fox)*

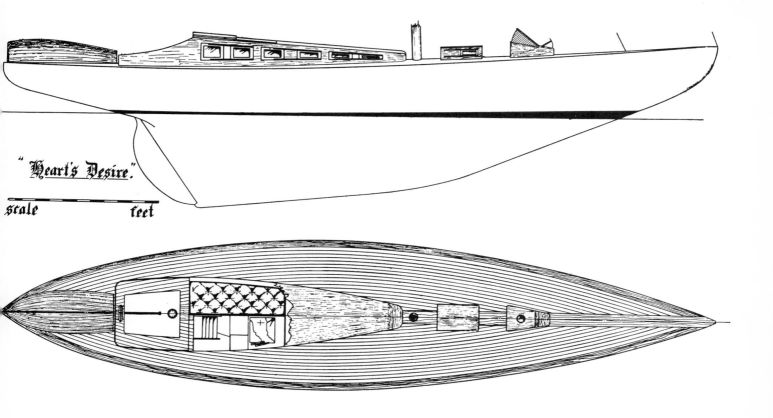

"Heart's Desire."

scale _____ feet

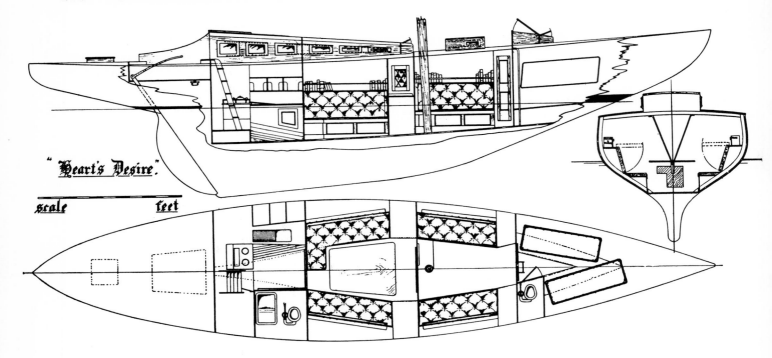

Though designed as a one- or two-person cruising boat, the Heart's Desire *could accommodate up to 10 folks overnight. (Sailing, Seamanship and Yacht Construction by Uffa Fox)*

Uffa Fox designed a square rig for his ultimate cruiser, with the squaresail having his one-man-limit area of 500 square feet and the square topsail having 200 square feet. The gooseneck on the lower yard extends the yard forward of the forestay so that the squaresail doesn't chafe on the stay as long as there's any wind in it. This rig also allows the sail to be braced up fairly sharp on a beam wind. And it would let you set the fore staysail as an anti-rolling sail.

The rig of the *Heart's Desire* is very well thought out and very versatile. Her pole for poling out the big ballooner when running, her lower yard, and her topmast are all interchangeable if necessary. So are her pole for the balloon staysail, staysail boom, and upper yard.

Mr. Fox was going to fit three-foot lifelines all around the cutter's deck with no fewer than four pulpits. Not only was she to have bow and stern pulpits, but she was to have a pulpit on each side in way of the shrouds. Uffa said these would be handy for the leadsman. They might also mean that her heads would grow rusty from lack of use.

The *Heart's Desire* has a small, shallow cockpit. Her helmsman, sitting in its forward end with the compass at his feet mounted under the floor, would be well protected by the high coaming, deckhouse, and 8-foot dinghy stowed neatly on the stern.

The fore hatch has side flaps so it can be left open most of the time without spray finding its way below. Her tapered deckhouse windows slide aft to open and jam forward to shut tightly. She also has shutters with small, heavy glass deadlights to go over them in heavy weather.

The deckhouse is practical and ingenious with its berth for the person off watch or the singlehander catching a catnap. It also has a chart table that slides aft so you can use it while sitting on the companionway ladder. The companionway can be shut off from the rest of the accommodation below, a nice feature in cold or heavy weather.

The cutter's arrangement plan is simple. The backs of the four transoms swing up to form upper berths, so although the *Heart's Desire* was intended for only one or two people for long-range cruising, she could accommodate a crowd of 10, with the use of the pipe berths in the fo'c's'le, overnight in a harbor. The headroom under the deck is six feet.

So the *Heart's Desire* represents Uffa Fox's

thinking for an ultimate cruiser for himself in 1934. Somebody ought to try her out, for she has many fine characteristics, in my opinion. At any rate, she represents the considerable sailing and designing experience Uffa Fox had already accumulated in 1934. He wrote, "For I have sailed in canoes, dinghies, all kinds of racers, from the smallest to the largest, and in every kind of cruiser, pilot and fishing boat, in all weathers fair and foul, and this design is the result of it all, a blend of every one, from square-rigged vessel to a canoe."

31/ The *Tamaris*

> **Length on deck: 28 feet 7 inches**
> **Length on waterline: 24 feet**
> **Beam: 8 feet 3 inches**
> **Draft: 4 feet 3 inches**
> **Sail area: 494 square feet**
> **Displacement: 6 tons**
> **Designer: Maurice Griffiths**

After 1945, English sailors could begin thinking about boats in terms other than their capabilities for patrol, rescue, and carrying a punch. One experienced English cruising man, Maurice Griffiths (also an experienced designer of cruising boats and an experienced boating editor), decided to design a boat in which he could cruise for peaceful purposes.

Not surprisingly, to anyone who knew Griffiths' designs, the *Tamaris,* as he called the new boat, turned out to be a husky canoe yawl with a raised deck. She is 28 feet 7 inches long on deck, with a waterline length of 24 feet, a beam of 8 feet 3 inches, and a draft of 4 feet 3 inches. She displaces just under 6 tons and has a sail area of 494 square feet.

At first glance she looks to be huskier than she really is; she has been kept narrow, and her waterlines are quite fine.

She has a well-formed run for such a narrow double-ender. And doesn't she have handsome wineglass sections? (I fall for that shape every time!) The tumblehome in her topsides, carried on into the raised deck, keeps the latter structure from looking too clumsy.

I think she has a good-looking profile, aided and abetted by her oval ports, reminiscent of the style of Sam Crocker on the windward side of the Atlantic. As a matter of fact, I think maybe Sam Crocker could be thought of as an American Maurice Griffiths, and vice versa, if you see what I mean. The designs of both show a great appreciation for and belief in the comfortable cruising boat.

The *Tamaris* is planked with ⅞-inch mahogany, copper-riveted to 1¼-inch by 1-inch Canadian rock elm frames spaced 7 inches apart. Her keel is of English oak. Her deck is pine, covered with canvas, on 2-inch by 1½-inch beams, increased to 2½ inches by 2½ inches in way of the mainmast.

Her nice long outside ballast keel weighs 4,000 pounds, giving a ballast-to-displacement ratio of just over one-third.

The yawl's sails are small enough to be easily handled. Her mainsail has an area of 212 square feet; the staysail, 106 square feet; mizzen, 56 square feet; and jib, 120 square feet.

With her loose-footed fore staysail, she has two headsheets to handle when tacking, but there are no running backstays. She'd shorten down to mainsail and jib, and then reefed main-

Maurice Griffiths.

sail and fore staysail. She'd also balance under staysail and mizzen, though there is not enough area in the latter to drive her to windward in a strong breeze if there is much of a sea running.

For light weather, she has a big overlapping jib. I'd also want a balloon fore staysail.

On the mainmast, the intermediate shrouds pull against the forestay, and she has a permanent backstay pulling against the headstay. I'd prefer the backstay to be independent of the mizzen mast, led to a bridle to the quarters.

Her bowsprit is short enough to be easy to work on, yet it gives enough separation of the headstays so you could work the jib through handily when tacking. It's also enough of a bowsprit to be a good anchor derrick. The bobstay is 5/16-inch rod.

I think the mizzen boom needs topping up a bit; although it's just about parallel to the main boom, it doesn't look it because of its surroundings, and there is nothing like a perked-up mizzen boom to give a yawl a jaunty look. Such a nicety also has the practical advantage of keeping the mizzen boom a bit more up out of a

heavy sea if she's scudding along under staysail and mizzen when it's really rough.

The yawl's lifeline arrangement looks well and makes sense; you'd want to add higher ropes between main and mizzen rigging each side in heavy weather, together with a piece of rigging running out to the bowsprit end.

The *Tamaris* has auxiliary power, a one-lung, four-cycle, five-h.p. Feltham gasoline engine, turning a three-bladed wheel with a diameter of 11 inches and a pitch of 8 inches. There is an 8-gallon gas tank right back in the stern. She also has a 20-gallon water tank under the bridge deck to port.

There is space up on the raised deck for an 8-foot pram, as shown in the outboard profile drawing. You hoist the dinghy on board with the starboard topping lift unshackled from the main boom. The hauling part of this lift makes up to a luff tackle; it's amazing how heavy even a small boat is to lift on board. The topping lift is hooked to a wire span going to rings on the outsides of the pram's bow and stern transoms so she can be turned over in mid-air when hoisting in or out.

In the cockpit, we find that the yawl has that admirable device, a tiller comb. Why isn't this handy gadget in wider use?

She has no seats in the after end of her cockpit; you'd want a camp stool. The bridge deck at the forward end of the cockpit is cut out amidships to give more leg room and a sort of three-corner seat each side. There's a flush hatch in the cockpit floor.

Note that nice "landing" in the main companionway. It doubles as a fine seat.

Her galley is aft to port. A folding chart table lets down over the quarter berth to starboard. There's a nice vertical pipe for a handhold at the after end of the cabin table.

The saloon berths extend forward under the lockers shown. You stow your blankets in these cubbyholes during the day.

I suppose the word "blanket" is a nearly anachronistic nautical term these days outside racing circles, where, I understand, it is one of those mean things you try to do to the other guy. The sleeping bag seems to be the great thing today. I suppose the bags do have their conveniences, and I must admit I had to sweep

The Tamaris *was Maurice Griffiths' design for his own use when World War II was over.* (The Rudder, *July 1949*)

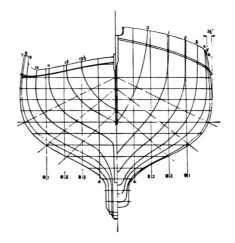

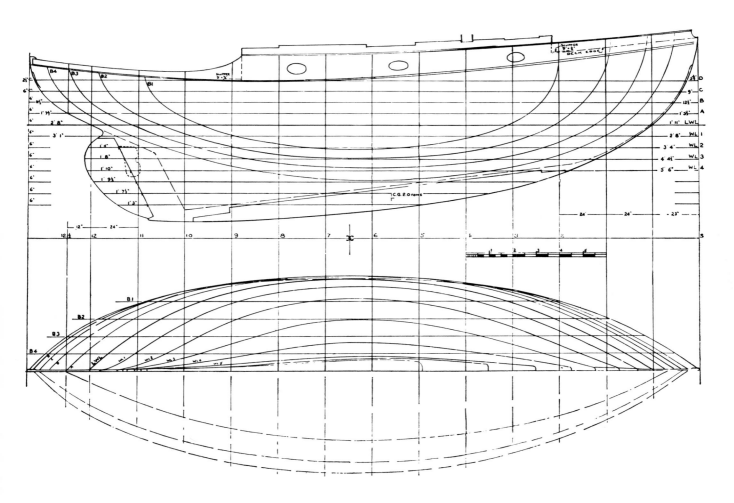

She's not as husky as she seems; as a matter of fact, her half-breadth plan shows her to be on the skinny side. (The Rudder, *July 1949*)

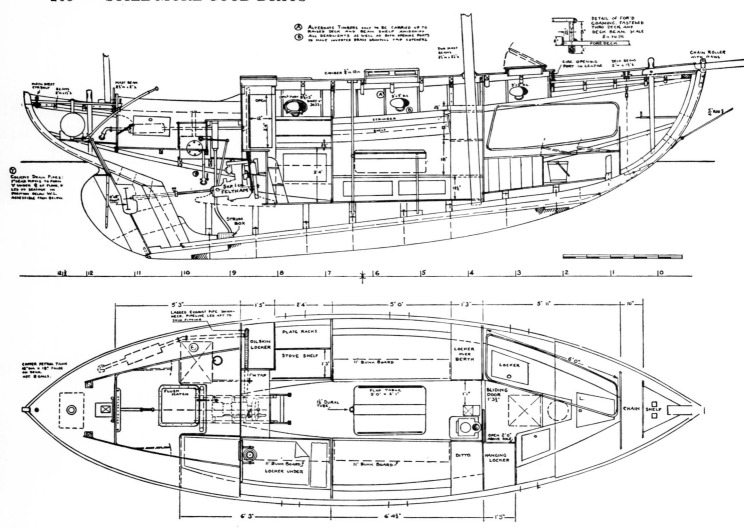

She's nicely laid out for short cruises for up to four people, or more lengthy voyages for a lesser number. (The Rudder, *July 1949*)

up a lot of red and blue lint from the blankets of the yawl that I grew up in. We'd start off in the spring using one lightweight red blanket and one big heavy blue one each. I can still remember the fun of crawling into my bunk clutching one of those red wool blankets by one edge up under my chin, rolling on my back and making myself into a ball with the big wad of blanket over upturned toes. Then when everything was just right, I'd shoot my feet down to the bottom of the bunk and if all went well, there I was with the blanket all stretched over me. Then I'd carefully pull the heavy blue over on top of everything, hoping not to dislodge the red in the process. Where's the challenge in a sleeping bag? By midsummer, we'd be down to just one

red (couldn't use just one blue, because they were too scratchy). The blues would be stowed away, not to be hauled out again until fall. By the time you had to have two reds and a blue — I never really did discover how to get under that combination smoothly — you knew it was about time to haul out for the winter.

But I fear Mr. Griffiths' blanket lockers have led me off course. She has a nice heating stove at the forward end of the cabin.

Of her six oval ports, the after two open and the forward four are deadlights.

There is a bucket in the fo'c's'le, a very sensible arrangement indeed.

The headroom in the yawl's cabin is 5 feet 2 inches under the beams and 5 feet 8 inches under the skylight. (Just recently one of my sons (6 feet 3 inches) and I spent a couple of days in a boat with a nice big cabin with less headroom than this, and I can't really say either of us would have been very much more comfortable if it had been seven feet.)

In the *Tamaris,* Maurice Griffiths achieved his objective, in my opinion, of designing a comfortable cruising boat. She wouldn't be fast, but she'd have no bad habits and would bring you home from a trip relaxed and happy. She's one of those pipe-smoking kinds of boats.

32/ The *Symphony*

> **Length on deck: 33 feet**
> **Length on waterline: 28 feet**
> **Beam: 9 feet 2 inches**
> **Draft: 4 feet 6 inches**
> **Sail area: 550 square feet**
> **Displacement: 7.6 tons**
> **Designer: Maurice Griffiths**

Many sailors, when dreaming of that ideal cruising boat, or when looking at a real boat they are tempted to buy, conjure up images of themselves sailing over the horizon single-handed.

The boat, then, whether real or imaginary, ought to have certain characteristics. She ought not to be so big as to be more than a handful, yet not so small as to be cramped, lack room for stores, or have too quick or tiring a motion at sea. She ought to be steady on the helm and she ought to have many small sails rather than a few big ones.

Singlehanded racing of late has broken these rules more than kept them, but we speak here of cruising. You used to see quite a few designs published labeled as "A Singlehanded Cruiser," but few designs are so designated to-day.

Here's a yawl that was so intended. The *Symphony* was designed by Maurice Griffiths in 1930. Mr. Griffiths presented her plans in his book *Dream Ships,* published in 1949. He has owned more than 20 boats and has seen more than 800 craft built to one or another of his many designs.

I think the *Symphony* is a handsome boat, with her high bow, canoe stern, flush deck, and good-looking deckhouse. Her overhanging spars give her a grace she wouldn't have without them.

The *Symphony* is 33 feet long on deck, with a waterline length of 28 feet, a beam of 9 feet 2 inches, and a draft of 4 feet 6 inches. She displaces 7.6 tons and has a sail area of 550 square feet. Her outside ballast consists of an iron keel of 2.3 tons.

One of Mr. Griffiths' objectives in designing the *Symphony* was to produce a boat with power to carry sail and stay reasonably dry in the process. The hull of the *Symphony* certainly looks powerful, especially her bow. Her sections look powerful, too — even a little chunky perhaps — but she has quite a long run and quite fine waterlines.

Looking back on this design, Mr. Griffiths said he would cut away the yawl's forefoot a bit more. I don't know about that. That fairly deep forefoot might help the singlehander to keep a grip on things at times.

Here's what Mr. Griffiths had to say about this design in regard to seakindliness and speed:

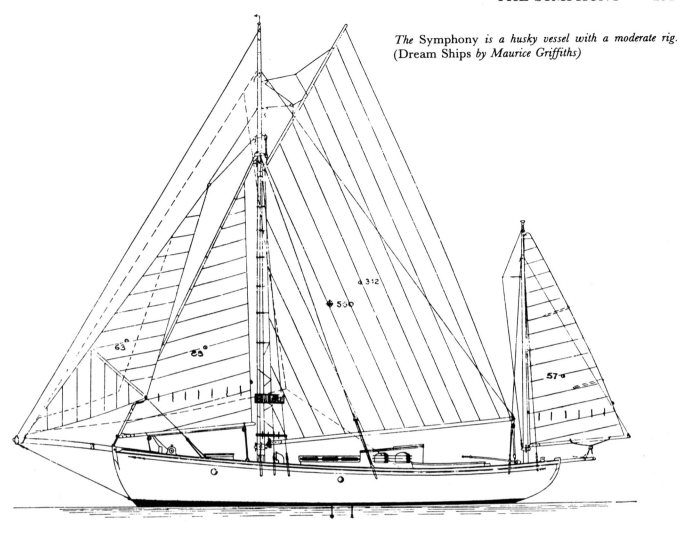

The Symphony *is a husky vessel with a moderate rig.*
(Dream Ships *by Maurice Griffiths*)

The lines were drawn to give above all things as easy and sea-kindly a motion, and an ability to stand up to canvas in a strong breeze and not lie down to sulk, as one has a right to expect from a nine-tonner [here he refers to Thames measurement]. When a man is making a long passage alone the question whether his boat will average five knots or six over a period of thirty-six hours or so does not mean a thing. If the singlehander is to be at sea for thirty hours or more whatever speed his boat can do, what makes it possible for him or just plain purgatory and exhaustion is the motion of his boat during all that time and the number of times she throws dollops of very wet and increasingly cold water over him.

If she is a dry boat and does not drench her helmsman and her motion is not unduly fatiguing, then it will not matter much if the owner takes forty hours over the passage. But if his boat is of the fast type that bashes into the seas, shakes herself continually in a wild

motion, and throws up heavy dashes of spray that drench him, the poor man will be wet, cold, aching with fatigue, and not in the least happy to do the passage in thirty hours.

To achieve this seakindliness, Mr. Griffiths gave the *Symphony* — above all else — "a fairly generous displacement." She wouldn't be fast (especially with her moderate rig), but she would have a good turn of speed. Another way to say it is that while you wouldn't be proud of her speed (as you would be of her easy motion), neither would you be disappointed with it.

It is interesting to compare the *Symphony* with some of the canoe yawls of similar size designed by Mr. Griffiths' countryman Albert Strange (see *Good Boats*). The *Symphony* is heavier than the Albert Strange boats. She is not as dainty and pretty — or as fast — as they are, but she is drier and more comfortable in a rough sea.

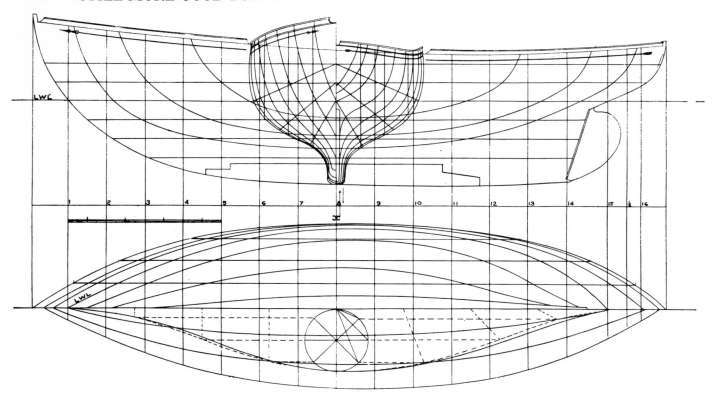

Above: *She was designed to be reasonably dry in rough weather and, above all, to have an easy motion at sea.* (Dream Ships *by Maurice Griffiths*). **Below:** *She has a conventional layout with some interesting twists: the head is around the corner, the fireplace keeps the books dry, and the engine box is a seat for the cook.* (Dream Ships *by Maurice Griffiths*)

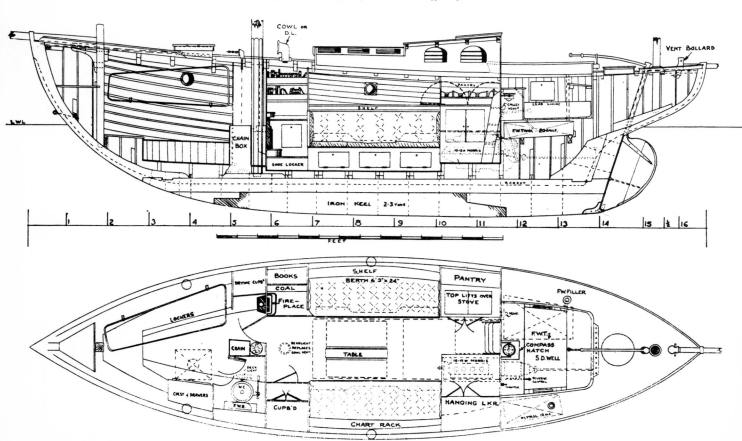

The *Symphony* was built very strongly for lying alongside working craft in crowded harbors and for taking the bottom, if need be, in estuary seas, an eventuality that seems to appear less catastrophic to English sailors than it does to Americans.

She has, as mentioned, a moderate rig. You'd probably want more sail in American waters.

Yet it might be as well to keep her rig as is, and have some big, light sails to play with. There could be a fairly lofty club topsail, for instance, and a huge, very light jib topsail cut flat enough so you could carry it on the wind in light going. These toys would necessitate setting up a preventer backstay to the masthead.

At the other end of the Beaufort Scale, you would first shorten down to jib and mainsail, and then to a reefed main and staysail. She'd balance better under jib and mainsail than under staysail and mainsail. The mainsail is cut vertically without battens for strength and for ease of roller-reefing. Its area is but 342 square feet. It would, of course, have a vang to the mizzen masthead.

The mizzen can be reefed, small (57 square feet) as it is. A sliding gooseneck would let you raise the boom when the sail is reefed to keep it out of the sea.

The staysail is self-tending on a club and can be reefed. The working jib, spitfire, and ballooner are all set flying. Note that the jib halyards all pull against the main halyards on the mast to help keep it straight.

The *Symphony's* engine is a 10-h.p. Morris. The propeller is off-center to port. She has a 12-gallon fuel tank on the port side outboard of the cockpit. Her 20-gallon water tank is under the cockpit.

The yawl has a flush deck for strength, there being deck beams throughout most of her length. She can carry an 8½-foot dinghy on deck over the skylight.

The cockpit is watertight and self-bailing. The English used to like their cockpit seats set athwartships, rather than fore-and-aft. I would think the crosswise seating would be far less comfortable than fore-and-aft when the boat is heeled.

Her compass is set in the thwartships locker at the forward end of the cockpit, a good arrangement. She has a tiller comb, an exceedingly handy arrangement, especially for a singlehander.

The *Symphony's* layout is tried and true. She has only one pipe berth forward instead of the usual two.

Her saloon looks like a cozy retreat. Mr. Griffiths had all the details worked out: she was to have a saloon with mahogany paneling, dark blue or red rep settee covers, oiled teak or mahogany floorboards, white enameled deck underside with varnished oak deck beams, teak skylight and hatch, and the Pascall Atkey open fireplace with blue or red tiles and polished brass fender and mantelpiece. Elegant.

Outboard of the Pascall Atkey is, in the saloon, a bookshelf, and, in the fo'c's'le, a hanging locker for clothes. The P.A. would fight clamminess in the clothes and mildew in the books.

Mr. Griffiths worked out a compact galley for this boat and others:

"The galley was an arrangement that I favored at that time, consisting of a fairly large locker 3 feet long fore and aft with doors opening in front at oven level and a hinged top which opened out to form a shelf.

"The two-Primus Clyde cooker swung on gimbals athwartships only, with its hot-plate just below this locker top. A ventilating shaft at the back of the locker took much of the fumes through the after bulkhead into the open air. On the whole this was a very satisfactory galley for a small boat, as when the locker was closed all smell of stale cooking was kept out of the cabin,"

The engine box doubles as a seat for the cook, a neat arrangement. The head is tucked around the corner in the fo'c's'le for privacy.

She has six feet of headroom in the deckhouse and a bit less under the skylight.

All in all, the *Symphony* would make a fine singlehanded cruiser. Or, of course, she would also be a good boat for two or three people, particularly for a couple with a child. But to my knowledge, no boat has been built to this design and she has remained true to the title of the book in which she originally appeared — a dream ship.

33/ The Derby Dory

> **Length overall: 11 feet**
> **Beam: 4 feet 1 inch**
> **Displacement: 200 pounds**
> **Designers: Garry Hoyt and**
> **Robert Henry**

One day there arrived in the office a rather elaborate brochure about something called "The proper seagoing dinghy." It described a boat called the Derby Dory, the creation of Garry Hoyt, the man who brought you the Freedom 40. On the back cover of the brochure was a picture of somebody rowing a small boat — presumably a Derby Dory — through the crest of a breaking sea, apparently in mid-ocean. An editor wanted to know if I'd try out the boat and write her up.

I agreed to do this but thought it only fair to admit that I had neither time nor inclination to row the boat out into the middle of the ocean and that my usual practice when in a small boat is to try to avoid breaking seas altogether.

With these caveats the assignment was still on, so on a gray day in May I went to the office of the builder of the Derby Dory, Tillotson-Pearson, at the former naval facility at Melville, just north of Newport, Rhode Island. It was good to see Dick Davidson again; he was Tillotson-Pearson's sales manager. He told me a bit about Garry Hoyt. Mr. Hoyt is a designer, not a naval architect, and his primary career is in advertising and marketing. He's an ex-

perienced small-boat sailor and has represented the United States at the Olympic Games.

The idea for the Derby Dory came from Garry Hoyt's fertile mind, a mind that is obviously tempered by considerable knowledge of what kinds of boat designs have worked well in the past but is also honed to cut through to new solutions for old problems. The man's ideas about boats deserve attention.

His idea about this boat was to create a yacht tender that would be a good lifeboat if the yacht it was tending should sink. He calls it "The proper seagoing dinghy," and he just happens to have Ten Commandments that he feels should not be broken in the design and construction of such a craft:

(1) The boat should be unsinkable. I didn't try to sink the Derby Dory. If I had that assignment, I'd lash a large, heavy cargo net to the little craft and fill it with many beach stones until the boat's flotation was overcome, in which case it would undoubtedly go to the bottom. It would take a lot of stones. I don't know any other way to get the thing under water.

(2) Be easily rightable. Didn't try this either, but the boat being fairly narrow (beam 4 feet 1

254

Garry Hoyt.

inch), fairly high-sided, (bottom of skeg to top of transom, 2 feet 7 inches), and having good big things to grab onto at each gunwale with hands and feet, I should think she'd be easier to right than most boats.

(3) Be bailable when swamped. Nor did I experiment with this feature, but my own dinghy is bailable when swamped and she has a centerboard trunk and less flotation than this boat.

(4) Be weatherly. More on this later.

(5) Be non-deflatable (this is not really a dinghy commandment, but is rather a disagreement with the dogma of another sect, the inflatable boat disciples). Needless to say, there is no way to deflate a Derby Dory.

(6) Have secure stowage and a built-in compass. Here Mr. Hoyt is giving us two commandments for the price of one, probably looking ahead — good ad man that he is — to the awkward situation he will face if he ends up with The Eleven Commandments. In any event, the Derby Dory does have dry, secure stowage in her compartments *and* there is a compass built into the vertical bulkhead of the forward compartment.

(7) Protection for her crew. Garry Hoyt believes it's important to be able to hunker down in the bottom of the boat while sailing. More on this later, too.

(8) Be self-steering. More later.

(9) Carry four adults safely. I wish I had known this was a claim for the boat before the trials, because it would have been interesting to try the Derby Dory so loaded. She'd certainly be cramped with four on board, and it seems to me she'd be a bit overloaded, yet dories do like weight. I really don't know about this one.

(10) Be able to stow on deck; handle surf; be beachable; and have a good fender. (Here Mr. Hoyt unashamedly gives up on the Ten Commandment idea and squeezes in four different ones at the end.) The Derby Dory will stow on deck if you have 11 feet of clear deck space. She's a heavy boat, the bare hull weighing 200 pounds. You don't just get a couple of people and personhandle her over the rail. You need davits or tackles on masts. A good halyard would do, but most modern halyards, strangely enough, are rigged awkwardly for hoisting heavy loads.

As promised, I didn't handle her in surf, but Garry Hoyt has, and he and the boat have come through more or less full of water but have been able to get rid of it and proceed.

I suppose any dinghy is beachable; with her flat bottom, the Derby Dory will certainly take kindly to beaches.

She has a fender system to make the mate of a towboat drool.

In all these commandments, there is no men-

tion of towing. This is because Garry Hoyt naturally doesn't want to tow a dinghy at sea. Nevertheless, most dinghies do get towed from time to time. The Derby Dory, like most dories, might need additional weight in the stern to tow reasonably well, though I should think her skeg would help keep her from sheering around. And of course any boat can be towed if her bow is snugged right up under the stern of the towboat, and here the Derby Dory's fender system would be a big advantage.

Dick and I finished drinking coffee and talking about the boat and I went outside with Bob Clark, Dick's assistant, to see what one looked like and try her out. Remembering that the Cape Dory turned out to be a Whitehall model, I wondered what the Derby Dory might turn out to be. I guess I was really kind of hoping she wouldn't really be a dory, because I was brought up to believe that dories had to be at least 14 feet long on top, and preferably more,

Left: *At rest with sails rolled up. (Freedom Yachts)*
Below: *Under oars in smooth water. (Freedom Yachts)*

to be any good, and though there have been some famous small dories, I'd always secretly suspected that they must be a bit crank.

The Derby Dory did turn out to be a dory, or at least a caricature of one. It's as if a political cartoonist wanted to satirize the dory, so when he drew her he gave her stubby, rather upright ends so nobody could say she was pretty. It's too bad this had to be done to this boat, but more overhang would simply mean she would take up more room on deck and blow around more when being rowed in return for more lift in the ends, which she probably doesn't need anyway, and mere beauty. And I suppose you can't go around asking for mere beauty in such a thing as a lifeboat. At least not in an 11-foot lifeboat.

Two other modifications to the traditional dory design are evident in the Derby Dory: her bottom is a bit wider than the usual proportion so she won't be so tippy, and her chine has a bit more than the usual rocker for ease of handling under oars.

And then there is that great fender. When I first laid eyes on the Derby Dory, I thought she was all fender. The thing doesn't help her looks a bit. It's practical, though. It gives her flotation if swamped and stability when heeled down to the gunwale, and it allows her to crash into things without hurting them or — more important in a lifeboat — herself. It also keeps spray and slop out of the boat. It's made of something called Spongex, a lightweight, tough, quite dense plastic. It's reputed to be four inches in diameter, though it seems more like a foot, and it is made up of 40 individual pieces, so that if it should get damaged, only the damaged sections need be replaced, not the whole thing.

The Spongex fender system is lashed securely to the Derby Dory's brim. The brim is a wide, outward-turning flange at the boat's gunwale molded into her heavy fiberglass hull. In addition to securing the big fender, it acts as a spray shield, stiffens the topsides, provides a lifting hold all around the boat, provides a righting hold for feet and hands all around the boat, and provides a strong base for oarlock sockets. And, of course, it gives the boat her name.

Garry Hoyt worked closely with Bob Henry, the naval architect, on the details of the Derby Dory's design, and Bob Henry was the one who drew her final lines and engineered the molding. This was in 1978. About a dozen of the boats were built. The idea didn't really catch on, so production has stopped.

I did want to try rowing her at the edge of the ocean if not out in the middle of it, so Bob Clark kindly drove, with the Derby Dory towing behind us on a trailer, to a protected cove I knew back of Price Neck out on the Ocean Drive. We launched the boat into perfectly calm water. Bob elected to stop ashore, so I set forth alone into the smooth water of the cove under oars.

I had been warned that the Derby Dory was exceptionally tender, but I didn't find this to be so. She's certainly not as tippy, for example, as a Phil Bolger light dory. You want to stay in the middle of her, all right, but you don't have to be constantly worrying about precisely which way she's tipping and how much, the way you do in some boats.

I ventured outside. There was a gentle breeze blowing offshore from the northeast, but there is always plenty of groundswell and surge coming in from the southward along that shore. The seas were breaking against rocky points and islets, and the biggest waves were breaking over ''sunkers,'' rocks too deep to show themselves but near enough to the surface to trip a big sea. I picked my way carefully among these welters of foam, having no desire to emulate the chap on the back of the brochure.

There was a confused sea with waves running in all directions reflecting off the irregular rocky shore. The Derby Dory bounced around plenty, but her motion was reasonable due to her weight, and she didn't take any water on board, except for a little through the port in the stern for the steering oar (used when sailing) when I backed her down into some steep stuff. A simple plug would keep that out.

I let her lie-to with the oars shipped and stayed sitting in the middle of the boat. To my surprise, instead of drifting off broadside, she headed off and ran straight before the wind. I assume this docile behavior is due to her skeg. I think it's an important attribute for a lifeboat; she'll make more leeway but will be far more

Under sail in smooth water. (Freedom Yachts)

comfortable and safe running before it than lying in the trough.

Back in the protection of the cove, I tried rowing standing up facing forward. She's not too tippy to do this in smooth water, and you could probably do it in fairly rough water once you got thoroughly used to her motion. Her higher-than-normal topsides for a boat her size makes stand-up rowing more comfortable than in most dinghies where you have to bend over farther. It's certainly important to be able to shift rowing positions on a long trip.

Wing-and-wing. (Freedom Yachts)

Like any dory, she is a bit hard to scull, because the sculling notch has to be on the centerline and she's too tiddly for the sculler to stand off to one side to scull. You have to get right forward of the end of the oar, not the most comfortable way to scull for any length of time.

Bob and I hauled her out and trailed her back to Melville for some sailing.

The earliest sailing boats must have had one mast, and then when more masts were thought of, the cautious thing to do was to add a smaller mast forward and another smaller mast aft to maintain balance, thus producing a three-master. The true genius, though, was the first sailor who tried two masts of about equal size, one forward and one aft, for he had wittingly or unwittingly invented a craft that could really be steered with just her sails.

This two-masted tradition was the heritage of a number of American small craft, such as the New Haven sharpies, Hampton boats, Chebacco boats, Block Island boats, and on and on. It's a tradition that Garry Hoyt has continued, and the people associated with Freedom boats say that it won't be long before something like 15 percent of each year's new boats will be cat

ketches. I hope they are right, for this is a sensible rig for cruising. As long as they believe in this tradition so strongly, I think the Freedom folks ought to use its terminology and talk about the foresail and the mainsail, rather than the forward sail and the after sail, which is the terminology they do use.

At any rate, the Derby Dory is a cat ketch. When you divide the sail area of an 11-foot boat in half, you have sails that are so small they are ridiculously easy to handle. As you rig the boat, manipulating mast, sail, and sprit — the sails are exactly the same size and are interchangeable — you feel as if you are at the most about to go skate sailing, or at the least just kite flying.

With the boat at rest and the masts stepped with their sails rolled up 'round them, you can just manage to get around the mainmast in the middle of the boat to go forward or aft of it; that is, when you get your weight far enough out to the side of the boat to get around the mast, you put her gunwale just in the water. (Come to think of it, I guess she *is* fairly tender.)

I shoved off in the basin at Melville and waited to see what would happen, holding the steering oar rigged out through the stern port

and the fore and main sheets. These sheets both led through cam cleats. I started to worry about not being able to slack them quickly and so unrove them out of the cam cleats. Once outside the basin, I laid her up on the same northeast breeze, now increased a bit to perhaps 12 to 15 knots. There was a little chop, but it was not rough. She went along with such extreme docility that within a couple of minutes I had the sheets rigged back through the cam cleats and all tied down snug so I wouldn't have to hold them and could concentrate on the steering oar. Then in another couple of minutes I found that that device required so little concentration that I shipped the thing. Now, having nothing at all with which to occupy myself, I decided I had better have lunch. That was nice, perched up under the weather rail on the midships compartment munching away at a sandwich and just watching the little boat sail herself very nicely to windward.

She is not what I would call fast, but she does all right for her size. I was devoting most of my attention to making and eating sandwiches and was just wondering about a third one when I looked up to see that we had gone almost all the way over to Prudence Island. I put the steering oar back in the water and steered her around onto the other tack.

Garry Hoyt says she'll do two things under sail that I didn't test. One is that she'll go to windward and can stay dry if it is blowing 50 knots. The other is that she'll go to windward without her dagger leeboards. I have a tough time believing either statement, but it wasn't blowing 50 knots and the leeboards I happened to have fit too tightly to remove while sailing, so I couldn't test either statement.

One of the points Garry Hoyt makes is that you don't have to sit up on the gunwale of the Derby Dory to sail her when it's blowing hard but can sit down inside for protection. Even in puffs of maybe only 15 knots, I certainly felt better about the boat when I was up on the gunwale. She felt as if she was going to ship water over the lee gunwale if I didn't stay up there, and she certainly felt as if she was going to slow down considerably if I let her just heel over to the puffs. Of course with more than one person aboard, that much weight to windward would make all the difference and certainly no rail perching would be necessary. Also, I had no ballast in the boat during my trials, and it is recommended that the middle compartment be filled with seawater, fresh water, or beer and ice.

Safe as I felt sailing this nice little Derby Dory, I almost became a boating fatality during this trial. I was going along minding my own business on the port tack, finishing off that third sandwich, when there came rapidly overhauling me a modern sloop with low-cut genoa and deck covered with people in yellow slickers. I assumed that, as the overtaking vessel, she would sail by me to leeward, possibly tack away before she got to me, or perhaps be a bit impolite and sail by to windward. Yet I could not ascertain that her helmsman had decided to do any of

Handsome is as handsome does?
(Freedom Yachts)

these things. I knew he knew of my existence, because more than one person on the bow of his boat had pointed at me and shouted something aft. Then somebody on the foredeck hollered at me that they were racing, apparently implying that that justified the destruction they were about to perpetrate. I know it was only one little boat and one person who was about to be run over, yet I decided to protest that person's fate. I announced in what I fully intended should be stentorian tones that they had better not run me down, with the clear — I hoped — implication that some mysterious, horrible fate awaited them if they should do this. I discovered, however, that the presence of a large, sharp, rapidly overtaking bow had converted me from a stentor to a milquetoast, and although terribly well-chosen words came out, they were so quavery as to be certainly drowned out by the ogre's roaring bow wave. Their utterer was next, but at the last second he was spared, for the racing sloop luffed just enough to go by to windward without hitting us. Trying to regain my composure, I continued munching and glared my worst glare, which appeared to do very little damage to the offensive vessel or her crew.

Anyway, it was time to run her off and get back to the Melville basin. I was curious to see if she would steer herself off the wind. Francis Herreshoff has written that a long-keeled boat is not a good self-steerer, for she takes sheers that are too powerful for the sails to counteract and bring her back on course. Yet I had never thought of an opposite kind of boat like a dory as being a good self-steerer either (until I went out in Sam Manning's big dory, which is a fine self-steerer).

The Derby Dory is a remarkable self-steerer. Close-hauled she follows the wind with considerable sensitivity, and if a sea throws her off, she gets right back to work on the right course with a quicker reaction than most helmsmen exhibit. With the wind on the quarter, it helps to trim the foresail in a bit flat. The quartering seas make her yaw around quite a bit, but she seems to maintain a good average course.

I ran her off dead before it, using the steering oar momentarily, and then flung the foresail over — this is basically a one-finger operation

— to put her wing-and-wing. In came the steering oar and away she went, steady as a church. Well, not quite. I didn't have the sails trimmed far enough forward (had them about square, and they ought to be even farther forward, which is quite possible with the sprit rig), so she rolled a lot — which, in turn, made her yaw a lot. She steered herself dead before it all right, but I had to jump around in lively fashion to counteract the rolling. I think the sails would have done this work for me if I'd had the sense to ease them forward of 90 degrees.

Although I used the steering oar to maneuver, you could probably sail her anywhere you wanted to without it once you got used to her.

I guess I do have a piece of general advice for Garry Hoyt: You have gone back to the basics on hulls and rigs, and I think your boats would be improved if you went back to the basics on rigging and fittings instead of using modern stuff like cam cleats — real cleats work better every time — and sails sleeved onto spars so you can't lower them — I'd want a halyard so I could strike the sails quickly and surely without having to stand up or go forward. You reef the Derby Dory by rotating the masts, but again, I'd prefer a vertical laceline to pull, like some of the sharpies had, so you could reef more quickly and without going to the bow.

At any rate, Garry Hoyt has created quite a boat in the Derby Dory. In an offshore disaster, I'd certainly prefer having one of these boats to climb into instead of a liferaft. I suppose the raft is more stable in ultimate survival conditions, but I'd prefer to take my chances trying to carry out a voyage to safety in a Derby Dory than waiting around for somebody to find my liferaft.

Is the Derby Dory a good boat for children? I think she's rather heavy for children to row, but I think she would be one of the greatest sail-training vessels for children, being forgiving yet sensitive. She'd show a youngster all about steering with sails and weight shifting.

So my report is that I think that brochure we got is perhaps a tiny bit presumptuous in claiming that Garry Hoyt has created *the* proper seagoing dinghy, in the sense of the only one or the ultimate one, but that it would certainly be correct to claim that he has created *a* proper seagoing dinghy.

34/ The Beetle Cat

> **Length on deck: 12 feet 4 inches**
> **Length on waterline: 11 feet**
>   **8 inches**
> **Beam: 6 feet**
> **Draft: 5 inches (board up)**
> **Sail area: 100 square feet**
> **Displacement: 450 pounds**
> **Designer: John H. Beetle**

The coast of Rhode Island between Watch Hill Point and Point Judith is a 20-mile stretch of sand beach interrupted by only three stony points, one at Weekapaug, one at Quonochontaug, and one at Matunuck. Right behind the beach, and running parallel to it, is a series of long, narrow, quiet salt ponds. The one that stretches along behind the beach from Weekapaug to Quonochontaug is called Quonochontaug Pond.

At the Weekapaug end of the pond, on a little, landlocked cove, is situated the Weekapaug Yacht Club. Some years ago the club succumbed to the idea of a clubhouse, but it is still a very modest building, having suffered only one addition, and there is, as yet, no bar. The geography of the place probably helps. There is no room for something that might reasonably be called a "yacht" on Quonochontaug Pond.

Both sides of my family have long and deep associations with Weekapaug and sailing on Quonochontaug Pond. I made my first single-handed voyage on the cove, a disastrous one-way trip to leeward across that great body of water in a big, heavy rowing skiff. It was at Weekapaug that I was taught, at an early age, to scorn the Beetle cat.

The boats that raced on Quonochontaug Pond were divided into three classes. In Class A, the big guys raced their Barnegat Bay sneakboxes. In Class C, older siblings and I raced in the *Popeye* against sister ships of the Cape Cod Nimblet class. In Class B, a variety of craft raced against each other under a handicapping system. At the very bottom of Class B, taking time from everybody, were two or three poor little Beetle cats, usually raced unsuccessfully by mere girls. Everything on the pond could pass the fat Beetles.

Thinking back on it now, I realize that Pop must have known that the Beetle cats were good boats, but he never bothered to contradict the notion popular among his children that they were "slow as blue mud." What we failed to account for, and Pop failed to point out to us, was that the Beetle cats were three feet shorter than all the other boats on the pond.

(In more recent years, more Beetles have arrived on the pond, enough to make a class by themselves, in which they have had some excellent racing and have even turned out, among both youngsters and adults, a handful of New England champs.)

At any rate, when Mother, a sixtyish widow

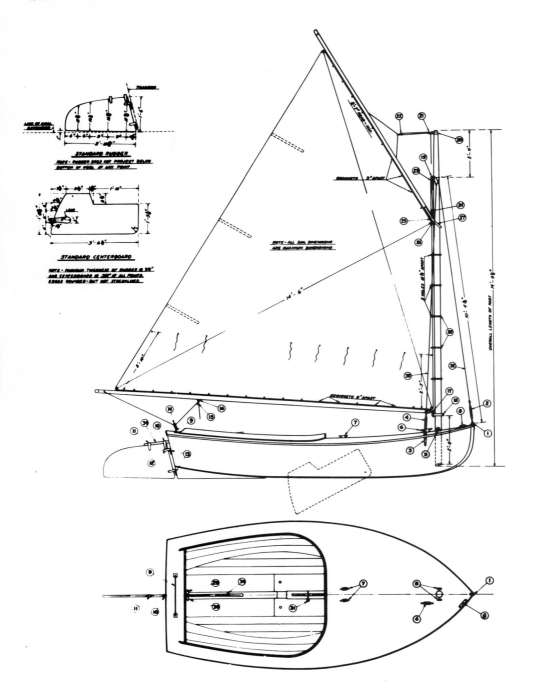

The sail and rigging plan of the Beetle cat, as drawn in 1947. (Concordia Company)

Beetle cats racing in a breeze, some reefed, some not. (Concordia Company)

looking for a somewhat more substantial vessel in which to get afloat on the Pawcatuck River than her seven-foot sailing pram, bought a Beetle cat, I was afraid she might be bored with the boat. She said the Beetle was really for her grandchildren anyway, but I noticed that the grandchildren had to make some rather elaborate plans to get their hands on the boat, because Mother always seemed to be out having great fun in her.

The new boat was named the *Rebecca* after one of the grandchildren, a nice old-fashioned name that probably fits the boat better than it fits the grandchild.

I sailed in the *Rebecca* some myself on visits back home, glad of a chance to get afloat again under sail in my old haunts, but not expecting much from a lowly Beetle cat. I still remember the shock I got the first time I put her up on a gentle breeze. I strapped her in cautiously and didn't try to head up too high, but she very quickly gave me to understand that she wanted no part of such condescension. Soon I had her jammed on the wind where she belonged, and she began opening my eyes to the way a well-

designed little catboat can point high and foot fast. Since then, I've had as much fun sailing the Beetle cat as any boat.

Another time the *Rebecca* opened my eyes (actually Mother's grandchild is way ahead of the boat in this department!) was when four of us adults went on board. Each chose a corner of the big cockpit and we beat down the river into a moderate-to-fresh sou'wester, went ashore at Watch Hill for ice cream, and ran back up the river, dry and comfortable both ways. Not bad for a 12-foot boat!

The Beetle cat was designed in 1920 and first built in 1921 by John H. Beetle, the son of James Beetle, who had set up as a boatbuilder in New Bedford, Massachusetts, and had built whaleboats most successfully. John Beetle and other members of the family reasoned that a small version of the Cape Cod catboat might make a popular craft to replace their dwindling business in whaleboats.

They were right. The company has built over 4,000 Beetle catboats, and there are 30 active racing fleets. The most active centers are Duxbury, Nantucket, Bass River, Falmouth, and

Youngsters seem to love her.
(Photo by Norman Fortier, courtesy Concordia Company)

Padanaram, all in Massachusetts; Edgewood and Barrington, on Narragansett Bay; Mystic, Connecticut; and Islip, on Great South Bay, Long Island. There is a New England Beetle Catboat Association to govern the racing of Beetle cats.

The Beetle cat is 12 feet 4 inches long on deck, with a waterline length of 11 feet 8 inches, a beam of 6 feet, and a draft of about 5 inches with the centerboard up. The boat draws about 2 feet with the board down. The sail area is about 100 square feet and the displacement about 450 pounds.

There is little or nothing to the Beetle cat under water. Thus the boat is quite fast for her length, my own early indoctrination to the contrary notwithstanding.

The Beetle has considerable stability at low angles of heel due to her great beam.

There's a nice little hollow in the waterline forward. Yes, the transom drags, and the sound of the bubbles right behind you is a nice musical speedometer. Racers always seem most concerned about this drag and are careful to get their weight forward to minimize it, and my impression is that they overdo this a bit, sailing the boats a bit too much down by the head.

Note that the rudder does not protrude below the skeg. Note also the nice curves in the forward end of the cockpit coaming.

The Beetle cat seems to me to be built just exactly right for her usual purposes. She's strongly and nicely built and has a wonderful warmth to her, especially after a few seasons of sailing and maintenance have given her a bit of patina. She's just fancy enough, with her varnished oak coaming, for example, so that you want to take really good care of her and never abuse her, yet she is just plain enough, with her painted gray ceiling to serve as cockpit floor, so that you don't need to feel guilty about traipsing a bit of sand on board after a beach picnic or being lucky enough to get some fish scales on her.

I love the look of the little round mast right up in the bow of the boat. This mast probably doesn't need shrouds, but they are offered by the Beetle folks as an optional item. The *Rebecca* has them. Few, if any, working cats had shrouds. The sail is held to the mast by five nice little mast hoops.

The halyards lead aft to cleats on deck just forward of the coaming. I always hoist the peak higher than shown in the sail plan, with the halyard all but chock-a-block. Thus the sail is quite high-peaked, approaching a triangle in shape, and the boom isn't too low.

The boom is just a bit longer than the boat's length on deck. When I got acquainted with the *Rebecca,* about the first thing I did was put a topping lift on her. Every boat with a boom deserves one.

The topping lift lets you control the boom whether the sail is up or down. It's no fun to have to have the boom in your lap when you lower the sail. It's handy, occasionally, to be able to start the sail down with the boom broad off, held up by the lift. You need the lift when reefing underway or when scandalizing the sail (more on this later).

When a catboat has her sail up, that's her whole, balanced sail plan you're looking at. So, unless you're very lucky, she may start sailing around her mooring just when you don't want her to. The easiest way to keep most of the wind out of her sail is just to top the boom well up.

Yes, the topping lift is a really great little piece of rigging on a Beetle cat. I think the Beetle folks should rig one on every boat. On the *Rebecca,* I simply led a piece of line from the end of the main boom through a single block at the masthead, down to a lead block on deck, and aft to a cleat just forward of the cockpit coaming, just the way the halyards are rigged.

The Beetle cat has a boom crotch that slides through a wooden bracket on the forward facing of the stern deck and seats in a slot at the bottom of the boat. The bracket has horns on it so it can double as a cleat for the main sheet. I do think the old adage about never belaying the sheet in a small boat has been a bit overworked. It's obviously good general advice, but that word ''never'' seems a bit out of place around the water. I figured lightning would strike me dead the first time I did it, but now I think nothing of tying down the sheet if I'll be on the same point of sailing for a while and if the breeze is steady and not too strong. The Beetle cat is more forgiving of such foolishness than most boats her size because of her considerable stability.

As a small daysailer, the Beetle cat needs little

gear on board. You want a good big bucket so that if you do miscalculate the stability factor you can quickly get rid of the weighty evidence. A little pump is handy to clear the bilge of rainwater. You want a big rag to take care of that sand and those fish scales. You want a small, unpatented anchor — say, a 15-pounder — and 100 feet or so of half-inch stuff for a rode, beach painter, or towline (I am assuming the Beetle cat will be the towing vessel, not the towed vessel, perhaps bringing in some hapless outboarder who figured his fuel a bit too closely). And you want an oar with which to sound and scull. For the latter, an oarlock socket mounted on the transom and a circular oarlock kept on the oar would work fine. That way the sculling oar wouldn't be bounced out of its fulcrum by powerboat wakes. Much better than paddling.

You may or may not want a cockpit tent. You would want one to keep the rain out if you needed to leave the boat unattended for days at a time, or if you wanted to use the boat for short-range cruising. In any case, the Beetle folks provide one.

I don't think I'd sail a Beetle cat a lot without building in a shelf on each side of the boat up forward under the deck for the storage of a ditty bag, the local chart, and whatever gets brought aboard for the day's trip.

But enough of this talk of hull, rig, and equipment; let's go sailing!

Rowing out to our Beetle, we see that it must have rained harder last night than we thought, for she is lying on her mooring quite far down by the head. Being a lot finer forward than she is aft, she changes her fore-and-aft trim when she takes water on board. We're impatient to get on board and pump her out to restore her to her proper, perky self.

That done, getting underway is the work of but a very few minutes. Drop the board, stick in the tiller, let go the main sheet, top up the boom, stow the boom crotch, and take the stops off the sail. Hoist away. Sweat up the throat halyard good and tight, slack the lift, and set up the peak halyard just so, being very particular to get only a suggestion of wrinkles from peak to tack, for the breeze, so far, is gentle. Cast her off and we're away.

Strap her down and let's go to windward. The boom stays out a bit over the quarter, but she points very high without slowing down too much.

Later, it breezes up, and we take some hard puffs. Not willing to reef yet, we press her a bit. Being a responsive boat, she lets us know exactly what she thinks of being pressed too hard. On the next hard puff, she heels right over and lets a few cupfuls of water in over the coaming, at the same time lifting her rudder enough so that press though we might she rounds up anyway, shakes her sail, and looks us right in the eye.

Well, we've gained plenty to windward, so let's run her off for a while. Of course she reaches and runs like a fool. Just takes right off and the bow is low enough so you get a nice view of a bone in her teeth of a size to be a big vessel's pride.

Her sail is big enough so that when now we press her off the wind we can just barely hold her off with the tiller, but we'd better hold her off, because if we let her broach in a puff, we may be in trouble.

Now we shift our weight as far aft as possible to keep the bow from burying. We wonder what a youthful, lightweight singlehander would do now. Maybe have a few 25-pound sandbags to pile up against the transom to sit on.

Of course such a sailor should be reefed down by now. Probably we should be, too. So we watch for a lull, find one, then round her up to tuck in a reef. Slack the sheet, let her lose way, and tie the helm down. She stays mostly docile, occasionally filling away enough to get steerageway and luff again. Top up the boom, slack the halyards, tie down the luff, haul out the clew earing. When she's on the luffing part of her cycle, reach out and tie in the after reefpoints. Tie the rest of the points, set up the halyards hard, especially the peak, slack the lift, trim her in, put the helm up, and we're away again, a bit of spray flying now as we drive her to windward.

Running home later, it blows still harder and we decide to experiment with a scandalized sail just for the fun of it. Take up a bit on the lift, slack away the peak halyard. We end up with a nice, well-setting trysail, but the upper part of

And fathers like to take the tiller, too. (Photo by Norman Fortier, courtesy Concordia Company)

The Rebecca *lying on her haul-off, waiting for her mainsail.*

the sail is thrashing quite a bit out there to leeward and the gaff is hardly docile. What it needs is a vang, so we capture the thing, put a rope on it, and tie it down to leeward of the "trysail." Not a bad rig.

Back home, under the lee of the point, we peak the sail up again, leaving the vang attached. Kind of fun to be able to haul it aft. We find we can slack the boom out farther than ever now that we have a way to keep the peak of the sail from going too far forward.

Round her up for her mooring. She's coming in just too fast, so shove the boom out, backing the sail. It makes a beautiful brake. Not too much. Now let it aft again and she coasts in just nicely. Tie her up.

Top up the boom, slack away the halyards and make them fast, leaving just comfortable room to shake out the reef. Let go the reef-points, slack the clew earing, and untie the tack. Let the gaff down some more and furl the sail, putting on plenty of stops good and tight. Put in the boom crotch and lower the boom into it. Take the slack out of the sheet, belay, and coil

down. Pull out the tiller and sit back in the cockpit to enjoy the peace and security of the place as seen from a good little boat. It's nice to be in a boat with your eye-level this close to the water. Amazing that such a diminutive craft can take you so far.

Yes, the Beetle cat is a mighty fine boat for any kind of protected-water sailing. Of course in a real sea she will pound, roll, or corkscrew — probably alarmingly — depending on whether she is close-hauled, reaching, or running. She's too small for rough water. She is, however, a substantial little vessel in which to explore ponds, rivers, estuaries, and even open bays — the latter provided the weather is moderate and settled. I have never seen a Beetle cat on a lake, but some of the 4,000 must sail in fresh water.

I am glad I've had my anti-Beetle-cat prejudice corrected. Mother doesn't use the *Rebecca* much any more, and most of the grandchildren seem to have gotten beyond her temporarily, but I certainly look forward to sailing her down the river whenever I go home.

35/ The Cape Dory 14

It seemed a good time to conduct the experiment. In a new town, no one would know that I had always had wooden boats, that I had joined in heartily with the makers of disparaging remarks about Clorox bottle boats and the kinds of sailors who would have such monstrosities. If I got a boat made out of fiberglass myself, new acquaintances might accept such an action as reasonably normal behavior. Old friends surely would have rushed to call for the little men in white suits. But old friends wouldn't have to know. Not for a while.

Such were the heinous thoughts swirling in some dark corner of my mind a dozen years ago while I prowled the waterfront of Camden, Maine.

The sight of a nicely shaped 14-foot Whitehall model pulling boat with a gunter rig for sailing, her hull cleanly molded in fiberglass, sitting demurely on the floor of the big shed at Carlton Dougherty's Harborside West, opened the circuits and brought the crucial question front and center.

"Okay, Taylor, here is a well-designed fiberglass boat. Are you going to live the rest of your life with prejudice, or are you going to see for yourself?"

With a definite sense that the sky was falling, I purchased the vessel.

I had seen prettier Whitehall models, but not a lot prettier. I thought she was a mighty good-looking boat when I first saw her, and now, after getting to know her rather intimately over 12 years, I still like the looks of her.

She turned out to be a Cape Dory 14, built by the Cape Dory Company in West Bridgewater, Massachusetts.

There was even a brochure about her! In the brochure was a Cape Dory 10, as well as the 14, but the 10-footer didn't have nearly as nice a model to my eye. The brochure said these were "classic rowing and sailing dories."

My world was crumbling fast. I had just bought a fiberglass Whitehall boat made by a company that thought it was making dories!

For the next few seconds I concentrated very hard on my boat's clean, sweet, decidedly un-dorylike lines and hoped that maybe it was only the Cape Dory Company's advertising man who thought they were making dories.

Carlton said the brochure came with the boat. I didn't want to be rude, so I just took the thing. It did have some nice pictures of her.

The Cape Dory 14 was designed by Andrew

Andrew C. Vavolotis.

Vavolotis. She is 14 feet 6 inches long, with a beam of only 4 feet 3 inches. Her hull weighs 200 pounds, and the area of her sail is 85 square feet.

She is long and lean, and I think she has a nice sheerline. I like the plumb bow with its beautiful hollow entry. She has a nicely shaped wineglass transom.

The first thing that appealed to me about having a fiberglass boat was that she has no seams. She's smooth. No wood boat can be so smooth. Inside and out. She's very easy to keep clean, even *polished.* There is something very satisfying about waxing the perfectly smooth hull of a small boat and actually polishing it. I couldn't believe the outside of a boat's hull could be that smooth.

I found that this nice, smooth hull had a weakness, though. There's a section of her bottom around the after end of the centerboard trunk where she's quite flat. Where a fiberglass hull is flat, it needs reinforcement. This boat had none, and the bottom "oil-canned" in a certain spot on each side of the centerboard trunk. Very unpleasant. And after five years of oil-canning, the joint between the bottom and the centerboard trunk began to crack and weep a little. Reinforcing the joint and installing a pair of short, fairly wide, flat "frames" on the

inside of the flat hull sections solved the problem. At least she doesn't oil-can any more, and the joint has stayed solid for seven years.

She has 600 pounds of flotation built in. She has a handy drain plug at the after end of the centerboard trunk, and when she's in the water with the plug out, she floods down until the flotation takes over, and she will float a heavy adult with the top of her centerboard trunk still out of water.

Her centerboard is a piece of steel that weighs 50 pounds. It's good ballast. It does get quite pitted and rough from corrosion by the end of the season. I give it a three-step Rustoleum treatment every spring and probably should pull the board and do it again mid-season. I'll try that this year, come to think of it. It's easy to pull the board. It pivots on a roller atop the trunk, so to take the board out, you do just that: lift it out.

Her bow and stern seats are formed by good-sized fiberglass air tanks. They are certainly functional, but I'd rather have wood in the ends of her for appearance' sake. She does have a nice mahogany midships thwart and heavy mahogany gunwales.

Her spars are aluminum. I don't like the looks of them. Yes, they're "maintenance free," but I enjoy varnishing spars.

*With the rig out and the ever-present
bucket on board.*

It's true the gunter rig is harder to handle
than the gaff or sprit, because when the sail is
being hoisted or lowered, the yard gets farther
adrift than does a gaff or sprit, but on this boat
the whole thing is so tiny that any rambunctious
ideas the yard may entertain can be quickly
curbed with a twist of the wrist.

The halyard runs through a masthead
sheave, which brings the yard snug to the mast.
It fits into jaws at the masthead that hold it
solid, a very good rig. I lead the halyard down
through a block on the stemhead so it doubles as
a forestay. Then the halyard leads aft and belays

beside the midships thwart. You don't want
to have to go forward to handle running rigging
in a little boat.

Even the smallest boat with a boom needs a
topping lift. Mine dead-ends on the boom, runs
through a block at the masthead, comes down to
a block beside the mast, and again leads aft to
belay on the gunwale just abaft the midships
thwart.

The boom has jaws, and there's a downhaul
to set up the luff of the sail. It's simple, and it
works well.

The sail had some kind of plastic nonsense fittings to hold it to the mast, but I had a nice little set of five mast hoops saved from some ancient craft, and they give more confidence and are certainly far better looking.

The main-sheet block was on a wire bridle across the transom fixed so it couldn't travel. I replaced the bridle with a rope traveler that lets you trim the sail better.

I found the aluminum boom so light that off the wind it wanted to lift right up at a 45-degree angle if it was blowing at all. So I put a vang on the boom about one-third of the way aft from the mast, leading down to a block on the forward end of the centerboard trunk. This holds the boom down nicely on a broad reach or running. I hold sheet and vang in one hand (I suppose something like a horse's reins?), which leaves another hand for the tiller. My running rigging isn't heavy, but it's a lot bigger than I need for strength, because the bigger line is a lot easier to handle. I like a piece of rope to clutch at, not little strings.

Her mahogany plywood rudder cracked the first time I sailed her. She was on a broad reach and it was blowing moderate-to-fresh in the puffs. I wondered if the guy who wrote the brochure made the rudder. But I wasn't really mad about it, because the boat did seem quite fast. In any case, a thin slab of oak on each side of the thin part of the rudder, through-bolted, has held for 12 years.

After a couple of years I put an extension on the tiller so I could get my weight farther forward and outboard when sailing close-hauled in a breeze.

She came with a red-and-white-striped sail with "CD 14" on it. It's a terrible-looking thing. I did take the CD 14 off and was careful to leave the sail bent on all the time and furl it the same way every time so that the same side of the foot would be well exposed to the rays of the sun constantly. By taking these careful precautions, I hoped the sail would rot quickly so I would have a good reason for getting rid of the red stripes. It was a nylon sail, so I didn't think it would take too long. I worked at this program conscientiously, and it took nine seven-month seasons to destroy the thing. But then I finally got a plain white sail. (It's also vertically cut with no battens.)

I have a little tan trysail for her, what the old-timers call a "traveling sail." I haven't used it a lot yet, but it does seem just right for a big breeze o' wind. It hoists on the main halyard to the masthead, I lash the clew around furled mainsail, club, and boom at whatever fore-and-aft point seems to give the right draft, and then trim it with the main sheet.

A couple of years ago, I discovered that aluminum spars in a small boat do fatigue. It was blowing maybe 15 and I was close-hauled, perched on the weather rail, not really hiking out, and she was almost rail down. We were roaring along in smooth water just inside Curtis Island. The first thing I noticed was that the bow wave had stopped. I found I had scurried inboard and that the boat was upright. There was a sudden silence. Then I noticed that the mast and sail were lying in the water to leeward. I wouldn't want you to think I'm an unobservant sailor; it takes longer to tell these things than they did to happen, but that's the order in which I sensed things. I always thought when you got dismasted that the first thing that would happen would be a great crash followed immediately by noisy confusion. Not at all. Dismasting (at least in this case) turned out to be the most peaceful imaginable experience. One minute we were roaring along and the next we were perfectly still and quiet.

So I gathered everything back on board and tidied up. No problem, I'd just row home. I reached in my jacket pockets to take out the oarlocks. Empty pockets. I didn't bother trying to reconstruct what strange chain of circumstances had conspired to make this the first time I'd ever been out in the boat anywhere under any conditions without oarlocks. I just grabbed one of the oars and paddled home "off the bow," Chesapeake Bay style, and was grateful that, all things being equal, I always stay to windward of home in a small boat.

Well, I thought, at least now I have an excellent reason to put wooden spars in this boat. I enjoyed that mental prospect for fully two weeks before I realized that such a simple pleasure would be foiled by the insidiousness of fiberglass. The "mast step" is a reinforced sleeve molded into the structure forming the forward air tank. A wooden mast would have to have a

Beached at the Lake. It's fun getting used to no tide.

bigger diameter than the aluminum mast. No go.

Okay, so I'll put another aluminum mast in her. Taking a circuitous route so as not to come anywhere near a boatyard, I went to a machine shop and got a nice piece of heavy-gauge aluminum tubing made up into a "mast" for $20. It's tougher than the old mast. It might go 20 years.

One very nice piece of gear I have in this boat I discovered by accident. As Pete Culler used to say, you use what's available. When I wanted a bucket, what was available was a cast-off horse bucket my daughter didn't need any more. It's a giant black affair, a little flexible, made of something I can only call "fiber-filled rubber," and apparently quite indestructible. I replaced its heavy, galvanized iron handle with a lashing tied permanently into the boat with plenty of scope so it doesn't restrict the use of the bucket

yet will ensure that the bucket stays with the boat. If it's cold and you're a little bit scared, you can get her from swamped to almost dry in less than a minute with absolute certainty using this device.

Another piece of equipment I always carry is an old towel. Nothing like it for cleaning her up and drying her right out. Much better than any sponge.

For snow removal, I use a hard rubber dustpan.

And now, after all these words about such a tiny boat, can you stand even more words, and in the form of a digression? Here we go. I was taught American history out of a textbook that we called "Muzzey" after its author. Many years before, our teacher had carefully underlined his copy of Muzzey, picking out the salient points he wanted us to memorize and regurgitate. He had a system of stars in the margin to indicate the relative importance of key points in the text. His classroom teaching consisted of reading us his underlining. We followed along doing our own. Anything rating one star you had probably better memorize for the test; two stars was almost a certainty to be there; and three stars meant you better know it absolutely cold or else. And then we came to the Lincoln-Douglas debates, and our mentor said, ''I don't care how many stars you put on this this one.'' Well, that's where we are right now — I don't care how many stars you put on this next item.

This next item is a very simple thing I discovered after sailing small boats for 40 years. It helps a great deal in sailing this particular boat we have been talking about, and I am sure it would help a great deal in sailing any small boat. I have never heard of it before, but it must have been invented hundreds of times already. I think you must know all about it and have been keeping it a secret from me all this time as a sort of joke. Well, I finally caught on.

What it is, is a board. You take a board sailing with you. I'll tell you the silly way I backed into this thing. I was thinking about a hiking board for this boat, something that would stick under the lee gunwale and extend well out over the weather gunwale to let me get my weight farther out to windward when sailing in a hard breeze. Like a sliding seat on a sailing canoe, only nowhere near as fancy. More like the hiking boards they use on the racing Chesapeake Bay log canoes. I had made this nicely varnished board to hold flower pots for my daughter at college. The board ended up back home for the summer, I spotted it, and said, ''There, I'll take that in the boat and just get a little feeling for what this hiking board ought to be like.'' So, for the first time in my life, I went sailing in a small boat with a board. The minute the boat filled away, I just about danced with glee and quickly forgot all about hiking boards. What I had with me was a movable seat stretched between the midships thwart and the after seat. Being completely loose, it could slide side to side across the boat, or take a diagonal angle, and, in short, be used to place my weight — comfortably sitting, mind you — in an in-

The CD 14 came off quickly enough, but the horrible red-and-white sail survived a decade of bad treatment. (Cape Dory Company)

Rowing in Camden Harbor. (Chris Cornell)

finite number of positions in the boat. Move to leeward, move to windward, move forward, move aft, move diagonally in any direction. With every puff of wind you can shift your weight just exactly where you want to, and you are taking a comfortable seat right with you as you go. A revolution.

You have certainly kept the sailing board a deep, dark secret for a long time. But I'm onto it at last. Now you can all bring yours out into the open.

The Cape Dory 14 rows very nicely. She's heavy enough to carry her way and goes through a head sea easily. Nor does she slew around in a quartering sea under oars. Seven-and-a-half feet seems to be about the right length for her oars.

Sailing, she's quite a fast boat. She's close-winded, and it's fun to beat her out of the inner harbor in Camden seeing how few tacks you can take. She reaches and runs fast. Off the wind in any sea at all, she really gets to shooting the waves. It's exciting. She even makes a good motorsailer. Lots of times I sail in through Camden Harbor in the evening on a dying breeze reaching along pulling on one oar just enough to keep her going straight.

I really like this boat. She rows and sails beautifully. Women and children don't like her, though, for they usually find that she's too cramped and tippy for them.

I have used her a lot in the last 12 years. At noontime, I often go out and explore Camden Harbor, under sail if there's a breeze or under oars if there's not, see what boats have come in overnight, maybe circumnavigate Curtis Island, maybe poke out into the Bay a hundred yards or so, or maybe go up to the head of Sherman Cove and back. Every time, of course, is different.

Or, with more time in the evening or during a weekend, I like to reach across a southerly to the islands if it looks as if it's not going to blow too hard. Or, maybe beat up under the Camden

Hills toward Lincolnville if it's northwest and then run back with the tide. It's also fun to beat 'round to Rockport, run up into the harbor and look the boats over, beat out again, and run for home.

All this Penobscot Bay work is for settled weather only, of course, in such a small boat as this. Caught out on the Bay in a rising breeze with a bit of a breaking sea building up, she could be quickly overwhelmed. I've not had her out in such conditions, and if I do, it will be through lack of judgment on my part as to what the wind is going to do. She'd probably do quite well shortened down to her traveling sail scudding off before it. Or with everything struck and under oars. But there'd be no way to get to windward. In a hard chance you could dump the rig over for a sea anchor.

But this is no boat to take in harm's way. She's a dainty little slip of a thing and I try to be quite gentle with her.

Epilogue

RACING THE DINGHY

The Camden Yacht Club is rather informal as such organizations go. Every summer, along with their standard racing events, they run a couple of what they call "Family Fun Races." Such editorializing in a title always puts me on my guard (just as you should be when reading a book that purports to present good boats), yet because such a race is the only one open to the Dinghy (described in the last chapter), on July 3, 1977, I decided to enter her.

She would compete against everything from a PJ forty-something-or-other on down — on a boat-for-boat basis. Handicapping was not to be part of the fun, a simplicity with which I heartily agree. After all, racing ought to be to see who has the fastest boat.

The fleet of some thirty sail was divided into classes according to length. The Dinghy, of course, was the smallest boat in the smallest class. There was a Cape Cod Bullseye next above us in the class; the biggest boat in the class was a Vertue.

For some reason, I had difficulty finding a crew for this event. No matter, the vessel had only one sail, a centerboard, and a rudder to fool with. I'd race her singlehanded.

I showed up for the pre-race briefing with a pencil over my ear and a chart under my arm, trying to look the part of a skipper or navigator of a racing yacht.

The race committee chairman ran down his list to see if all the entries were actually going to start.

"Calista?"

"Here."

"Gazella?"

"Present."

"Mary B II?"

"Yo."

Suddenly I realized the Dinghy had no name. A mere 14-footer that rowed as well as she sailed and vice versa and was in commission nearly all year, she seemed neither to deserve nor need one. There was enough knowing head-tapping about the little vessel being in the race, however, without the additional embarrassment of my having to argue my philosophy before the race committee and the assembled yacht captains about naming boats that already had perfectly good generic names. Clearly, the Dinghy was going to have to be named in the next few seconds.

I tried to calm down. It would be no good to blurt out *Miss Suzy Q* or *Taj Mahal* and then have to live with it. I got a grip on myself and tried to think of some reasonable comparison. What was like that little slip of a boat?

But now the chairman was addressing himself to me. "Roger, what's the name of your [split-second pause] boat?"

"The *Feather*," I replied, only then realizing I was in a cold sweat.

After the meeting broke, the skipper of the *Gazella,* whose brother is the skipper of the *Calista,* came up. "Glad your boat's name has seven letters," she said. "But it really ought to end in a vowel," she added reproachfully.

"Underway at 1130," the log reports. I stuck the chart in the folds of a jacket in the bottom of the boat, put sandwiches and beer in the bucket, hoisted the sail, and cast off from the Yacht Club float.

"Beat out to starting line off Curtis Island into a gentle and rising southerly." I was worried about the risingness of that southerly; the *Feather* could be overpowered if it blew hard. I'd hate to start, I thought, and then have to withdraw. "Did Not Finish," the race committee would record. Maybe it would be better to have them record, "Did Not Start." Somebody going over the records later might assume I'd been home in bed with a cold. At any rate, I hoped the southerly wouldn't rise any more.

On the way out of the harbor, Henry Scheel, the yacht designer, passed by in a big boat, looked at me lollygagging on the stern seat as I sailed along, and called over to me to shift my weight forward; he didn't realize I was saving my racing trim for later so as to make the competition overconfident.

"Hove to for lunch." I sailed off in a corner by myself away from the racing yachts beginning to charge around in the vicinity of the starting line, slacked the sheet right out, put the helm right down, and let her drift while I enjoyed a sandwich and a beer. It was all very delightful except for worrying about the rising southerly.

"Sailed round watching the big classes start." The excitement of watching big boats start a race never palls. I steered the *Feather* defensively, keeping well out of everybody's way.

"Breeze went westerly and fickle, some fairly hard puffs and some soft spots." So much for the rising southerly. It looked as if it would be safe to sail the newly named vessel around the course after all. Our class was to go to the bell buoy off Rockport harbor, back 'round The Graves, and so return to a finish line off Curtis Island. The whole thing was less than seven miles.

"Started at 1335 back in the middle of the fleet in a nearly flat calm." Starting a race is always a problem. I usually find myself on the starboard tack barging at the windward end of the line along with everybody else in the world. I used to be smart in the big Herreshoff *Aria* and just hit the line someplace in the middle, get clear air, and drive off to leeward, since the boat went to windward very fast by footing like an express train a half point to a full point farther off the wind than the other boats. Once I outdid myself completely when returning to Quonochontaug Pond years after my introduction to racing there as crew for older siblings. My son Roger and I arrived as experts from away and I felt constrained to show the locals just how clever out-of-state big shots could be. I decided we'd port-tack the fleet of Comets, ended up right in the middle of everybody, and was lucky to escape with the boat intact and a mere immediate disqualification to my credit. The most consistent starter I ever knew was Jack Martin racing his Herreshoff 23-footer down in Annapolis. He'd heave to nearly on the line with the boat on her normal course. When he saw the guy on the committee boat reach up to hoist the red flag, he'd trim everything in and be off. He never got really great starts, but he never got a poor one either, certainly never as poor as the start I gave the *Feather*. I simply got trapped by big sails all around me with little if any breeze to work myself out of the mess. The problem soon solved itself; the breeze returned and everybody got out of my way by sailing off ahead.

"First leg was a very close fetch to the Rockport bell." The breeze freshened, and I had to hike out for a bit to keep the *Feather* on her feet. Then, as we approached the buoy, it eased off again.

"Was eight minutes behind lead boat and last at the mark." It was a nice sail of three miles or so even if the bigger boats did go faster.

"Next leg a beam to broad reach to The Graves. Was 11 minutes behind the lead boat and passed the Bullseye." Being last, you can observe everybody else's mistakes and take full advantage of them. By the time I had rounded the Rockport bell, the breeze was quite light indeed. Nearly reversing course, we all changed a healthy fair tide into a healthy foul one. Many of the boats ahead of me were not making enough allowance for this head tide in the light breeze, and they were sagging off to leeward. I headed the *Feather* more up into the current and managed to sail a fairly straight line over the bottom to The Graves. Other boats sailed the great-circle route, including the only other competitor anywhere near my size, the Bullseye. The breeze came in a little more, and by then I was creeping up on the Bullseye's weather quarter, as my lesser distance sailed had its effect. I remember one particular puff when I leaned out and aft as the *Feather* reached along fast, surging right by the Bullseye down to leeward a ways.

"Finished just that way." The rest of the sail to the finish was a broad reach, and the *Feather* managed to stave off the Bullseye. Very satisfactory. As we crossed the line, the race committee wanted to know if we'd sailed the whole course. The idea!

"Hove to for a beer and then beat into the harbor." I must have been feeling like celebrating sailing 'round the course safely.

"Got a prize for trying at the party." There was an extra, tiny trophy, and the race committee chairman kindly presented it to me for sailing the smallest boat in the race.

As well as the *Feather* sailed that day, keeping much bigger boats at least in sight and beating a Bullseye, her name hasn't stuck. I still just call her the Dinghy. But if I get foolhardy and race her again, she'll go on the list as the racing yacht *Feather*.

Index